～ *Epistolary Histories*

Emory,

With thanks for your
transatlantic expertise —

Amanda & Wil.

Epistolary Histories

LETTERS, FICTION, CULTURE

Edited by Amanda Gilroy and W. M. Verhoeven

University Press of Virginia
Charlottesville and London

The University Press of Virginia

© 2000 by the Rector and Visitors of the University of Virginia

All rights reserved

Printed in the United States of America

First published in 2000

∞ The paper used in this publication meets the minimum requirements of the American National Standard for Information Sciences—Permanence of Paper for Printed Library Materials, ANSI Z39.48-1984.

Book design by Kachergis Book Design, Pittsboro, North Carolina

Library of Congress Cataloging-in-Publication Data

Epistolary histories: letters, fiction, culture / edited by Amanda Gilroy and W. M. Verhoeven.

    p. cm.

    Includes bibliographical references and index.

    ISBN 0-8139-1944-4 (cloth : alk. paper)—ISBN 0-8139-1973-8 (paper : alk. paper)

    1. English letters—History and criticism. 2. American letters—History and criticism. 3. Epistolary fiction, English—History and criticism. 4. Epistolary fiction, American—History and criticism. 5. Letter writing—History.
6. Letters in literature. I. Gilroy, Amanda. II. Verhoeven, W.M.

PR911 .E65 2000

826.009—dc21

99-089864

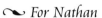 *For Nathan*

∿ Contents

ᥬ Acknowledgments

The editors wish to thank the British Council, the United States Information Service, the Royal Netherlands Academy of Arts and Sciences, the Rudolf Agricola Research Institute, and the Department of English at the University of Groningen, who sponsored the conference on letters at which earlier versions of some essays were delivered and which stimulated our enthusiasm for all things epistolary. Thanks are also due to the American Studies Program at the University of North Carolina, Chapel Hill, for providing a forum for the discussion of epistolarity. Cathie Brettschneider, our editor at the University Press of Virginia, has been remarkably supportive, and it has been a great joy to work with the managing editor, Ellen Satrom. We have also benefited from the incisive comments of the Press's readers. In particular, we appreciate Mary Favret's thoughtful reading of the manuscript, and her useful suggestions for its improvement. Our greatest debts are to our contributors, who, in addition to the work evident in these pages, have provided variously encouragement, accommodation, and friendship. Our understanding of correspondence has been immeasurably enriched by the cross-Channel and transatlantic communications engendered by this book. We especially thank Linda S. Kauffman for her loyal support and invigorating e-mails, and Gerald MacLean for his exotic letters. The book is dedicated to our son, Nathaniel Aran Verhoeven.

Epistolary Histories

∼ Introduction

The epistolary form, as we have come to recognize, is historically and culturally specific: the letters that come to us, and the fictions/histories that we write about them, rely on and bear the traces of particular historical practices. The essays in this volume focus mainly on Anglo-American texts from the seventeenth century to the present day, and they enter into an ongoing debate about the cultural history of the epistolary form. Crucially, they ask us, in Mary Favret's resonant phrase, "to read the envelope of contingency that surrounds any letter,"[1] and in so doing they annotate the ways in which each letter, however private and personal it may seem, is a letter marked by and sent to the world.

∼

The most historically powerful fiction of the letter has been that which figures it as the trope of authenticity and intimacy, which elides questions of linguistic, historical, and political mediation, and which construes the letter as feminine. Thus, P. D. James describes the dynamics of correspondence in Olga Kenyon's anthology *Eight Hundred Years of Women's Letters* in terms of "the intimacy of heart and mind speaking to heart and mind across distance and across time."[2] Kenyon's anthology enforces in its very title the association between women and letters, and the single text recommended for further reading is entitled *Writing the Female Voice: Essays on Epistolary Literature.*[3] Designed for popular consumption, Kenyon's text demonstrates the persistence of a rhetoric that equates epistolary femininity and feminine epistolarity, a rhetoric that derives largely from a particular view of the eighteenth-century novel and its association with women.[4] A brief survey will show how the female voice and the letter were put into circulation together, and how they became marketable commodities—not least, in critical writing about the eighteenth century.[5]

In traditional literary history, the letter has been read as the paradigmatic form through which the eighteenth century enacted what Peggy Kamuf calls "a collective obsessing about an idea called 'woman.'"[6] Though the epistolary form lent itself to a range of didactic purposes,[7] it was preeminently the favored mode of moral instruction for women, as evidenced by conduct manuals such as Wetenhall Wilkes's *A Letter of Genteel and Moral Advice to a Young Lady* (published in 1740, and into its eighth edition by 1766), Hester Chapone's *Letters on the Improvement of the Mind, Addressed to a Young Lady* (1773), and John Gregory's *A Father's Legacy to His Daughters* (1774).[8] Along with a strong religious emphasis (especially in Chapone and Gregory) and practical advice on domestic economy, such texts taught women "natural" femininity in the negative terms of silence and repression; they valorize women's capacity for feeling, so long as such feelings remain within the bounds of propriety (Chapone devotes two chapters to the "*Regulation* of the Heart and Affections" [emphasis added]). As the century progressed, the emerging middle-class ideology of affective individualism offered women the promise of romantic attachment and choice of partner, but social stability continued to be predicated on the subjection of women within marriage. The obsession with femininity and with the process of "feminization" that preoccupied conduct material spilled over into narrative fiction. Indeed, the generic and ideological boundaries between conduct writing and the "novel" were very porous, especially early in the period; there are striking family resemblances between the literature of moral instruction in letters, fictionalized conduct material, and the eighteenth-century novel.[9] While the multiple voices of Richardson's epistolary novels problematize the fixed moral message he wished to convey, his heroines Pamela and Clarissa nevertheless take up the pen to join a cultural correspondence, in which the plots of female seduction and betrayal, marriage and motherhood, were already in circulation.

It is not surprising that, during the same period, the form of writing most accessible to and acceptable for women was letter writing. Female letters traditionally focused on domestic life or on love; they spoke in the private voice appropriate to women whose roles were increasingly circumscribed within the constraints of bourgeois ideology. Of course, we know that women did engage in other modes of correspondence: Lady Mary Wortley Montagu's *Turkish Embassy Letters* were a sensational success when they appeared in print in 1763 (after the author's death), and went through multiple editions. In the early nineteenth century Jane Austen ironically undercut the cultural stereotype that gendered the familiar letter as female: Henry Tilney, in conversation with Catherine Morland, first claims that "Every body allows that the talent of writing agreeable letters is peculiarly female," then comments on the deficiencies of female writing, and finally asserts the equal distribution of artistic excellence between the sexes.[10] Austen critiques gender conventions in Henry's refusal to marginalize women to the gendered genres of journal and letter writing, and deconstructs the association of fashion and femininity in his ironic fascination with—indeed, fetishization of—dress fabrics (in his long conversation with Mrs. Allen on "the subject of muslins"). Nevertheless, until quite recently, critical discourse has on the whole accepted female epistolary skill as a truth universally acknowledged, and has subscribed to the fiction of the feminine, private letter.[11]

At the heart of this fiction is the notion of transparency, of both language and woman. Richardson's Pamela writes: "I have no reason to be afraid of being found insincere, or having, in any respect told you a falsehood: because, though I don't remember all I wrote, yet I know I wrote my heart, and that is not deceitful."[12] Clarissa, too, at least initially, believes in the transparency of the letter, seeing it as a type of written mimesis of the heart, a document that authenticates the self, and she is increasingly troubled by the "strange constructions"[13] put on her letters by others. Though readers from Fielding on have questioned such epistolary innocence, the dominant critical tradition equates letters and love, women's writing and the writing of the heart. Brockden Brown's epistolary heroine Jane Talbot confesses, with a textual self-consciousness that exposes the lineaments of the tradition, that "I have always found an unaccountable pleasure in dissecting, as it were, my heart; uncovering, one by one, its many folds, and laying it before you, as a country is shown on a map."[14] P. D. James supports her assertion of epistolary intimacy with reference to Dorothy Wordsworth's words to her brother William, in which we "see the beating of the inmost heart upon paper," and she gives the last word to Héloïse, for whom letters express "the transports of the heart."[15] In so doing, James takes her place with critics like Jean Rousset, who writes of the epistolary as the "literature of the cardiogramme"—that is, "the direct registering of the heart"—and like Janet Gurkin Altman, for whom the letter is "an apt instrument for transcribing the sudden switches and inconsistencies [of] a love-affair."[16]

However, since the early 1980s the critical concern with epistolary heart-strings has been subjected to scrutiny by commentators of various persuasions and has been considerably broadened. Critics have started to reflect on the letter as a cultural institution with multiple histories. Any account of these new histories must necessarily be partial (in both senses of the word), but it is useful to map significant trends and to position important works of epistolary criticism, always bearing in mind that what may seem at times like a linear narrative is more like an ongoing correspondence with a variety of overlapping critical voices. In 1982 two important books appeared on Richardson's *Clarissa* that emphasized the ideological resonances of epistolary writing: Terry Eagleton's *The Rape of Clarissa* and Terry Castle's *Clarissa's Ciphers*.[17] Eagleton demonstrates how sexuality and class inflect the power dynamics of any epistolary relationship, and argues that Richardson uses the epistolary form to challenge the dominance of the aristocracy: the novel is an agent of cultural revolution, for Clarissa dies to give birth to the middle class and the feminization of discourse that marked its consolidation of political power. Among the many wonderful insights of *Clarissa's Ciphers* is its crucial enlargement of the "fundamental correspondence" between the readers inside and outside the text. Showing how the novel thematizes interpretation, Castle argues that its "moral dimension" rests in the "self-examination" it compels in readers: *The History of a Young Lady* and the history of its interpretations expose nothing less than the politics of reading and of criticism. Castle advocates a feminist ethical reading that concerns itself with the "dynamics of oppression,"[18] and like Eagleton, she takes particular umbrage at William Warner's playful, politically uncommitted, deconstructive, and arguably misogynistic exegesis of the novel.[19]

Other histories of the letter emphasize the limitations of the traditional epistolary canon. The rarefied canon comprising *The Portuguese Letters*, the letters from Héloïse to Abélard, *The Life of Marianne, Pamela, Clarissa, The Sorrows of Young Werther, Julie; or, the New Eloise, Dangerous Liaisons,* and *Evelina* serves to equate the epistolary with the romantic/erotic and (in almost all instances) places a female figure at the center of a male-authored text.[20] The construction of female subjects by male pens produced very limited fictions of female authority and validated the plot of heterosexuality. Yet in Robert Adams Day's listing of English epistolary works prior to 1740, almost all the novels dominated by a female voice are written by women (or by "Anon").[21] It may have been precisely the success of such novels that contributed to the dominance, after 1750, of the public image of the epistolary novel as speaking in a private female voice. In other words, the commodification (if not fetishization) of this voice tells us much about eighteenth-century cultural anxieties about the place of women in the literary marketplace and taboos against women's writing, and more broadly, about women's public voice and their capacity to address a public readership. Susan Sniader Lanser convincingly proposes that "The eighteenth-century attraction to epistolarity through which the reader becomes the (privileged and permitted) voyeur may have as one of its agendas the restriction of oppositional voices to discourses privatized in both content and form and the simultaneous resexualization of the woman (and by implication the woman writer) as a secret to penetrate."[22]

Moreover, the established canon does not include novels written after 1790, and thus evades the revolutionary discourses ushered in with that decade. Nicola J. Watson's important book *Revolution and the Form of the British Novel, 1790–1825* examines "the fate of the letter" in British fiction after the French Revolution, particularly in the work of women writers.[23] Analyzing radical fictions by women including Helen Maria Williams, Mary Hays, and Mary Wollstonecraft in the 1790s, and then more conservative novels by the likes of Jane West, Maria Edgeworth, and Elizabeth Hamilton, before turning to the historical fictions of Sydney Owensen (Lady Morgan), Jane Porter, and Walter Scott, Watson tells the story of the gradual disciplining of first-person epistolary forms by third-person historical narrations attached to the patriarchal sphere of family and state. She argues that in the 1790s the plot of sensibility became confused with the plot of revolution, so that the sentimental novel, and especially the epistolary novel, paradigmatically represented by Rousseau's ambiguous plot of illicit passion in *Julie,* came to be seen as a marker of a dangerous, individual excess, a potentially revolutionary energy that had to be expelled or marginalized in the formation of a new national identity and political consensus. Significantly, like other epistolary critics, Watson also annotates an epistolary excess that cannot be contained by the rationalizing powers of the dominant culture, notably in her tracing of the "deformations" wrought on the sentimental letter in the extraordinary "cross-generic," and gender-bending, correspondence of Caroline Lamb and Lord Byron between 1812 and 1824, a correspondence rewritten and adulterated in

Lamb's novel *Glenarvon* and Byron's *Don Juan*.[24] In effect, their "literary duel" exposed the letter, and the body for which it was both substitute and supplement, to the exigencies of the amatory and commercial marketplace.

In addition to writing a new historical narrative of epistolarity, Watson provides a wealth of footnotes about little-known novels of the period, thus fueling the expansion of the traditional canon of epistolary fiction, an expansion made possible by the new editions that are crucial to real changes in epistolary studies. The University Press of Kentucky has established a series to republish eighteenth-century novels by women, and epistolary novels are well-represented in Broadview Press's eclectic list. Broadview has reissued Eliza Fenwick's novel *Secresy; or, The Ruin on the Rock* (1795) and Anne Plumptre's *Something New* (1801), the latter a text that challenges the female beauty myth and offers us that historically endangered species, a male epistolary subject.[25] Even as we write, these new editions are generating critical responses that push at the generic and cultural boundaries of epistolarity. Julia M. Wright, for example, reads Fenwick's *Secresy* in terms of its cross-Channel correspondence with Laclos's *Les Liaisons Dangereuses* and the "intergeneric" clashes that mark the parameters of cultural and generic disempowerment.[26]

A similar revival of interest in American epistolary texts has also taken place in recent years. Hannah Webster Foster's epistolary novel *The Coquette* (1797), with its subtle use of the letter form to explore the social constraints on female desire, has provoked many critical readings and two recent editions by major scholars, Cathy N. Davidson and Carla Mulford. It now has a prominent place in canonical fiction of the period and has helped to focus attention on other neglected epistolary works.[27] We have come to recognize, too, that many women in the late eighteenth and early nineteenth centuries, in both Britain and America, used literature and letters to create empowering friendships with other women, as one mode of resisting the isolation of domesticity. It is surely no coincidence that Jessy Oliver, one of the heroines of Susanna Rowson's 1798 novel *Reuben and Rachel; or, Tales of Olden Times* (not in itself an epistolary novel), escapes paternal oppression and sets herself up as a postmistress in a remote English village, where she is subsequently reunited with her old friend Rachel, after which they set off together for America—discursive emigration validating the sentimental plot (for Jessy subsequently marries her true love, Rachel's brother Reuben). As Christopher Castiglia argues, "That Jessy and Rachel reunite in a post office, the literal site of the circulation of letters, points to the central connection of reading and writing between women and the creation of female agency."[28] The significance of transatlantic modalities of epistolarity, especially during the late eighteenth century, is already proving a provocative area of critical investigation. Leonard Tennenhouse has shown that there was a specifically "American Richardson," that is, that the huge popularity of *Pamela* and *Clarissa* was founded upon texts that differed significantly from those published in England: specifically, abridged versions were published in the 1790s that crucially prioritized the seduction plot over letter writing. This research enables a revisionist perspective on letter fictions of the early republic, which no longer appear as pale Richardsonian imitations but as vigorous engagements with the colonial tradition in a new national context. In other words, if we abandon the attempt to read patrilineally, the expected prioritization of Richardson over Rowson, for example, is problematized, if not reversed.[29] Elizabeth Heckendorn Cook reads Crèvecoeur's *Letters from an American Farmer* (1782) as a text that "mourns the collapse" of the uneasy accord, or social contract, between public and private spheres, capitalism, and the nuclear family, which produced a "transnational ideal of a *literary* public sphere" during the eighteenth century. She demonstrates how the pressures of nationalism in revolutionary America ruptured "the Enlightenment ideal of a cosmopolitan civic exchange," an ideal whose various (re)constructions she traces in epistolary novels by Montesquieu, Richardson, and Riccoboni.[30]

The letter has gained a new lease on life both in and as theory, mapping the route of subjectivity for Jacques Lacan and encompassing all genres, indeed functioning as the paradigm of textuality (the dualism of correspondence enacting the duplicity of all language) for Jacques Derrida (though both Derrida and Lacan remain attached to the fiction of the letter's femininity). More recently, the concept of the "purloined letter" (derived from Poe's story), which functioned for Lacan as a parable of the primacy of the linguistic sign over the speaking subject, and for Derrida as a sign of the errancy of meaning and the intractability of the unconscious, has migrated into political and historical approaches.[31] Important epistolary critics have revised their engagements with correspondence to take account of the impact of New Historicism as well as the ways in which gender studies has reshaped feminist criticism's agenda in recent years. Linda S. Kauffman's early work focused on that powerful narrative of the letter engendered by Ovid's *Heroides,* in which women and letters give form to loss and pain. She "situate[s] critiques of mimesis within politics and history, delineating how discourses of desire have been disparaged or re-pressed by the structures of official thought from Ovid onward," but be-cause she attempts "to chart a typology of discourse," she is concerned with "the postal *agelessness* of intertwined motives and motifs in discours-es of desire."[32] In other words, she traces a desire that transcends history. Her later book *Special Delivery* satirizes the sentimentality on which amorous epistolary discourse depends and shows that, to quote (as she does) Atwood's (post)epistolary heroine Offred, "context is all" in the read-ing of epistolary texts. The meaning of desire is shaped by politics, eco-nomics, and commodity culture, and the epistolary mode—marked by dis-continuous narrative, self-referentiality, deconstruction of plot, character, and story, and defamiliarization of the distance between life and text—emerges as "a destabilized and destabilizing category in both twentieth-century fiction and theory."[33] Janet Gurkin Altman's illuminating struc-turalist analysis of epistolary fiction from the seventeenth to the twentieth centuries, *Epistolarity: Approaches to a Form,* in which she documents the most typical epistolary structures, such as mediation, confidence, and read-ing, has now been supplemented by her move toward a cultural history of correspondence. Altman prizes apart the chains that have linked women to love letters only, for her material on Catherine of Siena and Christine de Pizan shows that they helped to invent a lingua franca before the rise of the state. She also exposes the gap between the myth of letters as a fem-inine genre and the decline in the publication of women's correspondence (except love letters) between the sixteenth and eighteenth centuries in France, a period when, as she argues, "the consolidation of the absolutist sphere of public authority depended on mobilizing a relatively univocal army of visibly loyal male epistolarians."[34] She emphasizes the *public* face of letters, showing, for example, the alliance between officially sanctioned letter books and state leaders in France between the sixteenth and eigh-teenth centuries, and the ways in which the letter manual constructed pop-ular civic identity. Crucially, Altman examines a number of late-eighteenth-century French letter manuals, which printed women's letters alongside men's, and which reinforced a vision of the public sphere as inclusive of both sexes and dependent on their interaction as private individuals. As she puts it, "Women's letters were printed alongside men's as examples of verbal art cultivated and circulated in private, but which ultimately served to record, conduct, and criticize the state."[35]

Altman's work is part of a significant body of criticism that has been produced in recent years on French epistolary literature.[36] Though most of the material examined in this introduction, and in the essays that follow, is Anglo-American, and we do not have the space (nor the expertise) to examine in detail the cultural, textual, and theoretical specificities of French epistolary writings, we should note here some important work in this field, especially that which takes up the issue of cross-Channel correspondences. Elizabeth J. MacArthur's *Extravagant Narratives* shows how letters played a crucial role in seventeenth-century France in a codified system of social relations; she finds the seeds of the epistolary novel in epistolary manuals, and in a detailed reading of (primarily) the woman's letters in the Du Deffand/Walpole correspondence, she traces an extravagant multiplicity of relational models.[37] MacArthur usefully historicizes issues of narratology, embedding her discussion of the nonclosural dynamics of the epistolary form in the specific context of seventeenth- and eighteenth-century French culture. Like Nicola J. Watson, Elizabeth Heckendorn Cook rewrites the traditional critical narrative of the death of the sentimental letter at the reactionary end of the eighteenth century, but she does so by showing how the letter was always already political, and crucially transnational—she moves from Montesquieu to Richardson to Riccoboni to Crèvecoeur. She argues that "the categories of public and private work as an interlocking cultural system" (thus, "'scientific' epistolary treatises employ the tropes of subjectivity refined in the sentimental epistolary novel"), and that we need therefore to read the epistolary contract, which notionally regulates private, affective relations, as analogous to, and complicit with, the technologies of capitalism.[38] The texts she analyzes construct the citizens of the Republic of Letters. April Alliston works within a feminocentric frame, but similarly advocates a comparative approach to eighteenth-century women's writing. She shows the "secret correspondences" between French and British women writers, notably Lafayette, Boisgiron, Sophia Lee, and Staël, whose novels need to be "read across . . . the borderlines of national traditions." As Alliston points out,

"That eighteenth-century women novelists in England and France read each other at least as much as they read Richardson and Marivaux and Rousseau is indicated in part by the surprisingly large number of those who supplemented their literary earnings by translating each other's works, or who spent time on the other side of the Channel." Cross-Channel reading enables us to see how these writers resisted the patrilineal transmission of values within a national context, valuing instead maternal relations and developing protective paradigms of "female homosociality."[39]

∽

The work of critics like Altman, Alliston, Watson, MacArthur, and Heckendorn Cook confirms that the major contemporary trend in epistolary studies is away from thematic and structuralist criticism and toward meticulous cultural historicization: the epistolary generic contract is always revised in the light of changing historical contexts. Perhaps no critic has done more than Mary Favret, however, to historicize the letter in literature, and her work deserves to be considered in some detail here. Favret's *Romantic Correspondence* argues, as we have already noted, that literary notions of the letter as genre are based on analyses of a select group of epistolary novels, those that promote our understanding of the epistolary as personal, feminine, and preoccupied with interiority. She points out that the century which engendered *Clarissa* and *Julie* also produced Edmund Burke's epistolary political tract *Reflections on the Revolution in France* (1790) and the eloquent materiality of the letter in David's painting *Marat Assassiné*. Moreover, even if we stick to the terrain of fiction, "Any innocence attributed to the letter in literature is achieved only after a more worldly history has been erased"—a history that encompasses Aphra Behn's epistolary tale of incest and politics, *Love Letters from a Young Nobleman to His Sister* (1684–87), the generic wanderings of Smollett's *Humphrey Clinker* (1771), and all the "epistolary fictions dealing with court intrigue, international spying, social and political critique" that dominated the novel market when *Pamela* was published.[40] The enormously successful eight-volume *Letters Writ by a Turkish Spy*, for example, appeared in English translation between 1687 and 1694 and was avidly consumed by the British reading public during the first half of the eighteenth century, as evidenced by the many reprints, pirated editions, and imitations.[41] Favret provides illuminating readings of a range of texts outside the traditional epistolary canon to deessentialize the "personal" nature of the letter and show its disruptive potential: thus, both Helen Maria Williams's *Letters from France* and Mary Wollstonecraft's *Letters Written during a Short Residence in Sweden, Norway and Denmark* translate "the familiar letter into a public critique."[42] In the first case, Williams employs sentimental discourse as a political strategy to write (and make) history, and since her eight-volume collection includes letters of unidentifiable authorship, the confining envelope of authorial identity is unsealed. In the second case, Favret rightly avoids the biographical thrust of much Wollstonecraft criticism and directs our attention to how the published letters significantly revise Wollstonecraft's correspondence with her lover, Gilbert Imlay, so that the writer is less an erotic victim in the sentimental tradition than an agent of social criticism.[43] Favret's examination of Austen's letters, especially their materiality as objects of scrutiny and as signs of the social in her novels, shows how they function to confirm the importance of community, a theme of connection that she pursues in her analysis of *Frankenstein*. It is clear that the epistolary as a published mode enabled a range of female voices other than the intimate.

Favret's individual analyses gain significance within a specific interpretative framework, and the history she tells has far-reaching consequences for our readings of epistolarity: like Watson, she adopts a macropolitical approach, reading questions of genre and gender through the question of the formation of British national identity in the wake of the French Revolution. Favret shows how the "looseness" that made the familiar letter available to women writers in the eighteenth century, and that helped it cross class bridges in an increasingly literate society, also led it into the political realm: such promiscuity tainted its image, and this suggests one reason for the dwindling of epistolary fiction. Favret provides a convincing narrative of how the *public* face of the letter changed in the 1790s, when it was either castigated as the agent of conspiracy or celebrated for its democratic ability to transcend social barriers.[44] She gives details of the networks of radical correspondence such as the Revolution Society and the London Corresponding Society, which were dedicated to political reform and to friendship through correspondence, and which gave primarily working-class men a new sense of nationhood (and which forged connections with France); she documents the reactionary moves by which a hermeneutics of suspicion dominated the reading of correspondences, especially during the war with France. Thus John Hurford Stone's comments on millinery and fashion, in his correspondence intercepted in 1798, were thought to conceal treasonous double meanings.[45] The infamous "Gagging Acts" of 1794–95 effectively "produced a fiction of subversive, collective correspondence that, like the societies themselves, rewrote the letter's claim to privacy and to individuality."[46] The multiple, often contradictory, resonances of the letter in this period help us to understand why it continued to appeal to women writers from both ends of the political spectrum, being the form chosen for Mary Hays's *Letters and Essays, Moral and Miscellaneous* (1793) and Mary Robinson's impassioned *Letter to the Women of England on the Injustice of Subordination* (1799), as well as Laetitia Matilda Hawkins's *Letters on the Female Mind* (1793), a conservative response to Helen Maria Williams that placed politics completely out of bounds for respectable women; while Catherine Macaulay's enlightened *Letters on Education* deployed the epistolary form in order to create a dialogue between two women on a number of educational topics, from advice on primary child care to discussions about the social effects of education.[47] Importantly, letter texts enabled an informal register that suited polemical writers who wished to reach as wide an audience as possible.

As Favret points out, it was precisely the government intervention in personal correspondence that facilitated the development of the modern Post Office, which coordinated a system of national communication and surveillance. If the post-1800 development of postal bureaucracy was marked by an eruption of threatening letters from working-class protestors (such as the "Captain Swing" letters of the 1830s and 1840s), it nevertheless organized "a national fiction of correspondence" that erased "the story of traitorous correspondence and partisan activity" and delegitimated unregulated correspondence.[48] The penny post, introduced in 1839, transformed "the postal service into an ideological vehicle of 'progress' for both political economy and national education": it institutionalized the affective links between families, often dispersed for reasons of employment; its accessibility fostered the desire for literacy; and the postal service coordinated communication and commercial transactions.[49] Emphasizing the institutional network within which correspondence takes place, Favret shows how the image of the British Post Office in the early nineteenth century comes to envelop the discourse of the letter.

It should be noted that Favret's emphasis on the institutionalization of the epistolary is not incompatible with the concern with absence and with the body that preoccupied earlier epistolary critics, but it sends us a materialist account of these issues. Indeed, in another article Mary Favret argues that it was preeminently epistolary discourse that brought home the Napoleonic Wars to the British public and simultaneously shaped the experience of war for those engaged on foreign fronts. She demonstrates that, on the one hand, the mere fact of war correspondence kept the war at a distance, deferring its violence while appealing to domestic and national bonds; and, on the other hand, that war correspondence behaved according to the rules of traditional epistolary romance, translating the experience of global warfare into an interiorized and psychologized event that invaded the mind (and body) of the English subject.[50]

While recent epistolary critics have turned to new areas of concern, such as technology, cybernetics, and violence (see Linda S. Kauffman's essay in this volume), and while political and historical approaches to the letter are dominant, there remain significant absences within epistolary studies. Criticism on epistolary writing does not seem to have come to grips with those issues of race and postcolonialism that have preoccupied, and continue to preoccupy, broad sections of the academic community; regrettably, the power dynamics of colonization remain on the margins of the present book, and though American epistolary writing is well-represented, there is little discussion of the work of Hispanic or black Americans. Little attention has been paid in epistolary studies to the function of the postal service as one of the technologies of empire, which coordinated channels of communication and fostered Britain's imperial interests.[51] Perversely (or even predictably), it is an epistolary novel, written at the historical border between First and Second Empires, as increasing colonial expansion was matched by domestic class conflict, that offers one of the most trenchant early critiques of imperialism and makes the connection between different dynamics of oppression: the abject, amorphous identity of the creature in Mary Shelley's *Frankenstein* (1818) is made up from the bits and pieces of Britain's anxieties about otherness,[52] and the novel demonstrates the complicities between "hierarchies of race and class, ideologies of empire, and gender oppositions."[53] Consigning himself to a funeral pyre after the death of his creator, the creature imitates an Indian widow committing *sati,* an act much debated by colonial rulers during the early nineteenth century. In *Frankenstein,* the colonial subaltern is silenced in an act of self-destruction. In Alice Walker's *The Color Purple* (1982), the subaltern speaks back in an epistolary text that revises its own generic heritage as well as literary history.

As Linda S. Kauffman notes, *The Color Purple* "is the first known epistolary novel by an African-American, male or female."[54] Though Celie writes letters to God, they are nevertheless part of the mainstream epistolary tradition of a pathetic heroine (like Clarissa or Héloïse) writing to an absent addressee; also, like earlier epistolary texts, the novel documents the commodification of the female body in patriarchal society. But race makes all the difference to this narrative—indeed, perhaps the novel's most affirmative action is Celie's conversion from thinking of God as a white patriarch to finding divinity in the details of nature. Walker thus both invokes and subverts the type of slave narrative that depends on religious transformation. Moreover, other dominant features of slave narratives appear in Celie's letters (sexual and physical assaults, the abduction of children, hard labor), while "Nettie's letters to Celie memorialize" the slave narrative's focus on escape, freedom, and "moral uplift."[55] Ultimately, Walker creates a generic hybrid whose blending of the epistolary genre with the slave narrative radically revises literary history (by destabilizing the bourgeois credentials of the "rise of the novel," which was bound up with the rise of epistolarity). In other words, in showing that black women remain enslaved by their gender, she adds race to the history of a gendered genre, and gender to (slave) narratives of race.[56] Recording the rhythms of Negro spirituals and scraps of Stevie Wonder's songs, paying specific tribute to Zora Neale Hurston and in general honoring an oral tradition, the novel is a love letter to African American literary history. Future epistolary studies will need to attend to the cross-Channel and transatlantic correspondences mapped by Alliston and Cook, *and* to the issues of race and the mechanics of colonization so memorably explored by Walker (as well as in some critical readings of her work).[57]

The emphasis on cultural-historical readings of epistolary texts marks the essays that comprise this volume. Before discussing how individual essays contribute to this trend, a few preliminary comments on the organization of the book are in order. Because letters are crucially part of a dialogue, each responding to a missive received and directing itself to an absent addressee, a letter is always, in Bakhtin's terms, "half someone else's."[58] There are always (at least) two sides to any correspondence, two subjectivities telling and reading potentially different stories, two voices testifying differently in an "event of utterance" through which self and other define and redefine each other. Indeed, the situation is even more complicated, for, as Gerald MacLean argues in this collection, the public nature of epistolary writing should also alert us to traces of the third-person reader outside the traditional epistolary dyad. We have tried to emphasize the dialogic quality of the letter in the form of the collection itself, and thus the book is arranged so that contributors respond to each other's essays in a type of dialogic "postscript." We have adopted this format to avoid a sense of closure, to resist the notion that any one critical position represents the last word on epistolary texts, and to demonstrate that correspondence promotes dissonance and difference as well as connection and community. Indeed, the structure of critical correspondence is both intellectually productive and disruptive, often unsettling our notions of academic invisibility. The responses demonstrate the essential imbrication of the epistolary with both public and private discourses, for each is a personal and partial response that nevertheless enters, and is informed by, an ongoing cultural correspondence, a correspondence to which the readers of this collection will no doubt add their own critical comments.

As we have noted earlier, recent epistolary studies have significantly broadened the feminocentric focus of the letter, revising the critical fiction that equates epistolary discourse with the epistolary heroine and that keeps both firmly in the private sphere. The essays in part 1 return to the issue of women and letters, not in any essentialist way but as part of a materialist account of letters as a liminal form on the border between public and private spheres. Nancy Armstrong's essay shows how the cultural and historical codes at work in Richardson's epistolary novel *Clarissa* bring particular constructions of gender, class, and ethnicity to bear upon our understanding of letter writing. She argues that Richardson, while substituting the logic of class for that of race, adopts the structural tenet of American captivity narratives, whereby through reproducing her thoughts in writing, the captive woman construed her body as "the envelope of an individuated consciousness which could be understood as the unique source and ultimate referent of writing." This valorization of literacy and recoding of the female body has all sorts of implications for the organization of domestic economy, not least in that cultural capital and fiscal responsibility are tied to a set of ideals about conduct. Armstrong suggests that we might use *Clarissa* as a vehicle for understanding the middle class as an emergent culture, and that it is in her radical disembodiment that Clarissa so perfectly represents the new, imagined community of the English middle class.

Donna Landry reminds us of the distance over which the familiar letter traveled in the eighteenth century, examining the epistolary travel accounts of Lady Mary Wortley Montagu and Elizabeth, Lady Craven, and in so doing noting the "potentially nomadic relation" encoded by the materiality of the letter. Montagu writes as one who has fallen in love with the sensuousness of Turkish material culture, and through her descriptions she aims to make her epistolary audience back home associate her with this culture of aesthetic delight. Craven, "loving to correct Montagu's views and thus legitimate her own," writes to her married lover, the Margrave of Anspach. Landry argues that Montagu writes to attain the love and admiration of her friends, Craven of her lover, but both also make the private public and solicit the admiration of a wider audience through publication. Both must negotiate with the writings of their predecessors, which Landry calls "the irritation of influence." They wish to be remembered as clever travelers in an exotic landscape, and by association as women of beauty. Both Montagu and Craven articulate their epistolary skill as feminine desirability, in ways that reveal the traces of a historically specific cultural imperialism.

In the final essay in this section, Clare Brant analyzes especially eighteenth-century readings of the letters of Mary Queen of Scots and argues that epistolary history should include the history of readers as well as writers. Through a meticulous examination of eighteenth-century vindications and villifications of Mary Queen of Scots, in which she functions like a character in a novel (a seduced, romantic, or reeducable heroine), Brant exposes ideologically motivated readings of the Queen's letters, in particular the notorious "Casket Letters." Epistolary history is seen to be gendered: thus, homosocial history (by Carte, Goodall, Tytler, Stuart, and Whitaker) is compared with female sympathy (notably on the part of Eliza Haywood), and women's interest in Mary Queen of Scots's strength is balanced against masculine interest in common political causes (pro-Stuart) or romantic projections in which monarchy was linked to passive femininity.

Part 2 continues the discussion of the gender implications of epistolary epistemology: Martha Nell Smith explores the relationship between two women, and Richard Hardack is concerned with the homosocial bonds between men. But part 2 also asks us to consider epistolary borders and boundaries of various other sorts: the boundary between the fictional and the real, between letter writer and letter reader, between bodies and texts, manuscripts and print. The essays show how the epistolary genre can destabilize and defamiliarize such distinctions, while the individual analyses demonstrate the correspondence between the formal and the ideological in the letter-writing culture(s) of mid-nineteenth-century America.[59] Martha Nell Smith's essay takes the critical suppression of the highly productive literary liaison between Emily and Susan Dickinson, which has been ignored in comparison with Dickinson's relation with male mentors, as a starting point to interrogate what difference its recovery makes not only for reading Dickinson's poetic project but also for critical-theoretical understandings of literary history. Smith argues that study of the reciprocal relationship of these two writers, one of whom became a literary celebrity, reveals much about the ways in which theoretical inventions of the twentieth century, particularly those postulating spheres of "public" and "private" that are driven by the machine of the "Book," have inhibited understandings of the histories of literary production, reproduction, and exchange. She demonstrates how deeply embedded both of their writing practices are within nineteenth-century cultural exchanges of the love letter, of manuscript volumes of favorite poems, and of scrapbooks. Twentieth-century literary history tends to have amnesia about these hand-fashioned modes of literary exchange: it has remade Emily's writings to fit the contours and categories of the printed book, while Susan's projected volume would have given readers a much stronger sense of the manuscript culture in which Emily Dickinson's poetic project was rooted. Thinking about the epistolary context in which Emily Dickinson circulated and "published" her poems significantly historicizes our understanding of her work.

Richard Hardack's essay goes beyond the traditional critical view of nonfictional letters as merely supplementary to the novels or poems of the author in question, their own textuality erased in their deployment as interpretative props. Through a series of meticulous close readings, Hardack shows how, in Melville's letters, Hawthorne serves as a nexus for Melville's formulation of the boundaries of his own work and body. Hardack documents an ontology of intertextuality that is entwined with a homosocial (at times, homoerotic) bonding between men, derived from Melville's transcendental pantheism. The Melvillean model of male fraternity and textual interdependence subverts male self-reliance and textual closure. The intertextuality of letters and bodies functions as "a 'feminine' cure for the extremity of male individualism during the American Renaissance." However, while in Melville's novels male bodies must be dismembered to correspond, women's bodies are endlessly permeable, and it is this aspect of femininity that Melville appropriates: in his reading of *Pierre,* Hardack proposes that "letter writing dramatizes Melville's longing for a kind of male parthenogenesis," whereby epistolary intertextuality represents male reproduction.

Part 3, "New Epistolary Directions," focuses on the ways in which the epistolary genre may help us to think through those questions of critical address that have preoccupied theorists, especially feminist theorists, in recent years. Anne Bower proposes that the epistolary form can provide an alternative to the authoritative and often adversarial discourses of the critical article. Exploring letter texts by Virginia Woolf, Fay Weldon, Jacques Derrida, Gerald MacLean, Gloria Anzaldúa, and Robert Stepto, Bower argues that the use of the letter form within an academic article or paper replaces the impersonal with the interpersonal; it can offer the scholar opportunities for new levels of intimacy and engagement in critical writing. While acknowledging that this form can be misread, mislaid, or manipulated, Bower shows how the epistolary form questions the basis of critical authority and encourages entry to a greater range of voices, thus promoting the sense of community that has been valorized by much feminist criticism. Other critics might wish to construe such epistolary inclusiveness as democratic in spirit, that is, as an impulse that not only animates feminist thinking but that enlarges the academic community in general.

Gerald MacLean's analysis of epistolary evidence from two historical sites—central Anatolia from the Neolithic to Hittite eras, and England during the revolutionary decade of the 1640s—provides him a historical ground from which to engage with questions of the personal and the political as they are figured in current (feminist) work appearing under the rubric of personal criticism. The Anatolian material provides evidence of a link between correspondence and commerce, of the desire to signify ownership of mobile property and to inscribe self-identity. The political letters from site 2 extend and complicate these paradigms, especially in the case of the epistolary ventriloquizing of the intercepted, published letter that permitted the writer to expose insider knowledge from the enemy camp in a time of war, and was crucially a public mode of address in the guise of personal communication. MacLean reads the raiding of the king's cabinet and the publication of Charles's letters on matters of state, many of them directed to the queen, Henrietta Maria, as emblematic of the epistolary reconstruction of "categories of the personal and the private . . . into public and political terms by means of which war could be conceived and conducted." All letters, then, as Nancy Armstrong puts it in her response to MacLean, turn out to be "purloined letters" bearing the trace of a potential third reader outside the immediate epistolary interchange.

In her essay, "Not a Love Story: Retrospective and Prospective Epistolary Directions," Linda S. Kauffman revises her earlier thinking about epistolary discourse and desire, annotating the rage of the Portuguese nun, for example, that she had previously seen only as unrequited love. She thus charts a shift from perceiving women as epistolary victims to epistolary agents. She argues that if women have been enslaved by the ideology of romantic love, they may have the most to gain by endorsing an "anti-aesthetic," such as pornography, that defies it. Kauffman discusses the postmodern novelist Kathy Acker, who has seized letter fiction for antiromantic purposes, and she shows how Acker's signifying strategies resonate subversively within the climate of right-wing, repressive legislation in the United States, particularly on issues of sexuality. In exploring the sadomasochism of everyday life, Acker exposes the obscenity of power, redirecting the rage of the Portuguese nun at global politics, not just failed romance. Kauffman then takes a provocative glance at the migration of epistolary discourses into new forms in the "Post-Age," including Ken Burns's television series based on war correspondences, personal ads, fan mail, literary criticism, and phone sex, and in so doing she asks us to question epistolarity's traditional boundaries of genre, gender, and transmission. Finally, Kauffman looks to a new discursive realm from which the relics of the epistolary artifact have disappeared but which retains the traces of epistolary address: her subject is the performance artist Orlan, who is turning her face into a composite of the icons of Western femininity through plastic surgery, and whose interactive "performances" are viewed globally via satellite. As Kauffman points out, Orlan's scene of writing raises crucial questions about the construction of identity for theorists of epistolarity. The impact of computer technology and telecommunications moves us into the epoch of the "posthuman," an arena colonized by feminist artists for its antiromantic potential: Kauffman's "epistolary innovators" reveal the contours of the "environment that already invisibly envelops us."

ᴄᴡ

We have grouped the essays in this collection under certain headings in order to facilitate a focus on a number of crucial epistolary topics: women, cultural and generic borders, and new critical directions (though, of course, there are many overlaps between the sections). The volume is loosely chronological, moving from eighteenth-century British writing, through nineteenth-century American, to twentieth-century epistolary theories (as well as back to ancient history and the seventeenth century). It is possible to chart some broad historical shifts in epistolary writing: tracing the increasing politicization and institutionalization of the letter in the eighteenth and nineteenth centuries, we see how letters became attached to different forms of cultural capital at different historical moments, to the emergent imperialist middle class in eighteenth-century England, to the mechanics of popular culture in mid-nineteenth-century America, and to the currency of academic writing and new technologies in our late-twentieth-century global village.[60] But we see also how difficult it is to map epistolary history, not only because new historical contexts are constantly being opened for us that reinflect our readings of earlier texts but also perhaps because the very materiality of the letter, its imbrication in multiple cultural practices, its potentially nomadic trajectory, makes it a form resistant to the construction of grand narratives. Epistolary history is not, we think, a teleological, linear history but rather a narrative of historically specific cultural connections and disconnections. We hope the reader will pursue correspondences within and between the sections, following, for example, the fate of the love letter through the essays by Landry, Brant, Moore, and Kauffman, or the relations between epistolarity, monarchy, and feminized privacy explored by MacLean and Brant. What emerges from the essays in this collection is an account of epistolary *revisions*, so that we see, for example, how certain contemporary figures, notably Acker and Orlan, seize the power of horror to attack the vestiges of eighteenth-century romantic ideologies, revising together technologies of the epistolary and of the body. Most of all, the contributors show how the letter puts pressure on the distinctions between public and private, and the range of ideological practices this distinction upholds at different historical-geographical points. Indeed, they challenge us to rethink the boundaries of epistolarity.

Notes

1. Mary A. Favret, *Romantic Correspondence: Women, Politics and the Fiction of Letters* (Cambridge: Cambridge Univ. Press, 1993), 56.

2. P. D. James, foreword to *Eight Hundred Years of Women's Letters,* ed. Olga Kenyon (Harmondsworth: Penguin, 1992), viii.

3. One wonders if *Eight Hundred Years of* Men's *Letters* would have the same marketable resonances as Kenyon's book; Elizabeth Goldsmith, ed., *Writing the Female Voice: Essays on Epistolary Literature* (Boston: Northeastern Univ. Press, 1989).

4. In fact, Kenyon's anthology, with its wealth of fascinating material on war and travel, work and politics, as well as the more traditional subjects of love, friendship, and domestic life, lends itself to multiple histories of the letter; the framing material, however, especially James's foreword, pulls these disparate threads into a more homogeneous account (it is notable, for example, that James's comment, quoted above, is reproduced on the dust jacket).

5. The following provide much more detailed and nuanced discussions of the association between women and the epistolary novel in the eighteenth century, with reference to both British and French texts, than is possible here: Janet Gurkin Altman, *Epistolarity: Approaches to a Form* (Columbus: Ohio State Univ. Press, 1982); Nancy Armstrong, *Desire and Domestic Fiction: A Political History of the Novel* (New York: Oxford Univ. Press, 1987); Robert Adams Day, *Told in Letters: Epistolary Fiction before Richardson* (Ann Arbor: Univ. of Michigan Press, 1966); Peggy Kamuf, *Fictions of Feminine Desire: The Disclosures of Heloise* (Lincoln: Univ. of Nebraska Press, 1987); Linda S. Kauffman, *Discourses of Desire: Gender, Genre, and Epistolary Fictions* (Ithaca: Cornell Univ. Press, 1986); Ruth Perry, *Women, Letters, and the Novel* (New York: AMS Press, 1980).

6. Kamuf, *Fictions of Feminine Desire,* ix.

7. For example, while some of the 173 letters that comprise Samuel Richardson's *Familiar Letters on Important Occasions* (1741) are concerned with female conduct, and almost half of the letters deal with love and marriage, the range also includes model letters of condolence, business letters about the collection of rents, and letters detailing the duties of apprentices. The addressees include sons—one is warned against excessive drinking (letter 36)—as well as daughters—one is advised (like Pamela) not to talk back to her husband even is he is in the wrong (letter 146)—and miscellaneous family members and friends, with a special emphasis on the conduct required of upwardly mobile young men (*Familiar Letters on Important Occasions,* ed. Brian W. Downs [New York: Routledge, 1928]).

8. An extract from Wilkes is available in Vivien Jones, ed., *Women in the Eighteenth Century: Constructions of Femininity* (New York: Routledge, 1990); Hester Mulso Chapone, *Letters on the*

Improvement of the Mind (1773) [along with Dr. Gregory, *A Father's Legacy to His Daughters* (1774), and Lady Pennington, *A Mother's Advice to Her Absent Daughters* (1761)] (London, 1816); Dr. John Gregory, *A Father's Legacy to His Daughters*, in *The Young Lady's Pocket Library; or, Parental Monitor* (1790), rpt. with a new introduction by Vivien Jones (Bristol: Thoemmes Press, 1995).

9. Moreover, as Elizabeth Heckendorn Cook points out, there was "no consistent distinction between 'real' and 'fictional' letters" in the eighteenth century; as well as "the epistolary novel per se," Cook lists "poetical epistles, letters on botany, and monthly newsletters on literature, fashion, and business conditions . . . travel letters, letter-writing manuals . . . editions of the letters of classical authors and of a few modern political and literary figures" (*Epistolary Bodies: Gender and Genre in the Eighteenth-Century Republic of Letters* [Stanford: Stanford Univ. Press, 1996], 17).

10. Jane Austen, *Northanger Abbey*, ed. Anne Henry Ehrenpreis (1818; rpt. Harmondsworth: Penguin, 1972), 49. April Alliston, in *Virtue's Faults: Correspondences in Eighteenth-Century British and French Women's Fiction* (Stanford: Stanford Univ. Press, 1996), also reads this episode, and another famous passage on letters in *Mansfield Park*, in terms of Austen's "critique of conventional gender codes" (233).

11. For example, Henry Tilney's assertion about female letter writing, quoted above, is cited without contextualizing detail in the foreward to Kenyon's anthology (*Eight Hundred Years of Women's Letters*); thus are the complexities of Austen's episode occluded in the service of particular narrative about femininity and epistolarity.

12. Samuel Richardson, *Pamela; or, Virtue Rewarded*, ed. M. Kinkead-Weekes, 2 vols. (London: Dent), 1:203.

13. Samuel Richardson, *Clarissa; or, The History of a Young Lady*, introduction by John Butt, 4 vols. (London: Dent), 1:311 (letter 61).

14. Charles Brockden Brown, *Jane Talbot* [with *Clara Howard*], ed. Sidney J. Krause et al. (1801; rpt. Kent OH: Kent State Univ. Press, 1986), 255.

15. James, foreword to *Eight Hundred Years of Women's Letters*, viii.

16. Jean Rousset, qtd. in Favret, *Romantic Correspondence*, 57 and 228 n. 12); Altman, *Epistolarity*, 179.

17. Terry Eagleton, *The Rape of Clarissa: Writing, Sexuality and Class Struggle in Samuel Richardson* (Minneapolis: Univ. of Minnesota Press, 1982); Terry Castle, *Clarissa's Ciphers: Meaning and Disruption in Richardson's "Clarissa"* (Ithaca: Cornell Univ. Press, 1982).

18. Castle, *Clarissa's Ciphers*, 16, 29, 196.

19. See William Warner, *Reading Clarissa: The Struggles of Interpretation* (New Haven: Yale Univ. Press, 1979).

20. This is the list provided in Favret, *Romantic Correspondence*, 34.

21. Robert Adams Day, *Told in Letters: Epistolary Fiction Before Richardson* (Ann Arbor: Univ. of Michigan Press, 1966), appendix A.

22. Susan Sniader Lanser, *Fictions of Authority: Women Writers and Narrative Voice* (Ithaca: Cornell Univ. Press, 1992), 33.

23. Nicola J. Watson, *Revolution and the Form of the British Novel, 1790–1825: Intercepted Letters, Interrupted Seductions* (Oxford: Clarendon Press, 1994), 3.

24. Ibid., 177.

25. Eliza Fenwick, *Secresy; or, The Ruin on the Rock*, ed. Isobel Grundy (Peterborough: Broadview Press, 1994); Anne Plumptre, *Something New; or, Adventures at Campbell-House*, ed.

Deborah McLeod (Peterborough: Broadview Press, 1996); as we made final revisions to our manuscript, another epistolary novel appeared from this press: Elizabeth Hamilton, *Translations of the Letters of a Hindoo Rajah* (1796), ed. Pamela Perkins and Shannon Russell (Peterborough: Broadview Press, 1999).

26. Julia M. Wright, "'I Am Ill Fitted': Conflicts of Genre in Eliza Fenwick's *Secresy*," in *Romanticism, History, and the Possibilities of Genre*, ed. Tilottama Rajan and Julia M. Wright (Cambridge: Cambridge Univ. Press, 1998), 149–75.

27. Hannah Webster Foster, *The Coquette*, ed. Cathy N. Davidson (New York: Oxford Univ. Press, 1986); *"The Power of Sympathy" by William Hill Brown, and "The Coquette" by Hannah Webster Foster*, ed. Carla Mulford (New York: Penguin, 1996). There is much recent work on epistolary fiction in early American literature, especially *The Coquette*; for useful surveys, see Cathy N. Davidson, *Revolution and the Word: The Rise of the Novel in America* (New York: Oxford Univ. Press, 1986), and W. M. Verhoeven, "'Persuasive Rhetorick': Representation and Resistance in Early American Epistolary Fiction," in *Making America/Making American Literature: Franklin to Cooper*, ed. A. Robert Lee and W. M. Verhoeven (Atlanta GA: Rodopi, 1996), 123–64.

28. Christopher Castiglia, *Bound and Determined: Captivity, Culture-Crossing, and White Womanhood from Mary Rowlandson to Patty Hearst* (Chicago: Univ. of Chicago Press, 1996).

29. See Leonard Tennenhouse, "The American Richardson: Writing the English Diaspora" (paper presented at the "Revolutions and Watersheds" conference, University of Groningen, May 1997); we are indebted to the author for allowing us to read this work in manuscript.

30. Heckendorn Cook, *Epistolary Bodies*, 7, 11, 29.

31. See Jacques Lacan, "Seminar XX," chap. 6 in *Feminine Sexuality*, ed. Juliet Mitchell and Jacqueline Rose (Basingstoke: Macmillan, 1982), and "Seminar on 'The Purloined Letter,'" in *Contemporary Literary Criticism*, ed. Robert Con Davis and Ronald Schleifer (New York: Longman, 1989), 301–20; Jacques Derrida, *The Post Card: From Socrates to Freud and Beyond*, trans. and intro. Alan Bass (Chicago: Univ. of Chicago Press, 1980), esp. 48. Critical interventions in "the purloined letter" debate include Barbara Johnson, "The Frame of Reference: Poe, Lacan, Derrida," and Jerry Aline Flieger, "The Purloined Punchline: Joke as Textual Paradigm," in *Contemporary Literary Criticism*, 322–50, 351–68. Recent theories continue to reproduce, in however deconstructed a way, an erotics of epistolarity that elides the letter and the female body, as in Derrida's term "invagination." See, too, Luce Irigaray's use of letter imagery in her reference to the "enveloped and enveloping body" in "Sexual Difference," in *French Feminist Thought: A Reader*, trans. and ed. Toril Moi (New York: Blackwell, 1987), 155. Linda S. Kauffman surveys "Feminist Critiques of Barthes and Derrida," in *Special Delivery: Epistolary Modes in Modern Fiction* (Chicago: Univ. of Chicago Press, 1992), 119–30.

32. Kauffman, *Discourses of Desire*, 22, 314, 315 (emphasis added).

33. Kauffman, *Special Delivery*, xxi, 263.

34. Janet Gurkin Altman, "Women's Letters in the Public Sphere," in *Going Public: Women and Publishing in Early Modern France*, ed. Elizabeth C. Goldsmith and Dena Goodman (Ithaca: Cornell Univ. Press, 1995), 99–115 (quotation on 105). On the publication of real correspondences, see Altman, "The Letter Book as a Literary Institution 1539–1789: Towards a Cultural History of Published Correspondences in France," *Yale French Studies* 71 (1986): 17–62, and for letter manuals, see Altman, "Teaching the 'People' to Write: The Formation of a Popular Civic Identity in the French Letter Manual," *Studies in Eighteenth-Century Culture* 22 (1992): 147–80.

35. Altman, "Women's Letters," 114. Michael Warner is similarly concerned with writing and the public sphere in America, but his book is not concerned with epistolarity per se (though he occasionally writes of "real" letters), rather with the ways in which new technologies of print transformed the relations between people and power and mobilized the republican structure of government (Michael Warner, *The Letters of the Republic: Publication and the Public Sphere in Eighteenth-Century America* [Cambridge MA: Harvard Univ. Press, 1990]).

36. See, for example, Katharine Ann Jensen, *Writing Love: Letters, Women, and the Novel in France, 1605–1776* (Carbondale: Southern Illinois Univ. Press, 1995).

37. Elizabeth J. MacArthur, *Extravagant Narratives: Closure and Dynamics in the Epistolary Form* (Princeton: Princeton Univ. Press, 1990), 33–34.

38. Heckendorn Cook, *Epistolary Bodies,* 45–46.

39. Alliston, *Virtue's Faults,* 1, 4, 19, 23. On Anglo-French epistolarity, see also Lanser's *Fictions of Authority,* which places epistolary discourse alongside other narrative forms, and analyzes texts from France, Britain, and the U.S. from the 1740s to the present day, and Watson's *Revolution and the Form of the British Novel,* which traces the long shadow cast by Rousseau's *Julie* over British sentimental, feminocentric fiction in the latter part of the eighteenth century (chap. 1 is entitled "Julie Among the Jacobins").

40. Favret, *Romantic Correspondence,* 34, 35.

41. Robert Adams Day discusses this text and other examples of epistolary espionage in a chapter that assesses "The Importance of Translations" in the letter's literary history (*Told in Letters,* esp. 40–42).

42. Favret, *Romantic Correspondence,* 96.

43. In this context, see Heckendorn Cook's comment on Riccoboni's resistance to "the exploitational logic of the sentimental epistolary tradition": "After being abandoned by her lover, Fanni [in *Fanni Butlerd*] transforms herself from private victim to public author by publishing her own letters . . . [thus] [c]onverting a dangerous private passion into a public denunciation of social corruption through the Enlightenment technology of print" (*Epistolary Bodies,* 28).

44. Favret, *Romantic Correspondence,* 43. See, too, Heckendorn Cook on "how political transformations of the last quarter of the century in Europe and America complicated the idea of 'correspondence' in the cultural imagination" and placed unbearable strain on the epistolary form (*Epistolary Bodies,* 175).

45. Favret, *Romantic Correspondence,* 48.

46. Ibid., 30.

47. Extracts from these texts are to be found in Vivien Jones, ed., *Women in the Eighteenth Century* (quotation on 116), and Jennifer Breen, ed., *Women Romantics, 1785–1832: Writing in Prose* (London: Dent, 1996).

48. Favret, *Romantic Correspondence,* 203.

49. Ibid., 203–10 (quotation on 204). On the seventeenth-century postal service, see Day, *Told in Letters,* 49; and for a book-length discussion of the development of British postal institutions, see Christopher Browne, *Getting the Message: The Story of the British Post Office* (Dover NH: Alan Sutton Publishing, 1993).

50. Favret, "War Correspondence: Reading Romantic War," in *Correspondences: A Special Issue on Letters,* ed. Amanda Gilroy and W. M. Verhoeven, *Prose Studies* 19 (1996): 173–85. For a further discussion of the relation between epistolary writing and fighting, see Clare Brant's

incisive essay, "Dueling by Sword and Pen: The Vauxhall Affray of 1773," *Prose Studies* 19 (1996): 160–72.

51. A notable exception is the work of Mary Favret; see the final chapter of *Romantic Correspondence,* esp. 206–7.

52. We owe this formulation to Elizabeth A. Bohls's fine reading of the novel in *Women Travel Writers and the Language of Aesthetics, 1716–1818* (New York: Cambridge Univ. Press, 1995), 230–45 (quotation on 231).

53. Zohreh T. Sullivan, "Race, Gender, and Imperial Ideology in the Nineteenth Century," *Nineteenth-Century Contexts* 13 (1989): 21.

54. Kauffman, *Special Delivery,* 184.

55. Ibid., 190.

56. See Kauffman on how Nettie's ambivalent position as colonized woman and colonizing missionary further complicates the whole scenario of race and gender (*Special Delivery,* 196–203).

57. In addition to Kauffman, see, in particular, Carolyn Williams, "'Trying to Do without God': The Revision of Epistolary Address in *The Color Purple,*" in *Writing the Female Voice,* ed. Goldsmith, 273–86.

58. M. M. Bakhtin, "Discourse in the Novel," in *The Dialogic Imagination,* ed. Michael Holquist, trans. Caryl Emerson and Michael Holquist (Austin: Univ. of Texas Press, 1990), 293.

59. For further analysis of nineteenth-century American epistolary culture, especially the writings of Emerson, Dickinson, and Henry Adams, see William Merrill Decker, *Epistolary Practices: Letter Writing in America before Telecommunications* (Chapel Hill: Univ. of North Carolina Press, 1998).

60. Further discussion of new epistolary technologies is to be found in the conclusion to Decker, *Epistolary Practices,* 229–41.

PART I

Epistolarity and Femininity

⌀ Writing Women and the Making of the Modern Middle Class

Nancy Armstrong

During the period between the publication of *Clarissa* in 1747–48 and the Crystal Palace exhibition of 1851, the novel came into its own.[1] The extraordinary popularity of Richardson's fiction and the sentimental tradition he launched were but two of a number of clear signs that a new class of people were dislodging the aristocratic ideal of marriage and making their own way of life into the national norm. Yet as late as 1840 the people who could be said to belong to such a class, according to its loosest socioeconomic definition, amounted to no more than 5.5 percent of the population.[2] Does this mean that the modern middle class was little more than an outrageously successful fiction? My earlier work on the novel answered this question in the negative. I argued that fiction not only defined a woman's mastery of a specific form of literacy as the source and measure of her desirability but also made the woman who possessed this literacy essential to a well-regulated household and nation.[3] In support of this claim, we might simply recall that the virtues displayed in Pamela's letters are what elevates her to a station where she can win the heart of a gentleman and reform the domestic interior of his country house. Thus it appears that, in at least this one important respect, social practice eventually imitated sentimental fiction.

This historical discrepancy, however, is compounded by a second. *Clarissa,* too, is composed of the letters of an abducted woman who remains steadfastly determined to return home. In this novel, the seduction plot succeeds, and there is no marriage between captive and captor, even though he has intercepted and read each of her letters with care. This epistolary heroine comes from a prosperous and respectable if hopelessly bourgeois household, and her elopement and rape doom that family to live out their days in grief and humiliation. On what would seem to be the most important point ideologically, then, this novel reverses the conventions to which we customarily attribute *Pamela*'s enormous success. Yet Richardson's second novel was, if anything, even more popular than his first. This pair of discrepancies make sense, to my way of thinking, only if we are willing to read *Clarissa* not in traditional European terms but as the product of an emergent culture.

It is a fact not universally known that during the period when *Clarissa* was first enthralling European readers, accounts of Europeans held captive in America were flooding into England from the colonies. English readers evidently consumed these captivity narratives almost as avidly as they did Richardson's fiction. Readers knew what kind of narrative would ensue, once it had been identified as the testimony of a captive woman, almost as well as they knew how to receive the words of a woman who had fallen victim to rape rather than succumbed to seduction. Mary Rowlandson's personal account of her abduction and removal into Indian territory testified to the constancy of her belief in God, despite incredible physical hardships and without solace from anyone or anything connected to home.[4] In this way, Rowlandson's account also maintained the American captive's relationship with an English-speaking community. By simulating one half of the speech-act situation, namely, the activity of tale telling, this testimony implied the other half, a community of listeners with whom the letter writer could establish a relationship, as she recounted what suffering she endured while separated from them. The community that she addressed through the written word was *not* the same community, however, from which she had been forcibly abducted. Indeed, the mere fact of her writing ensured that the two communities would be fundamentally different. In writing to an English community, the captive defined that community as one made of readers rather than of speakers and members of a religious sect. Rowlandson's writing evidently found—or even founded— such a group, as her account was widely advertised and went through numerous editions on both sides of the Atlantic.[5]

Richardson tapped into the power of this written testimony when he organized a series of exemplary letters into a captivity narrative. He effectively translated the basis for English identity from nationality into class by having a gentleman of inherited wealth carry off a servant girl to his country house in Lincolnshire. In using a woman's letter writing to narrate the account of the indignities she suffered under these circumstances, Richardson eroticized the whole question of cultural identity. Where Mary Rowlandson's writing remained true to her New England origins by demonstrating religious devotion, Pamela remained true to her homespun morality by resisting seduction. Together these accounts encouraged the English readership to think of spiritual pollution in terms of sexual defilement. In that she eventually agreed to marry her would-be seducer, however, Richardson's heroine could be accused of violating the Rowlandson model.[6]

Indeed, there was an equally familiar though clearly residual tradition of captivity narrative in which the female captive assimilated and even married into the culture of her captor-suitor.[7] Despite all Richardson does to assure us that Mr. B underwent a moral conversion, Pamela's shift from resistance to complicity with her seducer would have been one and the same thing as "going native" in the tradition of the captivity narrative. For the very reason that *Clarissa* fails to reconcile contending households in marriage according to the sentimental formula, the novel could be said to fulfill the logic of the captivity narrative more perfectly than even *Pamela* does. From *Charlotte Temple* and *Uncle Tom's Cabin* to John Ford's *The Searchers* and Toni Morrison's *Beloved,* American culture has wrestled with the narrative assumption that a dead daughter is better than one polluted by another culture. It could even be argued that to maintain their identities within American culture successive diasporic groups have found it convenient to invoke this notion of purity.

For the very reason that one did not cease to be English when marrying up in rank, however, one might expect the logic of class to diverge from that of race on the issue of intermarriage. Where *Pamela* suggested that the amalgamation of two previously existing classes could indeed produce the basis for a new one and a new basis for Englishness as well, Clarissa said no and adhered to the logic of the captivity narrative more literally than perhaps any of her colonial counterparts did.[8] In place of the compromise formation that brought *Pamela* to such a happy conclusion, Richardson played out a relentlessly negative logic in the ending of his second novel. The colonial prototype required the heroine's return to the community from which she had been abducted. In returning, as I have suggested, the captive did not restore the community to its originary state of wholeness; she subtly but irrevocably modernized the early modern notion of community. Before English men and women were separated by an ocean from many of their friends and family, they presumably carried on most of their relationships in speech instead of writing. Before female captives began to reproduce their thoughts in writing, furthermore, the body of an English woman was part of a larger social body rather than the envelope of an individuated consciousness which could be understood as the unique source and ultimate referent of writing. Once enough accounts of captivity had circulated in print, however, members of the community of readers evidently began to think of themselves as similarly self-enclosed centers of consciousness and points of origin for language, and letters in turn became a way of conducting the most intimate relationships with others who understood themselves in similar terms. The rest is history. The most private self was the self expressed in certain kinds of writing rather than in speech, and this disembodiment of speech amalgamated local speech communities into a national readership.[9]

In *Clarissa,* Richardson made the well-to-do gentry and lesser nobility into the captors of a captivity narrative. His heroine comes from a prosperous and respectable family. She is not abducted from this family by savages but imprisoned in their house and with her father's blessing. Her brother James identifies her as a potential liability to the family, so long as she remains unmarried. Persuaded, her father confines Clarissa to her room until she agrees to marry a man whom she regards as well beneath her both in moral sensibility and in station. Deprived of a speech community, she writes to her father in the defiant voice of the captive: "can you think I am such a slave, such a *poor* slave, as to be brought to change my mind by the violent usage I have met with?" She naively agrees to run off with the relatively high-born Lovelace after "he solemnly vow[ed] that his *whole* view at present is to free me from my imprisonment; and to restore me to my own free will." To escape captivity, Clarissa turns for protection to a libertine aristocrat. But this move further removes her from the one position she claims she can occupy and still remain who she originally was, the position of beloved daughter. After Lovelace drugs and rapes her, the heroine addresses her captor thus: "tell me . . . since I am a prisoner as I find, in the vilest of houses, and have not a friend to protect or save me, what thou intendest shall become of the remnant of a life not worth the keeping?" As if to acknowledge their daughter's resemblance to colonial heroines, her family considers deporting her to Pennsylvania, "to reside there for some few years till all is blown over; and if it please God to spare you, and your unhappy parents, till they can be satisfied that you behave like a true and uniform penitent."[10] Remorselessly true to her own version of the captivity narrative, however, Clarissa takes a more direct route home.

So single-mindedly does she pursue this goal that she eventually recovers an exalted form of the position within her family that she would have lost through marriage to either Solmes or Lovelace. The novel leaves no room for ambiguity on this point, so overdetermined is the conflict for which it seeks and fails to formulate a resolution. By imprisoning the heroine in her father's house, Richardson equates the Harlowes' prosperous estate with the American wilderness. As her old nurse Mrs. Norton explains, "I am very seldom at Harlowe Place. The house is not the house it used to be since you went from it. Then they are *so* relentless! And, as I cannot say harsh things of the beloved child of my *heart,* as well as *bosom,* they do not take it *amiss* that I stay away." In contrast with Mary Rowlandson, then, Clarissa has no father and no home to return to, as she herself declares: "fatherless may *she* well be called, and motherless too, who has been denied all paternal protection and motherly forgiveness."[11] True to the captivity narrative formula, she comes home anyway. The fact that she has to do so in a coffin cancels out the equation between Harlowe Place and the kind of domestic sanctuary it took to resolve the conflict between household and family in both Rowlandson's account and *Pamela*. In making that home her mausoleum, Richardson locates salvation somewhere else.

Despite these pointed modifications of the captivity narrative, Richardson never allows his heroine to compromise what must therefore be considered its definitive trait: the captive's unswerving desire to return to her culture of origin—her refusal, in other words, to go native. In *Clarissa,* Richardson uses the logic of the captivity narrative to set one form of masculine authority (that of the father) against another (based on social station).[12] If her father believes his brand of authority is challenged when his daughter rejects Solmes, then Lovelace understands his rank is insulted when she rejects his advances. In holding them equally responsible for her rape, Clarissa reclassifies her father and her seducer as equally violent and thus as failures of masculine authority.

Despite the contrastingly negative ending that distinguishes *Clarissa,* the logic of reform nevertheless works hand-in-glove with the captivity narrative in Richardson's second novel, just as it does in *Pamela*. According to this logic, the male head of household gains social and even economic authority outside his household insofar as he demonstrates affection and good taste within it. No one embodies that logic in *Clarissa*. Her captivity could be said to challenge the authority of both groups—those whose money originated in business and trade, as well as the class of hereditary landowners—whom E. P. Thompson describes as contending for control of English society during the final decades of the eighteenth century.[13] Thus the novel calls forth a new category of masculinity and leaves that category conspicuously empty. By virtue of this omission, it can be argued, the novel makes an even stronger case than did its predecessor, the captivity narrative, on behalf of the necessity and power of reform. *Clarissa* extends the logic of reform to include those people whom modern historiography holds implicitly responsible for capitalism, even though historians are generally at a loss to prove the point demographically. Before suggesting how Richardson might have served the interests of an emergent middle class by having Clarissa perish for want of male protection, let me turn to a second body of information whose logic shaped and was shaped by the absence of a beneficent form of masculine authority.

In her essay entitled "Wife-Beating, Domesticity, and Women's Independence in Eighteenth-Century London," Margaret Hunt describes a transformation of domestic violence that suggestively parallels the penal reforms described in Foucault's *Discipline and Punish*.[14] The households supplying her data are those of small businessmen and their wives. In 73 percent of the cases, these women either worked at trades independently or in some way paid the lion's share of their own expenses. In addition, most of these households depended on buying rather than producing most of the goods they used, and in most cases the women negotiated for these goods with "a bustling society of female hucksters and small businesswomen." For information concerning the private lives of these women, Hunt went to the records of the Consistory Court, where a number of the women filed for separation on grounds of excessive domestic abuse. Among these records, she found evidence linking the economic independence of these women to the excessive violence within their households. As she explains, "conflicts over money, or more properly over the control of resources, reflected the particular dilemmas of a class that was both chronically short of cash and heavily dependent upon family connections and marriage to obtain it."[15] Hunt's research on the education of children among this same demographic group supplies another piece of the puzzle. As the century wore on, reading and writing apparently replaced violence as the culturally sanctioned way of resolving the economic conflict that tore these households asunder. Along with *Clarissa*, I believe, this historical information gives us privileged insight into what might be called the rise of writing: the process by which a certain form of literacy first provided the means of detaching the household economy from an extensive network of family alliances and—especially when embodied in an eligible young woman—provided a class marker and form of cultural currency in its own right.

In discussing what then constituted excessive or unusual domestic violence, Hunt reminds us that eighteenth-century English society was "one that saw violence as a necessary, if not always optimal, way of maintaining order in any hierarchical relationship."[16] The regular use of violence was considered legitimate when it was administered in the name of preserving hierarchy. Coexisting with this rhetoric of violence, however, was another rhetoric that those occupying inferior positions could on rare occasions appropriate for purposes of embarrassing those in power. A code that linked gentility to self-government as displayed toward others had been part of English culture since the first issues of *The Tatler* and *The Spectator*. Central to this concept of gentility was the proper respect for one's marriage partner. In one early issue of *The Spectator*, we find Richard Steele asking the following question in mock-incredulity, "Can there be anything more base, or serve to sink a man so much below his own distinguishing Characteristick (I mean Reason) . . . as that of treating an helpless creature with Unkindness, who has . . . divest[ed] her Happiness in this World to his Care and Protection?"[17] In order to elevate a kinder, gentler masculinity, the new standard of male conduct determined that the "creature" who found herself in the hands of such a gentle protector had to be a "helpless" one. One could invoke this code for purposes of condemning domestic abuse only when such violence clearly constituted a failure to exercise the responsibilities that came with a position of authority. Under such circumstances, violence just might undermine rather than reinforce masculine authority.

Inscribed within an early modern model of political authority, however, petitions written by women to the Consistory Court rarely operated like captivity narratives to empower the victims of domestic abuse. One case where a woman's writing might appear to work on behalf of the captive is the successful suit against John Spinkes, a practitioner in "physick," accusing him of beating his wife, Elizabeth Spinkes, with a whip and locking her up first at home and then in a lunatic asylum. Given its moment in the history of the middling household, however, it turns out that she had little chance of succeeding on the basis of the writing that disclosed the truth behind the scenes of her marriage. On the contrary, her freedom depended on her ability to stage an elaborate sequence of violent spectacles, during which she managed to gather enough allies to secure her release. In itself, the new code of civility invariably proved incapable of undoing the double bind that entrapped women and created disruptions within middling households. I mention the existence of such a code in order to call attention to the gap between writing that condemned the perpetrators of domestic abuse and the social authority that inhered in the exercise of violence up through the period during which *Clarissa* was first written and read. Written testimony that disclosed the secrets of domestic life appeared to have little or no power to countermand the authority of violence so long as the code of civility that condemned mistreating one's dependents lacked authority as well. How, then, did writing gain authority within the household, where it could help to make such public spectacles obsolete? This question is as much about the authority of the sentimental novel as about the high bourgeois code of civility.

Although Elizabeth Spinkes's determination to leave her husband may, from our perspective, seem worlds away from the hagiographic tenacity with which Mary Rowlandson clung to her English identity, the rhetorical objective of their respective narratives was remarkably similar. By simulating one part of the speech-act situation, namely, the tale teller, both endeavored to transform the community of listeners from one that accepted violence as the husband's prerogative into a community that felt paternal responsibility toward the victim. I find it significant that Elizabeth Spinkes's written petition to the court accused her husband of forcing her to turn over money that she owned in trust, which she claimed she did in hopes of eliciting more humane treatment from him. In making their complaints to the court, Hunt explains, it was not uncommon for such women to dissociate themselves from any economic motivation, much as Mary

Rowlandson renounced all worldly concerns, and petition for separation that would simply release them from confinement and excessive abuse. Their pleas to this effect rested on the utterly patriarchal assumption that even a husband could not have absolute authority over a woman's body if it still belonged to that woman's father. In forcing her to transfer her money to him, her husband forced Elizabeth to violate her father's trust, and by abusing her body, Spinkes abused her family's property. In agreeing to give away her father's money, then, Elizabeth used one brand of patriarchy against another. Such reliance on the more conservative brand of patriarchal authority cannot be regarded as politically regressive, however, not when these women used that logic to authorize their written testimony. Under these circumstances, they were representing themselves as property in hopes of claiming possession of their bodies through their writing and thereby achieving the status of subjects before the law.

Even so, for the women who filed complaints at the Consistory Courts, writing alone did not stand any chance against masculine prerogatives, any more than it did for the relatively well-born heroine of *Clarissa*. For most of the century, Hunt's examples suggest, violence was understood at most social levels as a spectacle that could be combated only by further violence. Witness the conclusion to Elizabeth Spinkes's ordeal. Locked in an upstairs room, she leapt out the window onto the street below, where a group of neighborhood women rushed to her defense. She had apparently planned the public uproar in order to secure her release from domestic incarceration. So long as hierarchy both within and outside the family depended upon public displays of violence, however, she was at a distinct disadvantage. Conflict within the household over the wife's claims to property were indeed likely to extend outside the household and polarize one family against another, neighborhood women against men, and even both at once. This was hardly a milieu in which the husband stood to lose anything by abusing his wife. Indeed, Spinkes apparently felt it incumbent on him to beat her into submission.[18]

By the 1840s, according to Leonore Davidoff and Catherine Hall, the relationship between masculine authority and the exercise of violence had completely reversed itself: "good taste, the capacity not to be vulgar, was replacing salvation as the mark of special status."[19] Middle-class men based their status on intellectual ability and associated violent behavior with a lack of education and refinement. However, such behavior was especially pertinent to middle-class women. Unlike her earlier counterparts among people of business and trade, the new middle-class woman had a physical presence, in Davidoff and Hall's analysis, "but that presence was only legitimated when it expressed a proper sense of belonging to a delicate, refined and gentle domestic world." For most of the eighteenth century, the independent businessman could represent his way of life as the truly English way only when that household was transported to the colonies and successfully reproduced there—Robinson Crusoe being the case in point. Nevertheless, during the years following the French Revolution, when the value of English currency was notably insecure, a relatively small group of people who could be called "the middle class" established their peculiar domestic customs as the measure of one's capacity for self-government. They also solidified their economic hold over England. Given the uncertainty over money and the fact that credit arrangements remained essentially local, Davidoff and Hall conclude, "personal reputation became a key to survival. The behaviour of the entrepreneur, his family and household as well as their material setting, were tangible indications of financial as well as moral probity."[20]

By calling attention to the striking change in what it took to be an exemplary head of household during the period from around 1780 to 1830 or so, I am not suggesting that we can chalk up the rise of the modern middle class to domestic reform. Rather, I want to consider how the ideology of reform caught hold: How did people come to think that England could and should be ruled from the inside out, household by household, and not from the outside through forms of political or economic violence? For those who supported themselves neither by inherited property nor by working at one of the traditional trades, the only way to make a profit and improve one's social position was to acquire capital from relatives and friends. To be a good family member, one had to venture capital, but doing so automatically put one's entire network of friends and relatives at risk from creditors who were entitled to take possession of their property with very few restrictions. It is not difficult to imagine why this conflict of interests might have reached an explosive pitch in the struggle over economic autonomy between husband and wife. If a woman brought family property with her into her husband's household, it would have served her interest to keep that entire network of alliances free of liability from debts her husband and his relatives might incur. He, on the other hand, required such capital in order to secure his household—including his wife and children—from creditors. If she brought money with her into her husband's family, it is fair to say that a wife was still marked as her father's daughter even after she had been incorporated in her new household.

Among the many ways in which the Harlowes believed that Clarissa would put the family at risk by marrying Lovelace, despite his superior rank, was the fact that marriage would give him access to the inheritance she brought with her into any such relationship.[21] Although she, like Elizabeth Spinkes, insisted on giving up that inheritance, the Harlowes nevertheless understood that Clarissa was giving away property that belonged to them, since they stood to lose the capital that would come to them from trading her to Solmes. Yet, as entangled as she was at the level of inherited income, the daughter's role in the economic business of the household had a much more immediate and practical impact at the level of the middling culture with which Hunt is concerned. There, any loss of capital or sudden liability to debt could strike "right at the heart of family survival, depriving people of the basic necessities of life, sending men, women and children into the street or into debtor's prison, crushing the innocent and charitable among one's kin as well as the extravagant or imprudent."[22] Thus the conflict between the need for capital and the fear of economic liability manifested itself within the middling household as a conflict between family and household. Before the term "family" could be attached to the kind of household whose apotheosis Davidoff and Hall describe, the established notion of kinship had to be displaced by a new concept of the self-enclosed household, a unit composed of the head of household and his immediate dependents. Marriage, in this case, was neither an extension of nor alliance between families so much as the founding of a separate household and the incorporation of a brand new family.

The people belonging to middling culture developed a discourse of time-discipline that belongs in the same tradition as both the English tradition of Dissent and New England Puritanism. If constant and immediate communication with God was a way of dealing with the colonial situation, then reading and writing began to offer people in business and trade a similar sense of control in a tumultuous economic climate where lightning could strike at any moment. According to Hunt, "The most characteristic 'middling' skill of all was bookkeeping, and the ability to keep accurate accounts soon became the centerpiece in the education of youths from trading families" or families destined for trade.[23] Accounting could calculate what went into the household against what went out, how many hours were expended, how much money owing, how much made. Under these circumstances, it is easy to imagine why the improvement of the household came to be linked to the education of children—male as well as female—in the language skills that represented economic control.

Through writing, time-discipline brought autonomy to the household in another sense as well. An advice book for women published in 1678 interlaced the language of economics with that of chastity to suggest not only that bookkeeping skills would stave off economic disaster but also that sexual "ruine" would lead to "poverty." Self-restraint was just as important for boys and just as likely to come from the right education. An advertisement from *Aris's Birmingham Gazette* in 1760 specifies "a sober steady young man of 18 or 20 of mean parentage but honest and unexceptional character, able to write a good hand and understand accounts."[24] Again, we see a moral lexicon ("sober") applied to economic competence. In theory, a middling education not only offered a method of predicting the relationships among credit, investment, labor, and the money that flowed back into the household but also provided a way of preventing the vices that were especially likely to put the family at risk. These vices were disowned by middling culture and associated with those who were protected by wealth from the consequences of undisciplined behavior, as well as with the lower classes who had little chance of self-improvement. In disowning these vices, this culture sexualized power. As Hunt explains, "power and rank held considerable erotic appeal for both women and men in the eighteenth century, and few middling people had illusions about that fact." This was the guilty knowledge that lay behind the fear that middling youths would be "'seduced' into immorality by associating with or attempting to emulate their betters. Middling people had to establish new, nonaristocratic definitions of 'manliness' that could 'seduce' (but more productively) in their turn."[25] Thus, one might say, the language that defined and oversaw the household as a discrete economic unit also provided the means of developing self-contained and self-regulating individuals.

As the figure that brought ties to her original family into her husband's household, the married daughter embodied the conflict between household and family. Since she was a source of both capital and liability, her body not only created a conflict between the internal economy of the middling household and the ties to friends and family but also offered the means of resolving that economic conflict and ensuring the household's survival. Her autonomy and well-being both represented and guaranteed those of the household. Before she could serve as such a guarantee, however, it was necessary for English readers to value her on some basis other than economics or family connections. Such a radical recoding of the daughter was most evident in the Creole culture of New England, where ties to England brought about the doubling of the English household into an original and its reproduction. In seeking to maintain its connection with the homeland, the colonial household replaced the original with another kind of family that conserved crucial features of that original. The bond between the two—and thus the value of the copy—depended on the daughter and the dedication with which she took up the task of cultural reproduction as the basis of her own desire and measure of female virtue. According to captivity narratives, a woman risked social if not physical death whenever she left that household. At the same time, the experience of being separated either by an ocean from England or by Indian territory from her family produced both her self-enclosure and that of the household she had left behind. In this respect, the degree of her devotion to Englishness in fact required her to transform the English model into a recognizably more modern version of the household.

Again resembling the captives of North America, Pamela and Clarissa defined themselves as bodies in peril, for which the only safe place was their father's house. When she finally succeeded in returning to Boston, Mary Rowlandson was quick to identify that location—and not England—as her true home and point of origin. In marked contrast with Rowlandson, however, Pamela and Clarissa could not be so reincorporated into their original families. Survival depended on their ability to produce a substitute for the family through an unwavering exercise of affection and good taste, virtues tested by their ability to stave off what are identified as aristocratic forms of sexual aggression. This is the logic of reform. It was according to this logic that Pamela converted the wilderness of Mr. B's estate into a household ruled by a form of time-discipline that testified to her affection for parents (in that she reproduced their values) and husband (in that she did it for him).

This same logic of reform was decisively thrown into question by *Clarissa*. Even though Clarissa overvalues family relations and indulges in extraordinary displays of self-discipline that culminate in death by self-induced starvation, no idealized substitute for the patriarchal family emerges. Nor does anything prove capable of regulating male brutality and lust. Indeed, Richardson makes a point of showing that his heroine's insistence on the letter of bourgeois propriety actually encourages her fall, since it incurs her father's wrath and arouses the desire of her seducer. Though governed by the conduct-book definition of family duty and good taste at every turn, her letters conspicuously fail to produce the kind of domestic male that Addison and Steele had encouraged readers to admire. Such a male is significantly absent from this narrative, and his absence leaves the heroine without a home to write home to.[26] As in the American captivity narrative, this absence creates the need for a household enclosed so as to render illegitimate competing claims upon a woman's body.

I have tried to suggest how we might use *Clarissa* to understand the modern middle class as an emergent culture. If it is reasonable to think of modern England in such terms, then we must also rethink the commonplace that the emergent middle class was responsible for writing novels and assume instead that novels were responsible for modernizing the middle class. If *Pamela* and *Clarissa* did anything at all to enhance the value that people from the middling classes had already begun to invest in literacy, it was because those novels added metaphysical flesh to their conviction that you are what you read and write. Thus we have the epistolary novel, in which women who have forsaken every other form of value manage to accrue extraordinary value to themselves exclusively through the act of writing. One can see this principle carried to its logical extreme in Clarissa's compulsive reconstruction of her violated self-enclosure: the frugality of her room, her liquidation of assets, her refusal to incur debts of any kind, her detailed management of time, her final words to friends and relatives, the careful orchestration of her funeral. She becomes progressively self-contained and dependent on writing alone as she descends in economic position to the barest of subsistence economies. This descent coincides with her retreat from Lovelace into smaller and smaller enclosures that he subsequently violates, until she occupies only the space between her narrow bed and her still narrower coffin. Purchased by selling off most of her things, that coffin provides her desk until the tiny gap between it and her bed closes and she exists nowhere but on the written page.

In this respect, it might be argued, Clarissa's dwindling capital exactly contradicts the principle of capital investment that created tension within households of the middling classes. Her every expenditure costs both her family and Lovelace dearly, because it not only diminishes her body but also exposes them to moral condemnation. Richardson indeed appears to have been thinking in opposition to any modern economic theory of value when he simultaneously devalues his heroine through rape and exalts her by having her remove herself from the exchange of women. How might this ultraconservative model of the family have addressed the economic double bind that people of middling households confronted on a daily basis?

The last third of *Clarissa* resolves the problem contained within the daughter's body. Because of the conflict between her father and Lovelace over her body, Clarissa feels compelled to cut herself off from her father's money and to refuse all economic support from Lovelace. Having no money at all, she perishes. In doing so, she makes the difference between private and public into a sacred spatial boundary guarding a secret whose violation is tantamount to self-destruction. Whatever money one spends, reading one reads, pleasure one enjoys, and people in whom one confides, they have to be contained inviolate within that sanctuary or one exactly like it. From a modern-day perspective, we tend to see this kind of domestic woman as by definition a captive within the modern socioeconomic world. Once married, she is cut off from friends and family. It is important to keep in mind, however, that in her husband's house she is in a household that reproduces that of her original family. In this respect, the modern English household resembled those of New England, where the contradiction between separation and home was first and most overtly dealt with as English settlers sought to makes themselves at home in the wilderness. A new kind of man was obviously required to define this home as a space of relative freedom, safety, affective bonding, and altruistic gratification that can never be mistaken for the kind of prison Clarissa fled in fleeing her father's house.

Among the middling classes, both women and men were educated to deal with money. To resolve the conflict between the competing needs for capital and protection from liability, however, the household would have to separate itself from the world where everything was on the market, especially women.[27] Contrary to the regular translation of affect into economic calculation and vice versa that we encounter, for example, in the novels of Daniel Defoe, this separation of household from what might be called "the rest of the world" was carried out in and through a division of writing into private and public. Among those who considered themselves "polite," the rhetoric of personal letter writing, for which *Pamela* was supposedly intended as a primer, avoided the taint of the profit motive. Even among the middling sort, household books were to be kept separate and apart from those of business and other income. Indeed, it is tempting to push the implications of the rise of the epistolary mode one step farther still.

Let us credit the development of a self-enclosed household among the middling classes in England with having limited the liability of loans and debt, in that such a household encouraged self-discipline among its members and disentangled personal life from outside business ventures. As soon as self-regulation and good economic management were considered interchangeable, then, it stands to reason that households displaying signs of violence would be stigmatized as bad economic risks. From these speculations, it does not require much of a leap to understand why that relatively small group of people who had managed their households and raised their children according to the new code of civility would grow increasingly prosperous during the period following the French Revolution, when wild fluctuations in the value of English currency made creditors extremely wary. Seeing their own households as the consequence and reward for their virtue and fiscal responsibility, those with money to invest apparently felt most comfortable extending credit to those with a house, garden, wife, children, and domestic help resembling their own.

If it makes any sense at all to read Richardson's epistolary novels as versions of the American captivity narrative, and if the historical material I have assembled actually supports the idea that the modern middle class was not one that already existed so much as one that consolidated itself in writing, then we have to reconsider just who was responsible for their so-called rise. Might it not be that we find it so difficult to describe the agents of modernity because they were the ones to tell the story? Thus they were the ones to determine how the victims and aggressors would be characterized and what would be required to create a nation where women and children could be safe from aristocrats and savages alike. I am not the first to describe the second half of the eighteenth century in terms of the vast reclassification of English society, or to argue that the novel was instru-

mental in carrying out this project, or even to suggest that the whole notion of class emerged out of this process and displaced the concepts of station and rank that had for centuries knit English society into vertical chains
of dependency. This essay simply supplements what is now a rather well
established argument by calling attention to certain similarities between
the modern middle class and a settler colonial culture. This comparison
suggests that the agency of an emergent culture rests not in the people
who embody power so much as in the disembodied power of the writing
that calls those people into being as a class and nation.[28] In her radical disembodiment, Clarissa can be considered the perfect embodiment of such
an imagined community.

Postscript by Donna Landry

Scholar Own Predecessor. Confirms Diagnosis.
Middle-Class Fiction No Fiction.

*One way of coping with the irritation of influence in scholarly writing, if not trav-
el writing, is the do-it-yourself plan. Commenting on one's own previously published
work, especially when confirming one's earlier findings, is a useful self-authorizing
strategy.*

Having, with Leonard Tennenhouse in The Imaginary Puritan, *attributed the
power of Pamela's writing to the influence of captivity narratives, Armstrong now
accounts for the even greater success of* Clarissa *by arguing for the later novel's
greater adherence to the logic of the captivity narrative, which resists assimilation. This is, as Armstrong says elsewhere of the flood of colonial captivity narratives into England at the time of* Clarissa's *publication, "a fact not universally
known." In refusing to submit her body to Lovelace, Clarissa repeats the "definitive
trait" of the captivity narrative, "the captive's unswerving desire to return to her
culture of origin—her refusal, in other words, to go native."*

*If only Armstrong had refused to "go native," in the wilderness of colonial
American literature, and stayed resolutely in British studies. She might then have
had more time for reading other kinds of writing besides novels and Margaret Hunt's
social-historical articles, as well as for reading novels besides Richardson's. But
Armstrong couldn't keep herself from traveling and "going native," exchanging her
English woolies for frontier buckskins (buskins?). Not only are all letters travel
writing; so also is most literary history.*

The cultural authority of writing, the power of literacy to displace both speech (oral communities) and violence (wife-beating): these are familiar themes. "Before English men and women were separated by an ocean from many of their friends and family," Armstrong writes, "they presumably carried on most of their relationships in speech instead of writing." Does Armstrong really assume that English people only began writing what Annabel M. Patterson calls "familiar letters" to each other after the founding of New World colonies?[1] The archives suggest otherwise. Internal travel, travel within Great Britain, was as necessary to capitalist development as colonial trade and was well-established in the late sixteenth and early seventeenth centuries.[2] And what of those narratives of Europeans captured by pirates and even enslaved, a tradition dating back some centuries? Special pleading seems to be going on here.

Critics of the novel often exaggerate the claims of their genre to world-changing status. Armstrong ends her essay by collapsing all interpellative situations into "writing," and implicitly all writing into novelistic fiction: "the agency of an emergent culture rests not in the people who embody power so much as in the disembodied power of the writing that calls those people into being as a class and nation." Might not other cultural forms, more highly "embodied" than novels, or print culture generally (this would not be difficult), serve this function in other times and places, even if we accept Armstrong's Foucauldian description of the interpellative apparatus of print culture here?

Self-authorization becomes self-fulfilling prophecy when Armstrong discovers the inevitability of the appearance of the epistolary novel in the story she is telling— about the epistolary novel: "Thus we have the epistolary novel," she observes, "in which women who have forsaken every other form of value manage to accrue extraordinary value to themselves exclusively through the act of writing." Not exclusively through writing, surely: what about that bit about keeping one's body virginally pure, knees together and so on?

The novel induces this sort of exaggeration, this sort of heroic advocacy. But then the problem with novels is that they cannot represent themselves, they must be represented.

Post-postscript *by Nancy Armstrong*

Letter to Ms. Landry

Dear Ms. Landry, obviously a woman of good sense and fine taste,

Her father and I echo your lament, "If only Armstrong had refused to 'go native,' in the wilds of colonial American literature, but stayed resolutely in English studies."

We too consider English studies much more polite than whatever Armstrong does. We entirely support your injunction that she remain true to the tradition of a national literature and bound to an ahistorical notion of the personal. As a child, she was warned of the perils of an overfondness for fiction. Alas, however, our daughter was never one to stay in her "woollies," intellectual or otherwise, an unfortunate tendency we trace to the branch of the family who migrated to the United States from Dublin. Of late, we have reason to suspect our efforts have been for naught, that she may indeed be an American.

Her Mother

Notes

1. At least this is Ian Watt's well-known contention in *The Rise of the Novel* (Berkeley: Univ. of California Press, 1957).

2. Norman Gash, *Aristocracy and People: Britain, 1815–1865* (Cambridge MA: Harvard Univ. Press, 1979), 21.

3. See my *Desire and Domestic Fiction: A Political History of the Novel* (New York: Oxford Univ. Press, 1987).

4. Mary Rowlandson, "The Soveraignty and Goodness of God . . . Being a Narrative of the Captivity and Restauration of Mrs. Mary Rowlandson," in *Puritans among the Indians: Accounts of Captivity and Redemption, 1676–1724,* ed. Alden T. Vaughn and Edward W. Clark (Cambridge MA: Harvard Univ. Press, 1981), 31–75. Rowlandson's account of her captivity is generally regarded as the best example of its type. It combined a modern authorial consciousness with early modern Protestant hagiography to produce a distinctively English experience and written testimony. Her abduction and captivity by a heathen people in a savage land put the author's faith on trial and, with her faith, her Englishness. Her testimony articulated unrelenting contempt for her captors and unwavering yearning for an Christian life among English people. For a biographical account of Rowlandson, see Mitchell Robert Breitwieser, *American Puritanism and the Defense of Mourning: Religion, Grief, and Ethnology in Mary White Rowlandson's Captivity Narrative* (Madison: Univ. of Wisconsin Press, 1990).

5. Within a year of its publication in 1682, Rowlandson's account of her abduction, captivity, and return went through three editions and several printings in British America. That same year, a fourth edition was published in England, and by 1720 a fifth edition appeared there. Encapsulated versions of the same story appeared in published sermons, in publishers' reports, and as advertisements included on the back pages of other books. By the end of the eighteenth century, almost thirty editions of the account had appeared, most in the last thirty years of the century, which suggests that the story was thoroughly familiar to the readership that devoured Richardson's novels. See Kathryn Zabelle Derounian, "The Publication, Promotion, and Distribution of Mary Rowlandson's Indian Captivity Narrative in the Seventeenth Century," *Early American Literature* 23 (1988): 239–61, and R. W. G. Vail, *The Voice of the Old Frontier* (Philadelphia: Univ. of Pennsylvania Press, 1949), 29–61.

6. For a discussion of the influence of British American captivity narratives on *Pamela,* see

Nancy Armstrong and Leonard Tennenhouse, *The Imaginary Puritan: Literature, Intellectual Labor, and the Origins of Personal Life* (Berkeley: Univ. of California Press, 1992), 196–216.

7. See, for example, James E. Seaver, *A Narrative of the Life of Mrs. Jemison, the White Woman of the Genesee* (Norman: Univ. of Oklahoma Press, 1992). It is worth noting that Jemison tells her story in the manner of a native informant to an Englishman who is responsible for the written version. As a captive who "went native" and married outside her nationality, she has set herself and family forever apart from "the rich and respectable people, principally from New England" (54).

8. It is to this apparently conservative logic of the narrative that Michael McKeon refers in saying that "Clarissa Harlowe . . . resists assimilation to the progressive model of her predecessor Pamela Andrews" (*The Origins of the English Novel, 1600–1740* [Baltimore: Johns Hopkins Univ. Press, 1987], 418).

9. See Benedict Anderson, *Imagined Communities: Reflections on the Origins and Spread of Nationalism* (London: Verso, 1991); David Cressy, *Coming Over: Migration and Communication between England and New England in the Seventeenth Century* (Cambridge: Cambridge Univ. Press, 1987); Ian K. Steele, *The English Atlantic, 1675–1740* (New York: Oxford Univ. Press, 1986); David D. Hall, *Worlds of Wonder, Days of Judgment: Popular Religious Belief in Early New England* (Cambridge MA: Harvard Univ. Press, 1990); and Richard D. Brown, *Knowledge Is Power: The Diffusion of Information in Early America, 1700–1865* (New York: Oxford Univ. Press, 1989).

10. Samuel Richardson, *Clarissa; or, The History of a Young Lady*, ed. Angus Ross (Harmondsworth: Penguin, 1985), 307, 349, 900, 1256.

11. Ibid., 979, 1176.

12. According to this most conservative interpretation of the daughter's body, not even the father can give her away. His identity descends to her and through her into another family of note, thereby ensuring the solidarity of his rank or station. Under these circumstances, the daughter functions as what anthropologist Annette B. Weiner has called an "inalienable possession"; see Weiner, *Inalienable Possessions: The Paradox of Keeping-While-Giving* (Berkeley: Univ. of California Press, 1992). Such an object is so vital to the identity of the group that it can neither be taken nor traded away without threatening that group's very identity. To protect against this threat, a group sometimes endows this kind of object with a metaphysical identity. Daughters who are so invested with the power of culture-bearers are incapable of assimilation. In folklore and fiction, they tend to die when they leave the family, thereby testifying to the fact that they cannot actually exchange hands.

13. E. P. Thompson, *The Making of the English Working Class* (New York: Vintage, 1966). Maxine Berg shows these groups locked in ideological opposition until the second decade of the nineteenth century (*The Machinery Question and the Making of Political Economy* [Cambridge: Cambridge Univ. Press, 1980]).

14. Margaret Hunt, "Wife-Beating, Domesticity and Women's Independence in Early Eighteenth-Century London," *Gender and History* 4 (1992): 10–33; Michel Foucault, *Discipline and Punish*, trans. Alan Sheridan (New York: Vintage, 1979).

15. Hunt, "Wife-Beating," 12, 17.

16. Margaret Hunt, "Time-Management, Writing, and Accounting in the Eighteenth-Century Trading Family: A Bourgeois Enlightenment," *Business and Economic History*, 2d ser., 18 (1989): 150–59.

17. Hunt, "Wife-Beating," 10.

18. Ibid., 21–22.

19. Leonore Davidoff and Catherine Hall, *Family Fortunes: Men and Women of the English Middle Class, 1780–1850* (Chicago: Univ. of Chicago Press, 1987), 191.

20. Ibid., 92, 208.

21. John P. Zomchik has proposed that "Richardson's narrative fashions the family into a corporate unity supported by economic interests" (*Family and the Law in Eighteenth-Century Fiction: The Public Conscience in the Private Sphere* [Cambridge: Cambridge Univ. Press, 1993], 69).

22. Hunt, "Time-Discipline," 151.

23. Margaret Hunt, *The Middling Sort: Commerce, Gender, and the Family in England, 1680–1780* (Berkeley: Univ. of California Press, 1996), 58.

24. Qtd. in Hunt, *Middling Sort,* 56.

25. Ibid., 67.

26. On the absence of such a male in *Clarissa,* Terry Eagleton offers these suggestive remarks: "Male hegemony was to be sweetened but not undermined; women were to be exalted but not emancipated. The recourse to the feminine was always problematical—for how could the public sphere of male discourse model itself upon values drawn from an essentially private realm? . . . The answer to this question is Richardson's last novel, *Sir Charles Grandison. Grandison* is not just a cashing in on the success of *Clarissa:* it is the logical culmination of Richardson's ideological project" (*The Rape of Clarissa* [Minneapolis: Univ. of Minnesota Press, 1982], 95).

27. As Davidoff and Hall explain, "For a middle-class woman of the early nineteenth century, gentility was coming to be defined by a special form of femininity which ran directly counter to acting as a visibly independent economic agent. Despite the fact that women hold property, their marital status always pre-empted their economic personality. The ramifications of this fact for their social and economic position were profound. It can be argued that nineteenth-century middle-class women represent a classic case of Parkin's distinction between property as active capital and property as possession" (*Family Fortunes,* 315).

28. Like James Clifford, not only do I consider what might be called "the story of development" to be the central narrative of modern culture but I also regard any specific allegory of development—whether of an individual or of a nation—as an allegory of a still more basic and pervasive narrative of writing. "[I]n the West," explains Clifford, "the passage from oral to literate is a potent recurring *story*—of power, corruption, and loss. It replicates (and to an extent produces) the structure of pastoral that has been pervasive in twentieth-century ethnography. Logocentric writing is conventionally conceived to be a *representation* of authentic speech." The historical emergence of this story had profound historical consequences, which were, I believe, fully anticipated in Clarissa's rather relentless displacement of all other forms of cultural inscription—including rape—onto writing. In Clifford's analysis, the primacy of the story of writing is at least partly responsible for writing the world: "the sharp distinction of the world's cultures into literate and pre-literate; the notion that ethnographic textualization is a process that enacts a fundamental transition from oral experience to written representation; the assumption that something essential is lost when a culture becomes 'ethnographic'; the strangely ambivalent authority of a practice that salvages as text a cultural life becoming past" (see "On Ethnographic Allegory," in *Writing Culture: The Poetics and Politics of*

Ethnography, ed. James Clifford and George E. Marcus [Berkeley: Univ. of California Press, 1986], 118).

Notes to Postscript

1. See Annabel M. Patterson, *Censorship and Interpretation: The Conditions of Writing and Reading in Early Modern England* (Madison: Univ. of Wisconsin Press, 1984), 211–40.

2. See, particularly, the introduction and the essay by Andrew McRae in *The Country and the City Revisited: England and the Politics of Culture, c. 1550–1850,* ed. Gerald MacLean, Donna Landry, and Joseph P. Ward (Cambridge: Cambridge Univ. Press, 1999).

～ Love Me, Love My Turkey Book: Letters and Turkish Travelogues in Early Modern England

Donna Landry

If we explore the spatial dimensions of the letter, the letter writer is always in some sense a traveler. An epistle documents what has happened to the writer since the last epistle. And so the letter writer is always traveling, explicitly through time, and either explicitly or implicitly across space. The eyewitness account as authenticating gesture belongs equally to the genres of letter writing and travel writing. Paradoxically, as Annabel M. Patterson has argued, it was the *"documentary* status of the letter, as well as its ability to personalize history, that first allured the writers of fiction to it."[1] Reproducing the features of the familiar letter as derived from Cicero, early modern writers appear to have been recycling not as a consequence of emulation-as-compulsion but out of what Patterson calls "'real' needs"; she wonders whether the letter might constitute a "natural genre."[2] The letter's "natural" construction of a self-authenticating self, capable of familiarity, is a convincing fiction. Indispensable in real life, and invaluable for promulgating fiction, might not epistolary form also prove intrinsic to travel writing?

Near the beginning of Rose Macaulay's novel *The Towers of Trebizond,* the narrator Laurie reports of Turkish traveling in the early 1950s: "Aunt Dot said she must get down to her Turkey book quickly, or she would be forestalled by all these tiresome people. Writers all seemed to get the same idea at the same time. One year they would all be rushing for Spain, next year to some island off Italy, then it would be the Greek islands, then

Dalmatia, then Cyprus and the Levant, and now people were all for Turkey."[3] So it also was, once upon a time in the eighteenth century, for English travelers. Like Aunt Dot, Englishwomen seemed to have found a peculiarly appealing combination of freedom and pleasure in Turkish travel. And like Aunt Dot, they felt compelled to write their Turkey books, in spite of the competing presence of all those other Turkey books. As Agnes Dick, wife of the eminent archeologist William Ramsay, admitted in 1897, it had by then become all too common for English travelers exploring "Everyday Life in Turkey" to experience "little but hardship and discomfort, varied by ruins." Based on her own experiences, however, she would nevertheless insist, "But the great charm of Turkish travel is that romantic and quaint experiences come almost daily to those who look for them."[4]

In the beginning there were letters from Turkey. Both the itineraries and the views of Anglo-American women travelers to Turkey have been remarkably repetitive since Lady Mary Wortley Montagu kept edited copies of letters to friends and relations in two small albums during her husband's ambassadorial posting to Constantinople in 1716–18. The same sights and sites are routinely reported across the centuries, often in rapturously similar prose, whether the traveler is touring the Ottoman territories of Bulgaria, the Black Sea, Constantinople, or the Mediterranean coast. But there being no repetitions without differences, subsequent travelers have often prided themselves upon correcting the reports and views of previous travelers. Montagu claims to correct George Sandys, Paul Rycaut, Jean Dumont, and Aaron Hill; Elizabeth, Lady Craven, asserts that she, in turn, is correcting Montagu; Byron's friend John Cam Hobhouse claims to reveal Montagu's untruthfulness once more, this time in the margins of his copy of her *Letters*.

Despite this constant repetition and correction, however, British and American travelers write as if they were the first ever to experience Turkey properly. Whether the traveler is a tourist on holiday, an amateur enthusiast pursuing some line of inquiry (botany, antiquities, Alexander's path), or a professional explorer or archeologist, each has a tendency to behave and record adventures as if entering some preciously personal terra incognita, however well-armed with guidebooks her expedition might be. Historical forgetting of the tracks inevitably left by previous travelers coexists, seemingly without any awareness of contradiction, with the conscious repetition of previous itineraries.

How does epistolarity collude in this construction? We might well conclude from the evidence that the letter writer is in a particularly good position to plead forgetfulness of past precedent and espouse an eyewitness brand of authenticity, both invaluable qualities in a travel writer.

Of Turkey Books

All Turkey books share a repetitive itinerary of places and incidents coupled with a straining after uniqueness. This double compulsion is not, of course, restricted to writers about travel in Turkey. Indeed, Mary Louise Pratt has suggested that the grid of national identity in the period of imperial expansion is so strong that it is hardly surprising to find "German or British accounts of Italy sounding like German or British accounts of Brazil." Since "related dynamics of power and appropriation" are at work in both situations, we might expect remarkable similarities: "The discourses that legitimate bourgeois authority and delegitimate peasant and subsistence lifeways, for example, can be expected to do this ideological work within Europe as well as in southern Africa or Argentina,"[5] or, we might add, the Levant. Undertaking so-called familiar letters as a form of travel writing appears to personalize the account of the foreign—*"I'm here,"* etc.—but cannot thereby escape the workings of ideology within the available discourses.

In spite of the peculiarly personal claims of the letter writer, there can never be a point of origin or even definable beginnings within a system of discursive citation, i.e., within a discourse conceived as an intertextual system. One is always "re-presenting" material, in the double sense of *representation* as described by Gayatri Chakravorty Spivak. The traveler is always simultaneously "standing in" another's shoes and yet failing to do exactly that—failing to produce the same without differences, without artifice and performance. The first sense of representation, my standing in your shoes, is the more literal as well as electoral-political, or "proxy," sense (*Vertretung*). Such a flat-footed form of "literal" representation always fails, because that act of being in the other's shoes involves representation in the other sense, of a theatrical performance or aesthetic production or "portrait" (*Darstellung*). There can be no literal identity between my feet and yours, no matter how well the shoes fit.[6]

Already by Montagu's day, reports of St. Sophia and the Seraglio had become de rigueur, inducing a sense of derivativeness and ennui. "Perhaps

I am in the wrong, but some Turkish Mosques please me better," Montagu writes of St. Sophia, going on to mention the Sulemaniye and the mosque of the Valide Sultan. Of the latter she writes, "St. Paul's Church would make a pitifull figure near it, as any of our Squares would do near the Atlerdan [*sic*] or place of Horses, *At* signifying a horse in Turkish."[7] Up against architectural discourse, even such a confident stylist as Montagu felt her powers failing. She feared she could provide only "a dull, imperfect description of this celebrated building," though her encounter was surely concrete or "hands-on" enough—the roof mosaic work was falling down, and she was presented with "a handfull of it": "I understand Architecture so Little that I am affraid of talking Nonsense in endeavouring to speak of it particularly."[8]

Repetition induces a foolish feeling in the travel writer of imitation without sufficiently personal sensory experience or knowledge—the "got" image or "achieved actuality," we might say, in the spirit of F. R. Leavis.[9] In the interests of this authenticity effect, this thereness of the "I was there" enunciation, it becomes necessary within travel writing to stage increasingly theatrical representations. The irony of all travel writing is that you can be damned sure someone else has already been there, exactly where you have just had an epiphany of uniqueness.

If we read Montagu according to her self-inscription, as "being the first" of a long line of English women travelers to Turkey, the injunction to cover old ground as well as to make it glitter with novelty becomes understandable. Montagu writes as if she were expected to reveal the whole truth of Turkey, including reporting on the previously reported, even sweating over the books of predecessors such as Richard Knolles (who never went there) and Paul Rycaut (who did) to get it right.[10] Here again, as with architectural discourse, she inscribes her failure, searching for a novel alternative. Perhaps a gender-specific alternative? Rather than repeat the already written, Montagu is more inclined, "out of a true female spirit of Contradiction," as she puts it, to correct the falsehoods of previous writers, such as Aaron Hill, who describes the sweating column in St. Sophia.[11] As her editor Robert Halsband notes, however, the sweating column is also mentioned in 1599 by George Douse and in 1610 by George Sandys, and, we might add, in modern guidebooks such as the Blue Guides.[12] I have seen it myself.

Because there can be no repetitions without differences, subsequent travelers have often prided themselves upon correcting the reports and views of previous travelers, which leaves them open to correction in turn. The impulse to contradict is as strong as the compulsion to repeat. Struck by the nakedness of her companions in the *hammam* at Sophia, Lady Mary searches for an art-historical referent: "There were many amongst them as exactly proportion'd as ever any Goddess was drawn by the pencil of Guido or Titian," and she notices that the ladies with "the finest skins and most delicate shapes" gain the "greatest share" of her admiration, though they may not have the most beautiful faces.[13] Nearly seventy years later, Elizabeth, Lady Craven, repeats Montagu only to contradict her: "Few of these women had fair skins or fine forms—hardly any," and "I think I never saw so many fat women at once together, nor fat ones so fat as these," and "The frequent use of hot-baths destroys the solids, and these women at nineteen look older than I am at this moment."[14] (Craven was thirty-six, and had borne six children.)

The "spirit of Contradiction," however, is not exclusively female. In 1813 John Cam Hobhouse, Byron's friend and traveling companion, annotated his copy of Montagu's letters so contentiously that he seems to have delighted in attempting to refute her point by point, especially with regard to Turkish manners, proclaiming that "her representations are not to be depended upon—Some of her assertions none but a *female* traveller can contradict but what a *man* who has seen Turkey can controvert, I am myself capable of proving to be unfounded—From what I have seen of the country, and from what I have read of her book, I am sure that her ladyship would not stick at a little fibbing; and as I know part of her accounts to be altogether false I have a right to suppose she has exaggerated other particulars."[15] Hobhouse's disputes with Montagu revolve around issues of taste, in which he figures as a traditional anti-Turkish Englishman. For instance, when Montagu praises the Turks for their "study of present pleasure," for their having "a right notion of Life" because "They consume it in music, gardens, wine, and delicate eating, while we are tormenting our brains with some scheme of politics, or studying some science to which we can never attain,"[16] Hobhouse adds a penciled note: "—vile music, bad wine & in such eating as would disgust any but a Turk." The emphasis on food is curious, suggesting that Hobhouse was experiencing a kind of culturally induced dyspepsia. However horrified they may have been by other aspects of Ottoman culture, travelers have often been pleasantly surprised by Turkish food. Perhaps Hobhouse had a peculiarly bad time in Turkey because he was traveling with Byron, one of Montagu's most avid readers and admirers. One further effect of travel writing as a discursive system, with which both travelers and travel writers must negotiate, might be called the irritation of influence, the sense that one's impressions must match or measure up to those of one's inevitable predecessors.

Epistolary Love, Epistolary Travel

What Montagu and Craven most strikingly share is a desire to represent Turkey as desirable, and themselves as especially desirable while representing it. As Robert Halsband observes, the "travel-memoir in the form of letters" had been "a literary genre popular since the Renaissance."[17] Montagu's and Craven's travelogues in letters render explicit a certain dynamic in epistolary discourse that might otherwise pass unnoticed: the materiality of the letter encodes a potentially nomadic relation through the separation-conjunction of the correspondents. Janet Gurkin Altman employs a cartographic metaphor to capture this sense of ever-shifting epistolary space: "To write a letter is to map one's coordinates—temporal, spatial, emotional, intellectual—in order to tell someone else where one is located at a particular time and how far one has traveled since the last writing."[18] To pursue this metaphor to its limits would be to conclude that all letter writers are in some sense travel writers. Might the reverse also be true? What would be the good of a Turkey book if there were no audience for it? Might not a travel book, a letter to the public, as it were, on the state of affairs in the Ottoman empire, bear traces of epistolary discourse even as it quite literally maps the traveler's spatial coordinates?

In the course of her travels to Turkey and back, Montagu wrote actual letters to many people in England and on the Continent, but she also prepared in those two small albums what she must have hoped would become a published "Turkey book." To save face, it would have to be posthumously published. Although her feminist friend Mary Astell urged her to publish, and even wrote an enthusiastic preface, Montagu was adamant about maintaining her aristocratic reserve. She could not quench her desire for literary fame, but neither could she openly pursue it because of her rank in society. She told Astell that the Turkish letters were "condemned to obscurity during her life."[19] Or, as Srinivas Aravamudan put it, she could "perish, and then publish."[20]

That Montagu meant to publish these letters, and that she meant this particular work to be her primary claim to fame, is evident from the fact that she took the two albums with her when she left England in 1739, and that on her way home twenty-two years later, while delayed by bad weather in Rotterdam, she gave them to the English clergyman there, Benjamin Sowden, "to be dispos'd of as he thinks proper." This was "the will and design of M. Wortley Montagu, Dec. 11, 1761."[21] Unfortunately, when the letters first appeared in print in May 1763, less than a year after her death, they were taken from a pirated and imperfect manuscript copy of the albums.[22] This corrupt text served as the basis of all editions until 1861, when the albums themselves were first used.[23]

Textual piracy, including spurious interpolations, did not interfere with the book's success, however. Extravagant praise from Smollett, Voltaire, Johnson, and Gibbon immediately followed its first appearance. Multiple editions were necessary to meet readerly demand. Halsband notes that the letters "were the only work Dr. Johnson read for sheer pleasure; and Edward Gibbon, when he finished reading them, exclaimed, 'What fire, what ease, what knowledge of Europe and of Asia!'"[24]

Montagu succeeded in circumventing the constraints of rank by going public posthumously with her literary talents. Her family had not given permission for publication, and her daughter Lady Bute's "sense of propriety was offended," as Halsband observes. Shortly before Lady Bute died, in 1794, she burned what Halsband calls "the voluminous diary kept by Lady Mary from her marriage until the end of her life."[25] Thus did the family have its revenge upon Montagu's adoring public, and future generations of readers and scholars eager to pursue intimate details of the life behind the fire, ease, and cosmopolitan knowledge.

The letters from the Turkish embassy are textured so as to solicit praise from the knowledgeable, but also to endear the writer to all possible readers. Sometimes the erotic structuring of this epistolary travelogue is made explicit. To her friend Lady Bristol from Constantinople in 1718, Montagu writes, after copying a Latin inscription from the serpent column in the Hippodrome, "Your Lord will interpret these lines. Don't fancy they are a Love Letter to him."[26] Going straight to the point, Montagu disavows ex-

actly what many readers *would* fancy. Lady Bristol's husband was John
Hervey, first earl of Bristol, and Montagu's sometime collaborator in scandalous satire.[27] The private joke that wittily binds Montagu to her correspondent Lady Bristol depends upon the fact that the classically educated
Hervey often quoted Latin tags in his letters.[28]

More powerfully solicitous of adoration than the explicit surfacing of
amorous discourse is the technique by which Montagu portrays her exotic surroundings as beautiful and herself as similarly, symbiotically beautiful. In the same letter to Lady Bristol, Montagu delivers this view of one
of Istanbul's most famous beauty spots, the Bosphorus—what is still today enthusiastically described by locals as "a Bosphor view":

> The Asian side is cover'd with fruit trees, villages and the most delightfull
> Landschapes in nature. On the European stands Constantinople, situate on Seven
> Hills. The unequal heights make it seem as Large again as it is (tho' one of the
> Largest Citys in the world), Shewing an agreeable mixture of Gardens, Pine and
> Cypress trees, Palaces, Mosques and publick buildings, rais'd one above another
> with as much Beauty and appearance of Symetry as your Ladyship ever saw in a
> Cabinet adorn'd by the most skilfull hands, Jars shewing themselves above Jars,
> mix'd with Canisters, babys and Candlesticks.[29]

After the practice of Turkish love letters, in which small natural objects
are sent to the beloved, accompanied by a traditional verse, Montagu finds
Turkey "a landscape where things metamorphose into meaning, where
objects are suffused with significances not to be found in dull, one-dimen-
sional English life," as Cynthia Lowenthal observes.[30] The exoticism of the
place translates immediately into rich descriptions and beautiful prose.
According to Lowenthal, Montagu "most fully exploits the romance of the
exotic character of Turkey in her rich and detailed descriptions of Turkish
beauty, descriptions that are the clearest instances of the particular kind of
'othering' found in the embassy letters."[31]

The othering of beautiful objects, including landscapes, but also the
beautiful Turkish women in the *hammam* at Sophia,[32] and Fatima, the
Kahya's lady at Adrianople,[33] is inevitable within Orientalist discourse. As
Meyda Yeğenoğlu has argued, Orientalism is not synonymous with "negative," as opposed to "positive," images of the Orient. So when Montagu
argues that she looks "upon the Turkish Women as the only free people
in the Empire"[34] or claims that "Nothing can look more gay and splendid"

than Turkish floor cushions, adding, "These seats are so convenient and easy I shall never endure Chairs as long as I live,"[35] she has not cast off the Orientalist lens. Rather, the power of Orientalism as a discourse and a system of representation stems "from its power to construct the very object it speaks about and from its power to produce a regime of truth about the Other and thereby establish the identity and the power of the Subject that speaks about it."[36] Montagu's may often be a utopian rendering of Ottoman otherness, but it is a rendering nonetheless contained with Orientalism as a system of representation, in the sense employed by Edward Said: "Every writer on the Orient (and this is true even of Homer) assumes some Oriental precedent, some previous knowledge of the Orient, to which he refers and on which he relies."[37] And Orientalist discourse perpetuates itself precisely as a system of citationality.[38]

Montagu's intricate "Bosphor view" becomes in Byron's citation of it in *Don Juan* "the very view / Which charm'd the charming Mary Montagu." Byron feels compelled not only to repeat the picturesque sight of the Bosphorus but also to remind us of this landscape's intended, because always-already discursively experienced (i.e., cited), effects:

> The European with the Asian shore
>   Sprinkled with palaces; the ocean stream
> Here and there studded with a seventy-four;
>   Sophia's cupola with golden gleam;
> The cypress groves; Olympus high and hoar;
>   The twelve isles, and the more than I could dream,
> Far less describe, present the very view
> Which charm'd the charming Mary Montagu.[39]

Not surprisingly, Byron leaves out the "babys" and the "Candlesticks," the dolls and other domestic curiosities of Montagu's well-wrought cabinet, and substitutes the names of buildings and places. If Montagu gives us the effect of a private view staged within a sumptuous domestic interior, Byron gives us the intimacy of offhand familiarity with the whole splendid scene, as well as an instance of his typically disingenuous use of the inexpressibility topos. Yet we can also hear that Montagu has managed to have her way with Byron, just over a hundred years after she first penned this description. He faithfully reproduces the view that had charmed her and now charms both Juan and Byron, and he also tells us that she herself was charming—at least, she was charming after writing this description of the view.

Not all followers in Montagu's footsteps have been so obsequious as Byron (remember Hobhouse), or so enamored of her representations. In 1786 Elizabeth, Lady Craven, bent on having her own adventure in Ottoman travel, dismissed Montagu's letters as so untruthful as to constitute forgeries, declaring that "whoever wrote L. M——'s Letters (for she never wrote a line of them) misrepresents things most terribly—I do really believe, in most things they wished to impose upon the credulity of their readers, and laugh at them."[40] Craven needs to have it both ways. She needs to avoid seeming to cast aspersions on the veracity of her predecessor and fellow noblewoman. And she also needs to clear a space for her own fresh perceptions of Turkey as the unrivaled truth. She is not far wrong about some few aspects of the *Letters* as they were presented to the public between 1763 and 1861, but the imperfect text was by no means so corrupt as to constitute a forgery, or to make it somehow not Montagu's work. Craven's dismissal of the authenticity of the *Letters* is transparently self-serving.

Having displaced Montagu by discrediting her book, Craven can now write her own description of a "Bosphor view" in deliberately wishful ignorance of Montagu's: "But I am certain no landscape can amuse or please in comparison with the varied view which the borders of this famed Straight compose—Rocks, verdure, ancient castles, built on the summit of the hills by the Genoese—modern Kiosks, Minarets, and large platane-trees, rising promiscuous in the vallies—large meadows—multitudes of people, and boats swarming on the shore; and on the water; . . . and a graceful confusion and variety make this living picture the most poignant scene I ever beheld."[41] Such a sensuous description of Turkish topography, flora, and fauna, I would argue, cannot *not* reflect back upon the writer as comparably, proximately, contingently desirable.

Montagu's most famous strategy for Turkifying herself was her donning her "Turkish habit."[42] Marcia Pointon has argued that, in combination with her written representations, the portraits Montagu had painted of herself in Turkish dress present her as "in possession of herself" and as "object of her own pleasure."[43] Dressed to kill off readerly skepticism, Montagu writes as one who has fallen in love with Turkish culture because the Turks' own appreciation of beauty indicates that Ottoman culture has itself been thoroughly aestheticized—that is to say, aestheticized first by the Turks themselves, in Montagu's account, and then doubly aestheticized by her appropriation. Claiming eyewitness authority, Montagu achieves this double vision through sleight of hand. She adopts a rhetorical survival strategy necessitated by the double bind of going Turkish in her mind and self-authorized representations,[44] a form of narcissistic pleasure, and yet, by continuing to be sensibly English, wishing to please as well as tease and provoke her English audience. Ottoman culture becomes both a stick with which to beat Englishness and an utopian alternative to it. Srinivas Aravamudan calls the process by which Montagu "places and then hedges her cultural bets" a form of "levantinization," or of "intellectual wagering without accountability": "To run or throw a levant was to make a bet with the intention of absconding if it was lost. My reading suggests that the aristocratic Montagu uses her ample intellectual 'credit' for the purposes of an utopian levantinization. The objective of Montagu's highly speculative intellectual wagers is the task of cross-cultural apprehension."[45] And so Montagu throws herself into minitreatises on how the Turks, so often despised by Europeans for being either terribly bloodthirsty or effeminately decadent, in fact "have a right notion of Life."

This opinion, which so infuriated Byron's friend Hobhouse, is offered not in an inflammatory way. Montagu definitely hedges her bets, rather than gambling recklessly on successful levantinization. To the Abbé Conti, a more cosmopolitan correspondent than many, she writes:

> Thus you see, Sir, these people are not so unpolish'd as we represent them. Tis true their Magnificence is of a different taste from ours, and perhaps of a better. I am allmost of opinion they have a right notion of Life; while they consume it in Music, Gardens, Wine, and delicate eating, while we are tormenting our brains with some Scheme of Politics or studying some Science to which we can never attain, or if we do, cannot perswade people to set that value upon it we do ourselves. . . . We dye, or grow old and decrepid, before we can reap the fruit of our Labours. Considering what short liv'd, weak Animals Men are, is there any study so beneficial as the study of present pleasure? . . . I allow you to laugh at me for the sensual declaration that I had rather be a rich Effendi with all his ignorance, than Sir Isaac Newton with all his knowledge.[46]

Praising the sensuousness and beauty of Turkish material culture, she aims to win her European audience to valuing a Turkish point of view on the desirability of pleasure—"Music, Gardens, Wine, and delicate eating." Of the actual *superiority* of pleasure to learning, and of the cultivation of beauty to commercial or political ambition, she is "allmost" persuaded, but not quite. Such a philosophy, in which the particularly English-sounding obsessions of partisan scheming and amateur science were displaced, would certainly make the position of upper-class English women easier to bear. I think this passage provides valuable evidence to support Elizabeth Bohls's claim that the "most painful, deeply repressed, inarticulate and virtually inarticulable longings of eighteenth-century British women" were "not sexual but finally political."[47]

Craven, loving to correct Montagu's views and thus legitimate her own, focuses her correspondence on a particular object rather than disseminating it among multiple readers. Having separated from her husband of sixteen years in 1783, she addresses all her letters to her married lover, the margrave of Anspach, as if they were brother and sister. Hers is a much more direct approach than Montagu's: love my letters, love me, marry me when your wife and Lord Craven are dead. The pair would indeed marry, in 1791, soon after the death of the margrave's wife and Craven's husband.[48] As we have seen, when Craven arrives at Constantinople via the Bosphorus, her prose becomes lyrical with admiration, just like Montagu's, though she would dispute any influence: "The Turks have so great a respect for natural beauties, that if they must build a house where a tree stands, they leave a large hole for the tree to pass through and increase in size, they think the branches of it the prettiest ornament for the top of the house; in truth, Sir, contrast a chimney to a beautiful foliage, and judge if they are right or wrong."[49] Once again like Montagu, but without acknowledging her as any kind of precedent, Craven singles out the relative freedom of Turkish women for astonished praise. She imagines Turkish women to be "in their manner of living, capable of being the happiest creatures breathing":[50] "I think I never saw a country where women may enjoy so much liberty, and free from all reproach, as in Turkey—A Turkish husband that sees a pair of slippers at the door of his harem must not enter; his respect for the sex prevents him from intruding when a stranger is there upon a visit; how easy then it is for men to visit and pass for women—If I was to walk about the streets here I would certainly wear the same dress, for the Turkish women call others names, when they meet them with their faces uncovered—When I go out I have the Ambassador's Sedan-chair."[51]

The irritation of Montaguian influence seems palpable here. From the declaration that Turkish women are freer than any other women, to the fantasy that Turkish women perpetually engage in heterosexual intrigues right under their husbands' noses, Craven echoes Montagu's observations as if she were the first to witness them. Yet she will not tag along after Montagu in the streets, shrouded in what Montagu called a "Ferigée."[52] Refusing to follow in Montagu's footsteps, she follows her unconsciously into the ambassadorial sedan-chair instead. It is as if Montagu were everywhere, as unavoidable as divinity.

But far from experiencing any desire to go Turkish, any wagering on cultural difference as enlightening transformation, Craven, writing to her German lover, becomes more English than Montagu, almost "more English than the English." Turkey, we are told, possesses natural beauties, but the local culture of ignorance and idleness has retarded its development: "Perhaps, Sir, it is lucky for Europe that the Turks are idle and ignorant—the immense power this empire might have, were it peopled by the industrious and ambitious, would make it the mistress of the world."[53] Untapped power has its own appeal. Craven writes as if cheek to cheek with a sleeping giant of possibility.

For the Turks themselves, she has little good to say. "I think of all the two-legged animals I have seen I should regret killing a Turk the least,"[54] she quips. To support her opinion of the national identity as ignorant and idle, Craven describes Turks making a pastime of doing nothing. The problem with this approach is that we have to wonder how long she herself watched the man watching the bottle in the stream: "The quiet stupid Turk will sit a whole day by the side of the Canal, looking at flying kites or children's boats—and I saw one who was enjoying the shade of an immense platane-tree—his eyes fixed on a kind of bottle, diverted by the noise and motion of it, while the stream kept it in constant motion—How the business of the nation goes on at all I cannot guess."[55] One can imagine the Lake poets engaging in just such contemplation of the forces of nature at work in everyday sights, even bobbing bits of litter in a stream, but Craven's notion of her own national identity is quite different from, say, Coleridge's. According to her, the problem with Turkish idleness is that it looks stupid to an English eye. She struggles to understand this inertia in terms of political unrest in the Ottoman empire: "[The Turks'] revolted pachas give them too much trouble, constantly, not to make them desire eternal peace with their foreign neighbours. . . . . The perpetual disquietude of the empire makes the thinking Turk find a comfort in the dull moments of rest he finds upon his carpet, spread under the lofty platane—and we must not wonder to see so many of them seemingly to enjoy moments, which to us would be death-like stupidity."[56] The upshot of the difference between Turkey and England is that Turkey is ripe for European intervention. In this respect Craven anticipates such British agents as Frederick Burnaby, actors in the Great Game to minimize Russian and French influence in the region and secure trade routes to India: "To some nations it would be very agreeable that the Turkish empire was to be driven from a situation which seems by nature formed as an universal passage for trading nations, which the inactivity of the Turks has too long obstructed."[57] In the next sentence, Craven puts herself firmly on the side of those nations to whom it would be agreeable if the Turks were driven eastward. All who "bear any respect to the best monuments of sculpture," we are told, must be in favor of liberating Athens from Ottoman rule, in order that "all it yet contains, might not by Mahometan ignorance be entirely destroyed."[58] Preserving the Elgin marbles for transportation to the British Museum, Craven attempts to win points with her readers by calling a Turk a Turk.

The presence of such prejudices in the writing of this bold and otherwise intelligent woman more than six decades after Montagu's sojourn in Turkey reveals the difference those decades had made—not only to the Ottoman empire, now perceived by Europeans as ailing and decadent rather than terrible in its power, but also to aristocratic English womanhood. Montagu was both ahead of her time and characteristic of a time in which it was possible for a woman to be so bold. In Bohls's terms, as the eighteenth century progressed, Montagu's claim to "the privilege of the aesthetic subject" came to seem "increasingly quixotic."[59] Yet her work continued to legitimate the authorship of women like Craven.

Nowhere are Montagu and Craven closer in their shared efforts to achieve cultural power through aesthetic representation than when showing themselves off on horseback. Part of the projection of beauty and desirability in epistolary travel is achieved through making oneself a spectacle, a sight. Montagu achieves this aestheticization by describing herself in Turkish dress, but there is also a notable self-representation on horseback.

Montagu figures herself as having astonished everyone in Adrianople with her sidesaddle, as if it were Columbus's ship seen by New World natives. Of Turkish horses Montagu writes: "They are beautiful and full of spirit, but generally little and not so strong as the breed of Colder Countrys, very gentle with all their vivacity, swift and sure footed. I have a little white favourite that I would not part with on any terms. He prances under me with so much fire you would think that I had a great deal of courage to dare Mount him, yet I'll assure you I never rid a Horse in my life so much at my command. My Side Saddle is the first was ever seen in this part of the World and gaz'd at with as much wonder as the ship of Columbus was in America."[60] Whether favorable or critical, all early modern English representations of Ottoman society negotiate a course within the discursive grid of Orientalism. Even in the act of praising the beauty and spirit of Turkish Arab horses, Montagu cannot help appreciating their subservience. This passage radiates a self-congratulatory sense of English cultural imperialism in feminine form. Lisa Lowe remarks how Montagu's riding sidesaddle emblematizes "the English command over and domestication of animals," while "her description of the natural hierarchy of beasts and horses might itself be understood to contain an allegorical defense of the 'natural order' of colonialism," dramatized in the comparison between the sidesaddle and Columbus's ship as objects of the colonized people's fascination.[61]

Through the white stallion's hot-blooded but sensitive, well-schooled Arabianness, Montagu is able to project herself as a spectacle of English cultural superiority. She can partake of English dominance as if she were reconquering the New World, rewriting Spanish imperialism as British. She is also a woman mastering an "Arab"—i.e., "Other"—stallion through her distinctively English gender machine.[62] Thus a history of European imperial conquest and colonial dominance enables one woman to script for herself a moment of powerful self-assertion and cross-cultural exhibitionism. The passage is also a fetching portrait of the letter writer, in command of something more phallic than a pen.

Craven, too, offers herself as an equestrian spectacle, both to the astonished locals wherever she goes and to her readers. While crossing Italy en route to the Ottoman territories, she takes a perverse pleasure in eliciting lamentations and prayers from the Italians, who, like the Turks, have never seen a woman riding sidesaddle before: "A lady on a side-saddle is an object of great wonder here—the peasants who pass me on the right side, when I am on horseback, the women, particularly, say, *Poverina—Jesu Maria—Povera—una gambia*—They actually fancy I have one leg only; their stare of concern always makes me laugh—and then they add *cara* to their lamentations."[63] Thus does the English traveler ride roughshod over the continent of Europe in the age of imperial expansion.

Such a sight does Craven present that even a fellow English traveler cannot stop himself from pursuing her rudely in the hope of finding out just who she is. But that is an impudence Craven's aristocratic reserve will not brook. Avoiding the public recognition of her face, especially by an English interloper, Craven literally stops the traffic:

I passed by a gentleman in an English phaeton, whose curiosity I suppose was awakened by an English horse and side-saddle—From an uncommon slow trot he flew after me full gallop—I was warned of this frightful operation by my servant, and had just time to turn my horse into a gateway—he could not stop his horses immediately—but being determined to see me, as soon as he could, he pulled up, and went as slow as it was possible—I thought this so impertinent, that I determined on my part, that he should not see me; . . . I passed by the left side of the phaeton as fast as my horse could go, with my hat and head so low, that the foolish man could not see me—My horse is a most excellent and fleet one, and I kept him on till my pursuer gave up the chase.[64]

How dare a mere Englishman interfere, by gazing at her, with Lady Craven's pleasure on the road? She sees him off with proper indignation, making it plain that national identity does not guarantee any fellowship of travelers abroad. But, like Montagu, Craven has managed through the relation of this incident to inscribe herself firmly in her readers' minds as a—literally—dashing figure on horseback.

After pages of scopophilic travel narration, the voyeuristic traveler revealing herself as exhibitionist could be said to constitute the ritualized climax of much travel writing. In the nineteenth century, Sir Charles Fellows complained that he found it "very difficult in travelling through this country to write a journal, or pursue any occupation requiring attention," for as soon as he arrived anywhere, he found his apartment "half filled with Turks, who, with the most friendly intention, bring their pipes and sit down, saying everything that is kind and hospitable, and watching every motion of my lips and hands. . . . A few years ago they would not even look at or speak to an infidel or a Ghiaour; whereas I now receive the salutation of all the gazers assembled to see me mount my horse, with its European saddle. The bridle is generally put on wrong, with the curb-chain over the nose, and the neck-strap buckled in front of the head, and the putting this right excites much curiosity."[65] Without their saddles and bridles, would these English people have seemed unremarkably normal to the locals? The European technologies of horseback travel provide the Englishman with a chance for unselfconscious exhibitionism. If the Englishwomen are appealing to their readers to fall in love with them, the men hope to be envied for their gadgets, and for their command of situations.

Montagu wrote to win the love and admiration of her friends, Craven of her lover. But both also solicited the admiration of a wider audience through publication. They wished to be remembered as clever travelers in an exotic landscape and, by association, as women of beauty, beautiful women. Montagu especially had an eye toward winning the love of posterity; her Turkish letters were the single work she most wished to have published. And since her letters are the single work of hers receiving the most critical attention today, courtesy of both feminist and postcolonial studies, it would seem that she succeeded. We might say that both Montagu and Craven, articulating their epistolary prowess as feminine desirability, succeeded in their designs.

The Afterlife of Turkey Books

What might have been the views of Turkish readers of English Turkey books? So far, the archives have been singularly unhelpful in this search. The closest I have come to an example suggests nothing so such as, once again, Montagu's pervasive influence. *A Turkish Woman's European Impressions,* published in 1913, is, not surprisingly, an epistolary work. In a letter written at Fontainebleau in September 1906, Zeyneb Hanoum ("my lady Zeyneb," a woman of good family), who is, according to the title page, also the "Heroine of Pierre Loti's Novel 'Les Désenchantées,'" has this to say about Montagu:

Amongst my favourite English books were . . . Lady Mary Montagu's *Letters.* Over and over again, and always with fresh interest, I read those charming and clever letters. Although they are the letters of another century, there is nothing in them to shock or surprise a Turkish woman of to-day in their criticism of our life. It is curious to notice, when reading Lady Mary's *Letters,* how little the Turkey of to-day differs from the Turkey of her time; only, Turkey, the child that Lady Mary knew, has grown into a big person.

There are two great ways, however, in which we have become too modern for Lady Mary's book. In costume we are on a level with Paris, seeing we buy our clothes there; and as regards culture, we are perhaps more advanced than is the West, since we have so much leisure for study, and are not hampered with your Western methods. And yet how little we are known by the European critics![66]

This text from the era of prerepublican reform in Turkish politics and culture comes to us mediated by its editor, Grace Ellison, who in her own roughly contemporaneous book, *An Englishwoman in a Turkish Harem,* sets the scene for Zeyneb's reflections: "Let those Western critics, who have taken such a deliberate stand against the present government and declared 'the new order of things worse than the old,' take into consideration such details as the opening of a restaurant for Turkish women. It is part of a great scheme of reform, and everything is going on in proportion. In 1908 more than two men sitting at a café together were 'suspect' and reported at headquarters; in 1913 Turkish *women* meet in a restaurant and discuss political subjects—certainly this is not the Turkey I expected to see."[67] The Turkey one expects to see is never, quite, the Turkey that's there, for there is always the presence of the Turks themselves to be accounted for, making their own history, even returning the Europeans' gaze. According to Zeyneb, unhampered by Western methodicality, but now also freed from those sumptuous but heavy Turkish outfits of yesteryear, modern Turkish women wish to be "known by"—not only read by, but adored by— "European critics." Wearing Paris fashions, these Turkish women are dressed precisely to kill off skepticism in their European readers. And still there is silence from Europe!

Once again we recognize the irritation of influence, the desire for the Turkifying Turkey to go native in: A pity about the Paris clothes, isn't it?

Postscript by Martha Nell Smith

Dear Donna:
Your exquisite essay, detailed with epistolary accounts of the Blue Mosque, a sweating pillar, and the Bosphorus, arrived on the greyest winter day, its re-presentations

shimmering before me, your wit tickling my self-reflexive fancy. My own coming to terms with the West's Orientalisms is not something I have invested enough time pondering, and your excavations of various layers of epistolary renderings to over-write previous imperial accounts and seduce private and public readers proved inspirational for a variety of reasons. Montagu had her way with Byron, and you certainly had your way with this reader.

Turns of familiar phrases—"dressed to kill off readerly skepticism" to describe Montagu's self-pleasures as she dons Turkish costume to go where no woman dared, and "in command of something more phallic than a pen" to recount the authority of her pleasure ensconced in her "sidesaddle" for Turkish eyes and to command powerful male equine flesh from an especial seat designed to accommodate the supposedly inferior sex—enact far more than readerly delight as they turn critical attention to the multiple levels of intellectual seduction. "Dressed to kill off readerly skepticism" aptly concludes this palimpsestic meditation as you recount Zeyneb's early-twentieth-century reading of Lady Montagu's Letters, *as she hopes to attract Western admiration, having shed the "Turkish habit" of costume that confuses the gendered rigors of European attire for the delineating styles of Parisian dress that relegate each sex to its "proper" place. When East moves West in cultural cross-dressing, possibilities for gender-crossing are lost, an irony that becomes palpable when one remembers the presumptions of Orientalist ideologies that emphasize veiling to persuade Western women of our good fortune and to elide critical reflection on customs that bind by the circumference of a skirt and that make females on horseback appear to be monopeds (which Lady Craven gleefully remarks with her "They [Italian observers] actually fancy I have one leg only"). Though their appetites for asserting "cultural power through aesthetic representation" are on prominent display, both Montagu and Craven exult in "a country where women may enjoy so much liberty," and thereby highlight just how complex are the machines of imperialism.*

You deftly account the "irritation(s) of influence" as Hobhouse and Craven correct Montagu in order to establish authority of impression and thus underwrite their own accounts by overwriting those of their predecessor. I found myself wondering, asking my colleagues and friends and creating great stirs in the university's hall and at the dining room table with the question, "In our technologies of critical writing are we all now part Englishman and part Englishwoman, trying to entice our readers both to fall in love with us and to envy our gadgets, our theoretical command, whatever our situations of study?" This seems to me not an especially astute observation on my part, so imagine my surprise at the immense irritation expressed under the influence of such a question about our "letter(s) to the World."

With quietly resonant simple declarations such as yours about the sweating pillar—"I have seen it myself"—your "letter to the World" also seems very much a let-

ter to me and every other individual reader fortunate enough to enjoy its deep and lasting pleasures. As did Lady Montagu, Zeyneb asserts "a right notion of Life," one with plenty of "leisure for study" and time for taking the "present pleasure[s]" of music, gardens, wine, delectables; and as you, Donna Landry, write from that notion at the other end of the century from Zeyneb and centuries away from Montagu, you present those pleasures and thereby bestow on each and every reader perpetual opportunity for taking up the subject of living fully in intellectual, emotional, erotic, aesthetic pleasures. No reader of your essay can possibly resist authoring, and in my book, that is the highest achievement of any work in letters.

Is it too imperial of me to ask that the next time you are easterly, you drop me a postcard of "a Bosphor view"? Since the postcard is by its very embodiment an "open letter," I should want that, for your generative insights are far too rewarding to be enveloped.

With warm regards & admiration,

Martha Nell Smith
Takoma Park, Maryland
Spring 1998

Notes

1. Annabel M. Patterson, *Censorship and Interpretation: The Conditions of Writing and Reading in Early Modern England* (Madison: Univ. of Wisconsin Press, 1984), 211.

2. Ibid., 212.

3. Rose Macaulay, *The Towers of Trebizond* (1956; rpt. New York: Carroll & Graf, 1995), 15.

4. Mrs. W. M. Ramsay, preface to *Everyday Life in Turkey* (London: Hodder & Stoughton, 1897), vii.

5. Mary Louise Pratt, *Imperial Eyes: Travel Writing and Transculturation* (New York: Routledge, 1992), 10.

6. See the discussion in Gayatri Chakravorty Spivak, *The Postcolonial Critic: Interviews, Strategies, Dialogues*, ed. Sarah Harasym (New York: Routledge, 1990), 108–9.

7. Montagu to Lady Bristol [10 April 1718], *The Complete Letters of Lady Mary Wortley Montagu*, ed. Robert Halsband, 3 vols. (Oxford: Clarendon Press, 1965–67), 1:399–400. Hereafter cited as *Letters*.

8. Montagu to Lady Bristol [10 April 1718], *Letters*, 1:399.

9. See F. R. Leavis, *Revaluation: Tradition and Development in English Poetry* (1936; rpt. Harmondsworth: Penguin, 1972), 25.

10. Montagu to the Countesse of —— [May 1718], *Letters*, 1:405.

11. Ibid., 1:405–6.

12. Ibid., 1:406 n. 1; Bernard McDonagh, *Blue Guide: Turkey* (New York: Norton, 1995), 89–90.

13. Montagu to Lady ——, 1 April [1717], *Letters*, 1:314.

14. Letters 56 [Athens] and 49, Palais de France, Pera, 7 May 1786, *A Journey through the Crimea to Constantinople. In a Series of Letters from the Right Honourable Elizabeth Lady Craven, to His Serene Highness the Margrave of Brandebourg, Anspach, and Bareith. Written in the Year 1786* (London: printed for G. G. J. Robinson, 1789), 264, 263–64, 226. Hereafter cited as *Journey*.

15. *Letters of the Right Honourable Lady M——y W——y M——e; Written during Her Travels in Europe, Asia, and Africa, to Persons of Distinction, Men of Letters, &c. in Different Parts of Europe. Which Contain, among Other Curious Relations, Accounts of the Policy and Manners of the Turks. Drawn from Sources That Have Been Inaccessible to Other Travellers* ["A New Edition, Complete in One Volume"] (London: printed for John Taylor, 1790), MS notes by John C. Hobhouse, A.M., 1813. British Library shelfmark: 1477.b.29.

16. Ibid., 149; in the Halsband edition of Montagu's *Letters*, this passage appears on 1:415.

17. Robert Halsband, introduction to vol. 1 of the *Letters*, 1:xiv–xv.

18. Janet Gurkin Altman, *Epistolarity: Approaches to a Form* (Columbus: Ohio State Univ. Press, 1982), 119.

19. Robert Halsband, *The Life of Lady Mary Wortley Montagu* (Oxford: Clarendon Press, 1956), 278.

20. Srinivas Aravamudan, "Lady Mary Wortley Montagu in the *Hammam*: Masquerade, Womanliness, and Levantinization," *ELH* 62.1 (spring 1995): 69–104; this passage on 88.

21. See *Letters*, 1:xvii.

22. See *Letters of the Right Honourable Lady M——y W——y M——e . . .* , 3 vols. (London: printed for T. Becket and P. A. De Hondt, 1763).

23. *Letters*, 1:xvii.

24. Halsband, *Life*, 289.

25. Ibid., 289.

26. Montagu to Lady Bristol [10 April 1718], *Letters*, 1:401.

27. In 1732 Hervey and Montagu would satirize Pope in *Verses to the Imitator of Horace*, and in 1735, Pope would pillory Montagu as *"Sapho"* and Hervey as the sexually ambiguous *"Sporus"* in *Epistle to Dr. Arbuthnot*. See *The Poems of Alexander Pope: A One-Volume Edition of the Twickenham Text*, ed. John Butt (London: Methuen, 1963), lines 101, 323–25.

28. See Halsband, *Letters*, 1:401 n. 1.

29. Montagu to Lady Bristol [10 April 1718], *Letters*, 1:397.

30. Cynthia Lowenthal, *Lady Mary Wortley Montagu and the Eighteenth-Century Familiar Letter* (Athens: Univ. of Georgia Press, 1994), 81.

31. Ibid., 101–2.

32. Montagu to Lady ——, 1 April [1717], *Letters*, 1:312–15.

33. Montagu to Lady Mar, 18 April [1717], *Letters*, 1:349–52.

34. Montagu to Lady Mar, 1 April [1717], *Letters*, 1:329.

35. Montagu to [Anne] Thistlethwayte, 1 April [1717], *Letters*, 1:343.

36. Meyda Yeğenoğlu, "Supplementing the Orientalist Lack: European Ladies in the Harem," in *Orientalism and Cultural Differences*, ed. Mahmut Mutman and Meyda Yeğenoğlu, *Inscriptions* 6 (Santa Cruz: Univ. of California, 1993), 45–80; the passage is on 69.

37. Edward Said, *Orientalism* (New York: Vintage Books, 1979), 20.

38. See Jacques Derrida, "Limited Inc.: abc," trans. Samuel Weber, *Glyph* 2 (1977): 162–254, and Gayatri Chakravorty Spivak, "Revolutions That as Yet Have No Model: Derrida's 'Limited

Inc.,'" in *The Spivak Reader,* ed. Donna Landry and Gerald MacLean (New York: Routledge, 1996), 75–106.

39. Lord Byron, *Don Juan,* in *The Poetical Works of Byron,* ed. Robert F. Gleckner (Boston: Houghton Mifflin, 1975), 5.3.1–8.

40. Craven, letter 28, Vienna, 14 Dec. 1785, *Journey,* 105.

41. Craven, letter 45, Palais de France, Pera, 20 April 1786, *Journey,* 199. (Note: "Kiosk means a summer-house with blinds all round.")

42. Montagu to Lady Mar, 1 April [1717], *Letters,* 1:326–27.

43. Marcia Pointon, "Killing Pictures," in *Painting and the Politics of Culture: New Essays on British Art, 1700–1850,* ed. John Barrell (New York: Oxford Univ. Press, 1992,), 39–72; these passages are on 70 and 63. In this sense the portraits serve as "reparation" (60) for Montagu's actual physical body at thirty-six, scarred by smallpox and aging (40).

44. This license of the mental traveler is captured in the old joke, "She's wandering in her mind again." "Don't worry, she can't go far!"

45. Aravamudan, "Montagu in the *Hammam,*" 70.

46. Montagu to the Abbé Conti, 19 May 1718, *Letters,* 1:414–15.

47. Elizabeth A. Bohls, *Women Travel Writers and the Language of Aesthetics, 1716–1818* (New York: Cambridge Univ. Press, 1995), 45.

48. *Dictionary of National Biography,* 1:508–9. Elizabeth, born in 1750, was the youngest daughter of Augustus, fourth earl of Berkeley, and Elizabeth, daughter of Henry Drax, of Charborough in Dorset. Lord Craven died in September 1791, and Elizabeth married the margrave the following month. In 1792, they moved to Hammersmith. He died in 1806, she in Naples in 1828.

49. Craven, letter 45, Palais de France, Pera, 20 April 1786, *Journey,* 199.

50. Craven, letter 50, *Journey,* 234.

51. Craven, letter 46, 25 April 1786, *Journey,* 205.

52. Montagu to Lady Mar, 1 April [1717], *Letters,* 1:328.

53. Craven, letter 46, 25 April 1786, *Journey,* 206.

54. Craven, letter 62, Varna, 8 July 1786, *Journey,* 295.

55. Craven, letter 46, 25 April 1786, *Journey,* 207.

56. Craven, letter 67, Vienna, 30 Aug. 1786, *Journey,* 326.

57. Craven, letter 48, *Journey,* 220.

58. Ibid., 220–21.

59. Bohls, *Women Travel Writers,* 45.

60. Montagu to [Anne] Thistlethwayte, 1 April [1717], *Letters,* 1:341.

61. Lisa Lowe, *Critical Terrains: French and British Orientalisms* (Ithaca: Cornell Univ. Press, 1991), 50.

62. See Gilles Deleuze and Félix Guattari, *Anti-Oedipus: Capitalism and Schizophrenia,* trans. Robert Hurley, Mark Seem, and Helen R. Lane (Minneapolis: Univ. of Minnesota Press, 1983), 32. A sidesaddle may not have moving parts (it is the woman using it who moves, grips, balances) but it functions as a social machine to generate gender difference. Deleuze and Guattari's notion that a "technical machine" is "not a cause but merely an index of a general form of social production" is useful. Outside Britain and France, sidesaddles were often unknown until well into the nineteenth century. Montagu was delighted to be liberated from one when she rode with Italian women in later life; see her letter to Lady Bute, 1 Oct. [1749],

Letters, 2:444. In most of the world, women rode astride. I have analyzed the history and significance of the sidesaddle extensively in an unpublished manuscript, *The Making of the English Hunting Seat*.

63. Craven, letter 22, Pisa-Baths, 20 Sept. 1785, *Journey*, 77.

64. Craven, letter 23, Florence, 28 Sept. 1785, *Journey*, 79.

65. Sir Charles Fellows, *Travels and Researches in Asia Minor, More Particularly in the Province of Lycia* (London: John Murray, 1852), 61.

66. Zeyneb Hanoum, *A Turkish Woman's European Impressions*, ed. Grace Ellison (London: Seeley, Service & Co., 1913), 38–39.

67. Grace Ellison, *An Englishwoman in a Turkish Harem* (London: Methuen, 1915), 5.

Love Stories? Epistolary Histories of Mary Queen of Scots

Clare Brant

cacher / to hide

A deliberative figure: the amorous subject wonders, not whether he should declare his love to the loved being (this is not a figure of avowal), but to what degree he should conceal the turbulencies of his passion: his desires, his distresses; in short, his excesses (in Racinian language: his fureur*).*

—Roland Barthes, *A Lover's Discourse: Fragments*

Barthes describes the lover's penchant for concealment under the witty heading *Dark Glasses,* a trope that also evokes, for me, the figure of the critic, as deliberative, as devious even, as the lover. Why do any of us work on what we do? Professional decorum screens out this question, but I suspect that the attractions, affinities, indifferences, and repulsions that mark our preferences as critics for one corpus of texts over another are kin to those drives that lead us to select love objects in our personal lives. There are certainly good reasons to spare academic writers, and readers, from discussions of these drives. But the study of love letters requires an acknowledgment that in this genre (perhaps above all), critics wear dark glasses, as if to disguise the glare of their involvements. For reading someone else's love letters is singular in several ways. The single figure of the critic gate-crashes a relationship between two people, in willful intrusion on intimacy. This snooping is sanctioned by scholarship, and the critic can expiate at least a little for trespass by self-consciousness. After all, critics, like lovers, understand solitude and its relations to writing; like lovers, they want words to seduce their readers, even as they are frustrated by the treachery of words. In reading love letters I am conscious of myself as a lover of words and an amorous subject. For my singular infraction of the writers' privacy, I pay with acknowledgement of my own secrets: so this is how you love! *me too,* or, *so do not I!* Intimacies collide and collude: mine with my lovers, theirs with their lovers, mine with their lovers and them.[1]

Reading letters raises questions about how readers become parti pris: to one side of a correspondence, to one correspondence rather than another, to one epistolary genre or a historical period rather than another. Love letters are especially relevant here because on the one hand we know love is a historical passion (though its variables are more clearly seen in histories of sex or marriage); on the other, we know love is timeless and the lover an archetype that escapes history, like the Lover in a tarot pack. Likewise, love, whether same-sexed or heterosexed, is perceived as historically continuous—lovers like the poor are always with us—and yet subject to ideologies of sex and gender that are always present, but also always altering. This pattern of constancy and change in what we understand love to be and do sets up turbulencies such that it is not surprising critics want a fiction of their own detachment. (And *dark glasses* is such an arresting image . . .) Moreover, though I have used the term *critic* loosely to mean a professional reader, one should distinguish between the literary critic and the historian, since each prefers its own brand of dark glasses (not least so as to put the other in the shade); different disciplines have different histories of reading letters, in which gender plays different parts. In eighteenth-century readings of Mary Queen of Scots's letters, for instance, homosociality between historians coexisted with chivalric sympathy; in contrast, women writers were more interested in establishing the queen as powerfully articulate and a Stuart monarch genealogically and emotionally connected to contemporary political interests.

I sketch in these parameters as preface to a history of the readings of a particular set of letters and the tangle of intimacies surrounding them because I want to argue that epistolary history should include the history of readers. The history at issue is not simply one of class or gender or race or profession or political or religious belief, though all of these elements come into it. Nor is it simply a paradigm of disclosure from private to public: although third-party readings and printing alter the intimacies of love letters, those letters can be resurrounded by secrecy—in the case I want to discuss, the letters were sequestered as state secrets and marketed within the genre of secret history. The history of readers and readings should consider not only when the reader is reading but what kind of letter the reader thinks it is, and with whom this reading will be shared. These are questions of literary history: what other kinds of letters has the reader read in order to be able to place this one? Literacy or publicity can be as important as identity in the history of epistolary readers.

The texts I want to discuss are two sets of letters written in whole or in part (and that is the question) by Mary Queen of Scots. All of the readers I discuss (myself included) wanted to make something of these letters and, in different ways, to naturalize their interpretations even as they cast them in discursively explicit genres such as history, biography or fiction. In order not to add autobiography to this list, I will keep my own history off the page, except for one story. I taught for a couple of years at Cambridge University in a college that was founded during the Reformation. On the site, appropriated by Henry VIII, had stood a nunnery famous for learning, and of which every trace was obliterated. The founder's emblem (a cock) was everywhere in evidence, but in the dining hall was one welcome image of a woman: a small portrait of Mary Queen of Scots. She was stuck high up in a dark corner, a queen's head in a frame the size of a postage stamp; her face had the complexion of Gorgonzola, and an air of regret as if at her neglect. The portrait's lack of expression was curiously compelling, given that its subject had starred in romance and tragedy, history and poetry, drama and legend. Its perverse lack of affect was probably what made me more alert to the excess of affect with which people seemed to read her letters, from her own time to mine. Hence my interest in Mary Queen of Scots, as an icon who was and is constructed from notions of women, texts, and histories. The specificity of these is masked by romance, so that the love story is also about our feelings for the queen as much as hers for any man; she is object as much as agent. Her epistolary voice, in consequence, gets read within this force-field of our desires. The associated discursive tensions are like borders—they divide us off from the subject—but they do not necessarily mark off one discourse from another. Oddly, in fact, they allow simultaneous topographies: so the letters of Mary Queen of Scots can be the terrain of both fiction and history, and without having to be placed in terms of the true and the untrue. My argument contributes little to the historiography of Mary Queen of Scots, but explores eighteenth-century readings of her story by a selection of male historians and female novelists in order to show how their interpretations of the letters employ differently gendered fictions.

Jane Austen observed famously in *Northanger Abbey* that history had few women in it. Royal women, however, have been unequivocally visible, and of all the queens in British history none have been more fascinating to historians and general readers alike than Mary Queen of Scots. "QUEEN *Mary of Scotland* had a reign of so much Action, and her Sufferings in the End of it, were of so extraordinary a Nature, that 'tis no Wonder that so many have attempted either the Whole or Part of her Story."[2] Her life "from the beginning, seem'd to be under the Direction of no friendly Planet," wrote one admirer;[3] her reign, wrote another, was "a chain of very extraordinary events, every link forg'd by dark contrivance."[4] Many agreed that "Her virtues were great, her misfortunes greater."[5] The timeless lover attracts tragic narratives. As Michael Lynch puts it: "the perennial fascination with the most famous of all Scotland's monarchs is also explained by the fact that here history shares—and can seemingly be explained by—the essential ingredients of popular fiction: sex, murder and intrigue, with a dash of religiosity."[6] Modern genres map onto older ones: comparing Mary Queen of Scots to her enemy John Knox, the late-twentieth-century artist John Bellany evokes fairy tales: "She's the beauty; he's the beast."[7] As Patrick Collinson observes of her "piebald press," "The Mary who is regarded with sympathetic admiration as tragic heroine, and if not sainted martyr then at least resolute victim, is the Mary of the English captivity, who is reborn once every hundred years."[8] High and low structures also mesh thanks to stereotypes of gender that can be updated. Victorians lent Mary fashionable fragility: "among the turbulent nobles by whom she was harassed, there was at least one on whose strong and steady arm she could lean," wrote John Stuart,[9] whose investigation of Bothwell's divorces was otherwise unromantic; Joseph M'Arthur, like many Romantics an "advocate of a poor helpless female," was excited by the tears of women persuaded by his researches.[10] Eighteenth-century critics, who not coincidentally were more interested in her letters, noted the lure of emotions more explicitly. Gilbert Stuart regretted that the subject "has engaged the passions rather than the candour of our Historians";[11] William Tytler admitted it was hard to stay "cool and unconcerned";[12] John Whitaker, torn between judgment and "compassion for a highly injured woman," decided they could be reconciled by "historical gallantry, advancing to the rescue of an oppressed Queen."[13] Borders between different layers of the past dissolve through figures of romance that make acts of interpretation on the body of texts, like the body of the woman, subject to constantly gendered fictions.[14]

At 1,300-odd pages, Whitaker's defense seems obsessive. But the materials under scrutiny were open to a wealth of interpretation, while providing a testing ground for historical method. Historians were drawn to the area because the fishing was so rich. There were several mysteries involving Mary Queen of Scots. Was she privy to the murder of her second husband, Darnley? Did she collude with Bothwell in his abduction of her, and what exactly were her relations with him? Did she in fact write the letters that the earl of Murray and his party produced as evidence of her guilt on the above charges, and that gave Queen Elizabeth a nominal excuse to imprison her in England? And, after languishing there, did she correspond treasonably with Thomas Babington in a Catholic conspiracy partly engineered by Elizabeth's minister Walsingham?

The answers served various agendas. If the first set of letters was genuine, Mary was guilty. If they were forgeries, Mary was absolved and Murray was guilty, and if Murray had not personally committed forgery, fingers could be pointed at various of his associates. If Mary was guilty, the Scottish Parliament was justified in deposing her, and Elizabeth had a case for determining her fate, either as the murderer of an English noble or, more shakily, as a woman who had by her immorality forfeited the protection due to her as a queen. As for the Babington correspondence, if innocent of treason, Mary was unjustly executed; if guilty, she might still seem wronged, or a victim—either of Elizabeth, fearful or envious, or of her spymaster Walsingham, the man whose craftiness defined Elizabethan statecraft.

Lines were not drawn as simply as one might expect. The severest accusations were laid by the Scots historians Robertson and Hume. It was no coincidence, suggested one contemporary, that both of these writers of popular history vilified the queen: men who were eloquent on women's failings found a ready audience.[15] The critical division was political rather than national: "Republican writers, equally averse to monarchy and to the house of Stuart, have drawn her picture in the blackest colours."[16] Both sets of letters supplied a regicide and a cause. The first made Mary kill Darnley for personal reasons, or the Scottish Parliament destroy Mary for political reasons. The second pitted queen against queen, making visible the rights, powers, and weaknesses of royalty. The letters were thus neither public nor private but proofs of how the personal was simultaneously social.

For all the excitement the letters induced in eighteenth-century historians, two factors made them proceed with caution. One was that readers demanded reasoning: "Every person now expects to be convinced by proof only, such as from the nature of things may be expected."[17] Legal paradigms had become powerful; authors plumed themselves and their age on a lack of credulity. Second, although the arguments were intricate and perplexed, the evidence was helpfully documentary. With careful analysis of the linguistic and literary aspects of the letters, hypotheses could be supported. Here letters were ambivalent. They could be trusted over oral sources: "Letters are more manageable than witnesses. They will never relent, recede or retract." But this would make them attractive to forgers: "They will always speak, whatever their prompters choose they should speak."[18] Ghastly cases of forgery were evident in history as well as everyday life. Thomas Carte, for instance, offered a chilling story from seventeenth-century Portugal. A minister loyal to John IV sent to his son signed papers left blank for filling up with letters of credit or recommendation. These were intercepted by a Spanish enemy, who filled them with copies of secret letters to Portuguese ambassadors. When this classified information was exposed, the minister appeared to be plotting. The real plot was revealed too late to save him from execution.[19] That Mary had not been allowed to see the Casket Letters at her trials encouraged those eighteenth-century historians seduced by legends of her attractions to do her justice retrospectively, as if the absence of the author's rereading encouraged later readers to become rewriters on her behalf. The borders between reading and writing were thus no firmer than those between fiction and fact.

Literature on the deposition and death of Mary Queen of Scots, like that on Kennedy's assassination in Dallas, abounded with conspiracy theories and irreconcilable details. The letters play a role analogous to the magic bullet or the grassy knoll. But if, as Tytler remarked, the probable was not always what happened, historians made doubtful narratives more plausible by refracting them through gender paradigms. Their inquiries into whether Mary Queen of Scots could have written the so-called Casket Letters were colored by assumptions about what any early modern noblewoman might write or do about desire. These assumptions, however, could be shifted or jolted, as at midcentury when Catherine of Russia was widely believed to have had her husband murdered. For eighteenth-century historians, the first set of letters were magnetic not just for their intimate contents, dubious provenance, and dramatic consequences, but because the different constructions to which they were open gave freer play than the Babington letters to ideas about class and gender. The Casket Letters also seemed to set Mary Queen of Scots's fate in motion, a more interesting prospect to eighteenth-century historians than the Babington letters that sealed it, and which seem to interest twentieth-century minds more.

Carte, Goodall, Tytler, Gilbert Stuart, and Whitaker, all sympathetic to Mary, show how variously eighteenth-century historians handled letters as sources. They also span various types of historians. Thomas Carte was the most professional—biographer of the duke of Ormond, collector of papers, and author of a physically huge (and unfinished) history of England. Hostile to regicides, he was lucid and thorough, especially on the Elizabethan sources. His account of Mary appeared in his third volume, published in 1752; the Casket Letters were treated separately in an appendix.[20] Walter Goodall was the keeper of the advocates' library in Edinburgh. A scholar whose forte was philology, he wrote a history of early Scotland in Latin. The second volume of his study of Mary, in 1754, printed various documents and the Casket Letters in full. William Tytler's background was similarly learned: he was vice president of the Society of Scottish Antiquaries. His 1760 study was indebted to Goodall for sources, but written more accessibly. By 1790 the work was in a fourth, revised edition. In 1782, Gilbert Stuart, another Edinburgh antiquary, praised Tytler but claimed his own inquiry was more impartial; in 1787 John Whitaker praised Stuart, but claimed to be more inspired in his eloquently deranged three-volume *Mary Queen of Scots Vindicated.*

To take the Casket Letters first: as Antonia Fraser has observed, "In the four hundred years since their appearance, more ink has been spilt on the subject—textual difficulties, language difficulties, theories of authorship, theories of interpretation—than on almost any other textual mystery."[21] Ink-spilling was especially prolific in the eighteenth century, however, for two reasons. First, the importance of letters in eighteenth-century culture meant historians had a high consciousness of epistolary practices. Second, the monarchist bias of many historians made them keen to explore the rights of wronged royalty.

The Casket Letters comprise eight letters and twelve poems allegedly written by Mary, and two marriage contracts between her and Bothwell. They were produced (not all at once) by the earls of Murray and Morton and their associates when Mary was in England, and offered as evidence to Elizabeth's commissioners first at York, then at London. Supposedly they showed Mary had known about the plot to kill Darnley, and had been complicit with Bothwell's abduction of her. Murray's ostensible reluctance to produce them, and the oblique nature of their contents, supported rather than proved the case against Mary; their subtle shame was more damning than crudely obvious proof. Had Elizabeth been neutral in the case, which she clearly was not, the letters might have been dismissed as too dubious rather than being used as a cover for dubious behavior of her own. There were several lines of investigation for historians: the material appearance of the letters; from whom, to whom, and about what they purported to be; what became of them; and whose interests, short- and long-term, their appearance and disappearance served.

Materially, there were many questions. The letters were without any of the signs usual in authentic correspondence: as Carte and others observed, they had no date of time or place, were unsigned, had no superscription or address, and made no mention of the bearer, which was particularly surprising since they were unsealed. (Normally a writer would reassure a recipient that the bearer was trustworthy.) These obviously suspicious omissions did not necessarily prove the letters were forged—eighteenth-century readers knew that illicit lovers often dispensed with regularities in their letters. But eighteenth-century historians—who, like forgers, were careful about sources—saw that the omissions could be explained by a picture of forgery. For example, Mary Queen of Scots was known to have kept her seal about her, on her person; if the forgers had been unable to steal or fake it, they would have had to have left the letters unsealed. The handwriting could not be proved, in the legal sense, because the letters lacked signatures, and because at least one woman was known to have written a hand difficult to distinguish from the queen's. Hence the Scottish Parliament, backing Murray, had had to describe the letters as being in Mary's hand rather than conclusively by her.

Matters were complicated by an intricate textual history. The originals were supposedly in French; translations and copies were provided for Elizabeth's commissioners. It was just about credible that they might prefer an English version: though they personally would have understood French, it made propaganda easier, as the letters circulated beyond the commission. When Murray returned to Scotland in January, 1569, he took the originals, though a further set of copies were supplied via Morton in January 1571. These later vanished, and the originals were never seen after 1584. What historians had to work with were texts potentially marred by copyists' errors and translators' corruptions. Here some impressive detective work was done by Goodall. In 1571, three letters in Latin appeared in Buchanan's *Detection,* and elsewhere in print, a Scots version of all eight, and seven in French. (The missing French one had a separate murky history.) It had been supposed, following Murray, that the originals were French and the other versions were translations. Instead, proposed Goodall, someone had composed texts in Scots, Buchanan—a moderator of the Kirk and no friend to the Catholic queen—had translated them into Latin, and somebody else put them into French. Goodall pounced on discrepancies that supported his theory: "Here it is obvious that the Latin is somewhat confused, and doth not express the *Scottish* sufficiently, whereby the *French* translator has been misled almost into nonsense."[22] If the French always followed errors in the Latin, they were not originals but spurious. Supporters of Murray writing after Goodall had to concede this might be so, but suggested there had been other originals, since lost—a suggestion regarded as desperate by Mary's supporters.

Class metaphors were emotive here. Both the letters and the translations were described by Mary's sympathizers as servile and base, whereas anything known to have been written by the queen was praised as elegant. The sonnets accompanying the letters, for instance, were discredited as vulgar by comparing them to Mary's elegy for her first husband, Francis II. According to Gilbert Stuart, the elegy had "a fancy, a delicacy, an elegance, a character in it, which give it the greatest charm, and the sonnets to Bothwel [*sic*] are in a strain and manner altogether opposite."[23] Tytler agreed: the elegy's thoughts were "natural, and simple, well connected, and elegantly expressed," whereas the sonnets were so unrefined he could not bear to discuss more than the first stanza of the first.[24] Historians also pondered the story of the letters' discovery. Murray said the casket containing the letters had been taken from one of Bothwell's servants, Dalgleish, sent back to Lochleven to get the letters after Bothwell left in a hurry. Nobles usually burnt incriminating letters: why had Bothwell gone to the trouble of keeping these, and then forgotten them? He was hardly the sentimental type, and it was unlikely he would use the letters in the future against his ally Mary. Supposing his forgetfulness to be natural, why had those who interrogated Dalgleish after his arrest asked him not a single question about the box they alleged was taken from him, in spite of numerous opportunities to do so? Here eighteenth-century historians were hampered by their attitudes to class. Loyal servants and condemned criminals alike could be trusted to tell the truth, they thought. Hence the majority believed those servants who, about to be executed for their part in Darnley's murder, expressly exonerated the queen. There were legitimate doubts about the confession of one, Hubert, who had implicated Mary: it was made two years later, and probably under duress if not torture. But it was also discounted by Mary's admirers as too low a picture even of lowered royal morals. Hubert claimed Bothwell said he was fetched every night to the queen's bedchamber. Tytler, appalled, rebutted this with a tangled argument that gave a genuine value to the genteel aspects of false letters. Discrepancy must be due to the forgers' misunderstanding of class: "Their caution, in not making the queen, in her letters, speak such plain language as this person does, was wise: Here they forget themselves, by putting the grossest words in his mouth. His character, they knew, was low enough to bear it."[25] Selective memory thus afflicted the forgers (as well as Bothwell); if their text was grossly sexual, it deflected their charge that Mary was grossly sexual.

More difficulties were apparent with the letters' chronology, which was intermittently inconsistent with known events. Historians were also suspicious that, after the letters' supposed seizure in June, Murray's party made no mention of them until 4 December, when Murray produced them at a special privy council meeting. Why did they not invoke the letters earlier, when it was in their interest to do so? "It is impossible that this could have been their line of conduct, if the letters had been genuine," concluded Stuart.[26] This silence could be explained as the rebels' hesitation over whether to gun for Bothwell or Mary or both. The proclamation for apprehending Bothwell described him as a regicide, but not as an adulterer, although the letters had allegedly been found by that date. A little later,

Bothwell was proclaimed a traitor for murdering the king and ravishing the queen, though the letters would absolve him from rape. In July, Mary was still described as an innocent object of Bothwell's murderous schemes. Only in December were the letters produced as evidence that both Bothwell and Mary were guilty of adultery and regicide.

These inconsistencies could be explained by the murky light of Scottish politics. Historians noted that the letters gave alibis to two groups: those nobles who had signed a bond supporting Bothwell's marriage to Mary, and wanted to be let off the hook, and the ruthlessly ambitious earl of Murray and his associates, who sought to seize the kingdom. "The forged letters were to prove, that, even if the resignation was *not* free, yet the deposition was just and reasonable."[27] The nobles needed the letters: "Their ambition, the murder of the King, their protection of Bothwel [sic], the bond, the marriage, their rebellion, their subversion of the government, the regency of the earl of Murray, and the letters are all linked together in an inseparable connexion."[28] More particularly, the letters were critical in persuading the English to support Murray's regency. As Whitaker colorfully put it, echoing terminology used about Parliamentarians in the Civil War, "They were considered as the sacred palladium of rebellion; as the holy image, which was only to be seen by the priests of anarchy, and on the keeping of which from the general eye, depended the fate of the whole empire of mis-rule!"[29]

One might ask why, if the case for the letters as genuine was so full of holes, historians bothered with it. The arguments were not all shaky—the letters had been accepted at the time and published all around Europe. Robertson pointed out that one of the letters was written on a sheet with a list of headings drawn up by the queen, and although the letters might be spliced texts from other sources, they were genuinely in the know on some matters. Mary's attraction to Bothwell was hard to deny (though Stuart argued Bothwell had used a love potion). Here historians enthusiastically promoted character as a historical force. Each writer offered a grand narrative of betrayal: Murray was the favorite villain, though Morton was also nominated as "the most unprincipled man of a most unprincipled age."[30] Goodall used the correspondence between Elizabeth and Murray to argue they had struck a deal to destroy Mary; the letter protesting Murray and friends' reluctance to publish the Casket Letters struck him as either "the height of assurance, or depth of hypocrisy."[31] Whitaker thought

Lethington, Morton's ally, was "the boldest and the mightiest forger, I believe, that the world has ever beheld." Mostly he denounced Elizabeth—"that MACHIAVELL IN A RUFF AND FARTHINGALE"—though he also blamed her commissioners for accepting the letters as evidence. They, like the translations of Mary's letters, were servile—"mere *gentlemen-ushers* to her hypocrisy, and mere *running-footmen* to her revenge." Also using correspondence between Murray and Elizabeth to prove underhanded dealings, he too failed to consider whether these letters between hypocrites might themselves be hypocritical. Whitaker mixed naiveté with literary consciousness, noting that if readers were predisposed to find Mary guilty, they would read documents with bias: "we lengthen the imperfect hints into intimations." Interpolating the unsaid was as important as reasoning away discrepancies; only then were historians able "to reconcile all the jarring parts of the story to each other, and to lend that historical smoothness to the whole, of which it is dreadfully devoid at present."[32]

In dealing with these gaps, historians became literary critics. They tried to analyze how forgers composed (putting in too many details, for instance), and how conspirators lied. That Morton and his commissioners swore so emphatically the letters were Mary's was for Goodall a sign of their guilt; Mary's equally vigorous denials were for Tytler proof of her innocence. Whitaker bombastically claimed, "Every author knows the difference, between a work traced and delineated on the mind, and the same work drawn out and completed on paper." But many historians constructed pre-texts with confidence. Strangely, this confidence was drawn from fiction. If the opposite of historical truth was romance, untruths in history would sound like romance. Liars could be detected by their resemblance to fiction—or, by their inability to get the fiction right. This confusion can be explained as the disorientating effect of returning both actual and literary women to the historical picture. Classical examples of iniquity occurred to some—"Mary must have been a Messalina indeed, to have written as they dictated to her," declared Whitaker.[33] Writing earlier, Eliza Haywood was untroubled by the distinction: the Mary Queen of Scots story is simply "not a *Romance*," yet "as surprizing as any Romance."[34] But for most male writers, romance was the constant sign of erroneous texts. Mary's alleged passion for Bothwell "would be shocking to credibility in a romance"; historians who believed it "must form their ideas of womankind, not upon the models of nature, but upon the characters exhibited by Madame and Monsieur Scudery, and other writers of romance."[35] For historians inclined to romanticism but not romances, proprieties of class offended: the forgers "knew not how to paint a queen in love with one of her subjects. They therefore represent her, as acting with all the sneaking humility of a cottager to a peer." Moreover, because the forgers were presumably male, "The natural indelicacy of their *masculine* minds, disabled them from giving us one touch of love purely feminine."[36] An absence of romance proved forgery too.

Surprisingly, modern fiction was less threatening. Tytler wrote of Mary as a seduced heroine: her marriage to Bothwell was a "fatal step" that "had hastened her ruin."[37] In 1726 a version of the letters appeared that made Mary unequivocally guilty but sympathetically passionate along modern lines: "ungenerous *Bothwell!* well are you convinc'd I have no Eyes for Charms but yours."[38] Whitaker thought the first, long letter must be fictional, because it had "all the length of one of Richardson's conversational epistles." He explicitly compared Bothwell to Lovelace as a rapist who used drugs; Mary is like Clarissa, "a sufferer from the dissimulation of others." His (otherwise positive) references to Richardson would remind eighteenth-century readers generally of forgery.[39] Jane Austen playfully took up this note of extenuating Mary as a reeducable heroine: Mary was guilty of nothing more than "Imprudencies into which she was betrayed by the openness of her Heart, her Youth, & her Education."[40]

Literary frames were also in place for discussion of Mary's captivity in England, and the Babington plot for which she was executed. Again letters were involved, this time found in a hole in the wall at Chartley.[41] Mary was removed to Fotheringay Castle, and all her correspondence scrutinized. The way Carte describes the seizure of Mary's papers mimics the titillating equivalence of female bodies and correspondence in popular fiction: "*Mary's* private closet was broke open; her cabinet and papers seized, sealed, and sent up to court."[42] One exchange was construed as treasonable: Babington offered to liberate her, and asked her to reward the conspirators for an attempt to kill Elizabeth. Cannily, Mary replied she would reward them for helping her to escape, and she suggested several practicable plans. This letter impressed even wily English politicians, who described it as "the most artful and cleverly written they have ever seen."[43] There were in fact two texts: the authentic letter, later destroyed, to which either

Walsingham or his agent Phelippes had added a false postscript asking for the names of Babington's fellow-conspirators, and second, a deciphered copy of the original, plus postscript, which Babington attested. Of this critical letter Patrick Collinson has observed, "I do not think we know, or ever shall know, for sure, whether those critically incriminating passages in the 'gallows' letter of July 1586 were Mary's own or inserted by Phelippes, or Walsingham."[44] Mary disputed, on every syllable, an interpretation of treason. Blame could be cast on her enemies, now as before forging letters to blacken her, or on her secretaries, who might be bribed into disloyalty. "Letters might come to their hands, which she might never see; they might insert things in her letters which she never dictated." Such epistolary lese majesty could mean the death of both queen and monarchy: "there was an end of the majesty, as well as the safety of princes, if they were to depend on the writing, and testimonies, of secretaries."[45]

This was a bold defense because it made integrity of correspondence a symbol for the security of the monarchy, and at the same time made the democracy of letters a threat to the monarchy. The promonarchist Carte, who was more interested in the Babington letters than other historians, sympathized with this argument. It was also a shrewd defense for Mary: conviction could hardly turn on her words if the writing and translation were done by others. (Mary had read Ronsard's arguments against the authenticity of the Casket Letters, and evidently learned some legal moves.)[46] The English, however, had an answer to this. Mary and the conspirators were convicted under an old statute that made imagining treason a capital offense. Whitaker's notion that works delineated in the mind could be traced by other minds was just old-fashioned by the Enlightenment. To the early modern mind it was not a problem: "'How then,' asked the solicitor, 'can the secret cogitations, which lie in the minds of traitors, be proved by honest men?'"[47] By letters: the instabilities that made letters unreliable *as texts* ironically made them a clearer index to hidden thoughts.

In dealing with concepts, old and new, of text as volatile, some eighteenth-century historians turned to panegyric as an older rhetorical way to display what they saw as exemplary aspects of majesty. "I will die a queen. My royal character is indelible," said Mary on her way to the block.[48] Both Carte and Stuart end their accounts of her with a rhapsody in which monarchy and femininity become signs for each other. In order to see the significance of gendering royalty this way, one must first look at how

Elizabeth was represented. She was a relatively popular monarch: even if, as Carte sorrowfully noted, civil liberties contracted in her reign, she was much to be preferred to Mary Tudor before and James I after her. Typically, Elizabeth's public successes were attributed to "masculine" ambition, and her personal vulnerabilities to "feminine" traits such as envy.[49] In particular, she was thought to be jealous of Mary's beauty. Without Weberian or Foucauldian analyses to explain how government controls could make a state successful, anti-Machiavellian eighteenth-century historians denounced Elizabethan polity as immoral. As Whitaker grumbled, "The Elizabeths and the Murrays, the children of artifice and of violence, will generally be the heroes and heroines of the mass of mankind." Conversely, elevated minds could appreciate Mary—as lofty and pure as "the snows of Caucasus."[50]

Popular support accounted not only for Elizabeth-worship but also for Mary-hating. The Casket Letters, Whitaker suggested, were designed by the lords to inflame the people: "The idea indeed had been started by the multitude." This was a good guess. Sir Nicholas Throckmorton, envoy in Scotland during Mary's dispossession, wrote to Elizabeth that "the women be most *furious and impudent* against the Queen"[51]—specifically, working-class women, who believed Mary had no more right to commit adultery and murder than any private person.[52] This vocal mass had to be separated from the queen who might otherwise be taken to resemble working women in sexual appetite. Hence the historians' efforts to turn Mary Queen of Scots into a silent icon, whose ideological charge could be secured by a stress on her exceptional beauty. The normally dry Carte grew damp in her praise: "Every part of her body was so justly proportioned, and so exquisitely framed, that people, lost in the admiration of each, were apt to imagine upon her whole form, that she was something more than human; a majestick air mixed with an incredible sweetness, sate upon her brow."[53] Gilbert Stuart ran a similar eulogy at the same narrative point: "The incomparable beauty and expression of her countenance, the exquisite propriety of her stature, and the exact symmetry of her shapes [*sic*] attracted and fixed the admiration of every beholder. In her air, her walk, her gesture she mingled modesty and grace."[54] Femininity gives an erotic charge to the monarchy. Both panegyrics follow an account of Mary's death: the queen is silenced as a real person, then resurrected as an em-

blem. Adoration of Scots monarchs, made dangerous by Jacobitism, becomes a "natural" tribute to the power of female beauty.

There were voices that dissented from this romantic appropriation of
Mary—not just among anti-Mary writers, but also among pro-Mary
women authors. Jane Austen mocked that self-centeredness that let male
onlookers share the stage with a royal spectacle. Of Burleigh, Walsingham,
and other ministers, she declared "these boasted Men were such Scandals
to their Country & their Sex as to allow & assist their Queen in confining
for the space of nineteen years, a *Woman* who . . . had every reason to expect Assistance."[55] The ironies are multiple: she reverses the moral tests
by which historical women were usually found wanting; she introduces
gender gratuitously; she warps narrative—most of the account of
Elizabeth's reign is given over to discussing Mary. Elizabeth's crime is to
have denied help to a deserving woman; friendship rather than rivalry gov-
erns relations between women. It is hard to tell how much of Austen's parody is ironic, and how much complicit, but clearly she satirizes the paradigms of Mary's defenders. The whole purpose of the *History* is "to prove
the innocence of the Queen of Scotland, which I flatter myself with having effectually done, and to abuse Elizabeth." Although the text is, ironically, by "*a Partial, Prejudiced, & Ignorant Historian*,"[56] the emotive power
of this championing discourse makes it distinctive enough to parody.

In contrast to Austen, Eliza Haywood makes Mary Queen of Scots a
figure from heroic romance. Her *Mary Stuart* of 1725 recognized Mary's
sexual and literary charisma; she quotes Brantome's view that "No man
ever beheld Mary's person, without admiration or love, or will read her
history without sorrow." Haywood emphasizes Mary's power as a writer:
her poems show "a certain Sublimity of Sentiment, a Vivacity of Wit, and
Strength of Judgment, which few of our Male Poets can equal."[57] Above
all, the Queen has spirit. Haywood's narrative of Scottish history alter-
nates between amours and foments, and interlocks them. Men keep falling
in love with Mary: their ambition leads them to love her, and love leads
them to be more ambitious, to impress her. Mary does not reciprocate
these passions, though she cannot help noticing them; she would be less
of a queen if she did not attract such attention. Violent love repeatedly explains political violence; men die because their passion leads them to mad-
ness the law cannot tolerate. As Scottish nobles lose their hearts and their

heads all around her, Mary contemplates choosing a husband—French? Scots? English?—and determines to satisfy both personal desire and state duty. History is a history of passions, noble and petty, among the nobility the world over. Genuine letters from Mary supply a voice at least in control of her texts, if not of events. The Casket Letters are breezily dismissed as an infamous pretense; she is cleared once Murray is proved to have forged her handwriting. Much more attention is given to the love letters written by the duke of Norfolk, whose possible marriage to Mary had indeed been contemplated as a diplomatic way to dispose of this surplus queen. When Elizabeth, here represented as subtle and wary but not condemned for it, acquires these letters, the duke justifies his love as no threat to the polity. Here the text is uneasy: the Catholic duke conveniently fails to mention he is also corresponding with the Pope. The power of address smoothes over tensions between personal and social roles for both sexes, though for women, beauty makes it easier.

Haywood suggests women manage this reconciliation better than men. Babington becomes simply another hopeful youth smitten by the "Heroick Virtues of so great a Queen," who proves active—and successful!—in her own defense. She sees off Elizabeth's chancellor, for instance: "it is wonderful how wisely and clearly she answer'd all his Quibbles." At issue here is a performance rather than a science of texts. She defeats the legal traps set by Walsingham: "she plainly shew'd him the Contradictions in his own Objections he made against her; and all that he could say against her, only shew'd her Innocence the clearer . . . she plainly prov'd, that she had been betray'd by her Secretaries."[58] Somehow, she is still executed. But Mary has discursive powers, and they outlast her life. Their demonstration is so plain as to be iconic. The narrative borrows from figurative drama: Mary's end is still a tragedy with spectators, but she is a speaking figure who speaks up for herself. This is the reverse of the silent icon promoted by male historians. Different treatments of the letters were important here: if forgery caused Mary's downfall, the Casket Letters demanded attention as documents on which historians' skills could be exercised for exoneration. The speaking subject thus disappeared into the subject matter. If, on the other hand, Mary was executed because her oppressors were afraid of a spirited and beautiful woman, the letters were relevant rather as they showed that woman as an active writer, and writing as evidence of the sex appeal of queens.

Through the figure of Mary Queen of Scots, eighteenth-century representations of royalty changed from heroic romance to a new kind of romanticism, in which monarchy was linked to passive femininity. This was
a little odd, given that actual royalty was becoming more accessible. In
1767, for instance, George III went out of his way to chat with Samuel
Johnson in the royal library.[59] Silence might project a reverential view of
the monarchy in reality eroded by familiarity (a familiarity in part encouraged by reading royal letters). Or it might covertly signal a dawning real-
ization that what historians had to say mattered more than monarchs. That
admiration for royalty did not always fit comfortably with progressive
scholarship can be seen in a striking episode in Carte's *History*. He men-
tions some recently discovered letters of Mary's, whose aggression must—
of course!—be answering some provocation from Elizabeth. These letters
charge Elizabeth and the woman of her bedchamber

with a course of wanton amours, and naming the very persons that ministered to
their pleasures. The lord treasurer *Burghley* took care to keep these letters from
coming to *Elizabeth's* hands: but preserved them; and they were afterwards buried
two feet under ground in his son the earl of *Salisbury's* house at *Hatfield* in
Hertfordshire. They were there found a few years ago, in a stone chest, rolled up in
woollen: and were shewn, by the publisher of *Burghley's papers*, to the late master
of the rolls at his seat of Belbar in that neighbourhood, and to another gentleman
still living.[60]

The significance of buried letters as an emblem of repressed sexual
knowledge is familiar from Victorian fiction: Carte seems, understandably,
not to know how to fit these earthy letters into his chivalric portrait of
Mary. So he reburies them. Discussing their origins and circulation rather
than their contents, he rhetorically returns them to the grounds of Hatfield
as historical treasure. He passes over the irony that Mary makes the same
slanderous charges about Elizabeth as Edinburgh laboring women had
made about her, passes over Mary's proactive charge of female disorder,
and offers instead a story about the erratic transmission of historical documents, which are still not quite in a scholarly domain. They have been
seen by gentlemen, which give them some kind of authenticity, but Carte
is unsure how to proceed beyond this class and gender solidarity.
Metaphors of historical discoveries as fossils and gems randomly extract-
ed suddenly look less fanciful. Unearthing letters, taking them across the
border from darkness to light, served to bind the semiprofessional com-

munity of historians. For once, a critic can see the spectacle of love letters reflected in the dark glasses of the critical reader.

Postscript by Linda S. Kauffman

Sunglasses, Portraits, Letters: Framing Mary, Brant, and Barthes

Mary Queen of Scots is an insoluble enigma, enmeshed in a web of significations surrounding women and letters, loyalty and royalty. Clare Brant's elegant essay is an intriguing meditation on the volatility of the epistolary text. Like Roland Barthes, Brant does not so much write about literature as to literature, which is, as she shows, inextricably interwoven with history.

What role did Mary play in Darnley's murder? Was she complicit in her own abduction and rape by Bothwell? Did her subsequent letters nurture a Catholic conspiracy and assassination plot? Were her letters authentic or forged—in whole or in part? A patchwork of authentic and false letters seems to have been cobbled together to convict her and justify her beheading. Brant argues that all readers construct the subject of their own desires, and then validate their interpretations by "close reading" of the evidence. Reading is never innocent, however, for it inevitably invokes conventions of genre, stereotypes of gender and class. What one sees depends upon the frame, and Brant's essay is all about framing: how fact and fiction are framed within narrative expectations; how scholarship frames one queen's "masculine" successes and "feminine" failings; how another queen is simultaneously praised for her chastity and damned for her sexuality; how political intrigues are subsumed by conventions of romance and mythology. Brant enumerates myriad cunning devices used to frame women. The framed woman is always in a double bind.

The first effect Brant's essay had was to drive me back to my history books, for, as an American scholar long steeped in postmodern literature, what I remembered about Mary Queen of Scots from my undergraduate history courses would fill a thimble. Mary, Catholic by birth and French by culture, was first married to Francis, King of France. The rumors of her unbridled sexual appetites seem to have originated either during or following her four and a half years of widowhood. Those rumors seemed to be confirmed by her impetuous marriage to Henry Stewart, Lord Darnley—against the express wishes of her own court and Elizabeth I, her half sister, who saw the marriage as a direct threat to her throne, since, as the great-grandson of Henry VII, Darnley had his own claim to the throne. Mary seems to have loved Darnley vehemently, although her dissolute husband contracted syphilis and plotted against her. In 1587 they produced an heir, James I, whom Mary saw for the last time when he was ten months old, and who subsequently repudiated and be-

trayed her by forming an alliance with Elizabeth I. Several factions of Scottish noblemen wanted Darnley dead: Bothwell's gunpowder plot failed, but Douglas succeeded in murdering Darnley. The Casket Letters are the only direct evidence of
Mary's alleged adultery with Bothwell before Darnley's death, but all the evidence
is circumstantial, and the letters may well have been forged by the same noblemen
who murdered her husband. Mary was never permitted to see the letters in order to
mount her own defense. Yet on the basis of these letters, Mary was branded a mur-
deress and a scarlet woman who deserved the vengeance of society.

Bothwell subsequently abducted Mary and raped her, knowing that consummat-
ing their union would force her to marry him, which she did. According to Antonia
Fraser, from the age of twenty-five onward, Mary lived a life of total chastity. Illegally
detained for nineteen years in captivity, she was further smeared when the Babington
plot (led by Walsingham) to assassinate Queen Elizabeth was thwarted; here, too,
officially reconstructed and partially forged letters were used to convict Mary of conspiracy. Fraser insists that Mary did not more than tacitly accede to such a plot, and
even then her actions must be read in the context of a captive seeking to escape her
jailors. Elizabeth I signed her death warrant and Mary was executed in 1587.

Should Mary have been reviled as a scheming whore, or revered as a misunder-
stood martyr? All the letters sealing her fate had a checkered history, copied from
French to English, always unsigned and undated; hastily collated; sometimes copied
with postscripts, sometimes without; allegedly written by a queen whose handwriting was notoriously easy to forge. Mary lost her heart to Darnley; her hand to
Bothwell; her handwriting to the forger Maitland; her head to Elizabeth. Ultimately,
her body in pieces parallels the epistles in pieces; Brant's aim is to re-member her in
a way that makes sense.

Brant argues persuasively that epistolary history should include the history of
readers. That entails analysis of texture and context, as well as consideration of
complex, often contradictory political and religious allegiances and of conflicting
attitudes toward gender and class. These broad considerations must be augmented
by other equally broad ones, for reading a letter drags along the whole history of
epistolarity with it: What other kinds of letters (and literature) has the reader read
in order to place the ones in question in context?

Brant approaches this question in two ways. First, she examines it through the
lens of literary history, analyzing the differences between the reading of letters for
an eighteenth-century, nineteenth-century, and twentieth-century audience.
Eighteenth-century readers of Mary's letters emphasized both the lure of emotions
and the lure of letters. The analogies to Samuel Richardson's Clarissa instanta-
neously sprang to mind for the eighteenth-century readers: Bothwell's seduction and
ravishment of Mary inevitably reminded them of Lovelace. They drew parallels be-

tween Clarissa's inexperience and Mary's, and even recalled Richardson's compli-cated subplots: the role of forged letters and found ones; the use of a love potion to facilitate the rape; the possibility of being bewitched. Nineteenth-century readers emphasized the frailty of womankind (morally and physically), as well as symboli-cally equating buried letters with repressed sexual knowledge. Twentieth-century readers would find the Babington letters more interesting than the Casket Letters, which appealed more to eighteenth-century readers weaned on Richardson. And twentieth-century readers, including Brant herself, rightly emphasize the enormous implications of class struggle: Mary becomes a scapegoat as an object lesson for the masses.

Second, Brant juxtaposes the severe condemnation by male historians like Hume and Robertson with the kinder views of Eliza Haywood and Jane Austen. Haywood transforms her into a figure of heroic romance, but stresses her literary talent, too. Austen is more ironic, particularly about the sexual politics involved. It is she who sees most clearly the kinds of double binds in which Mary was entrapped. Austen's wit and parody can be seen even in her title, which implies that all history, like her own History of England, should be viewed as being written by partial, prejudiced, and ignorant historians. Austen satirizes Mary's defenders as well as her attackers, for all these writers put literary frames around Mary's story. Once deposed, she can be resurrected as an emblem of ideal monarchy: the passively feminine, eternal Type.

Finally, Brant's own essay epitomizes the tensions that the two different strains of history hold for us all. These two strains (in both senses of the word) exist simul-taneously: the synchronic history of the Type, which transforms the Lover into a timeless, eternal icon; and the treacherous material history that unfolds diachroni-cally. Ironically, Roland Barthes valorizes the first kind of history throughout A Lover's Discourse. *We are fatally attracted to the Lover as Type: "Werther identi-fies himself with the madmen, with the footman. As a reader, I can identify myself with Werther. Historically, thousands of subjects have done so, suffering, killing themselves. . . . A long chain of equivalences links all the lovers in the world. In the theory of literature, 'projection' (of the reader into the character) no longer has any currency: yet it is the appropriate tonality of imaginative readings . . . I cling to the image of the lover, shut up with this image in the very enclosure of the book."* Werther *was written a year before Jane Austen was born, but it amply encoded the kind of romanticism Barthes invoked. Barthes's famous motto, "*larvatus prodeo,*" is relevant: "I advance pointing to my mask: I set a mask upon my passion, but with a discreet (and wily) finger I designate this mask."*[1] *Barthes is wearing* multiple masks here. For not only is he the avid reader of literature but he is the defiant rebel against one of the major tenets of structuralism and poststructuralism: "Thou shalt not refer or respond to literary characters as if they are real people!" *Indeed,* *his subtext throughout* A Lover's Discourse *is that Desire directly contradicts Theory.*

But perhaps such projection only applies to literary characters, not historical ones. Brant's point is precisely the opposite: historical figures cannot even be conceptualized without reference to literary typology. Consciously or unconsciously, historians, journalists, and novelists cut their patterns from the shapes of fiction. As Barthes asks, "How do History and Type combine? Is it not up to the type to formulate—to form—what is out of time, ahistorical? In the lover's very tears, our society represses its own timelessness, thereby turning the weeping lover into a lost object whose repression is necessary to its 'health.' In Rohmer's film The Marquise of O, *the lovers weep and the audience giggles."[2] So when Mary is silenced as a historical figure in order to be resurrected as the iconic, passively feminine monarch, her repression is "necessary to society's health."*

Antonia Fraser tells one story I wish Brant had included in her own narrative web: how Mary may have woven her own portrait for posterity into the figure in the carpet. Once the Babington conspirators were vanquished, Mary wrote a letter to her cousin, the duke of Guise. Her final aim was to die being perceived as a martyr rather than a traitor, as Fraser notes: "It was Mary's triumph that by her deliberate behavior in the last months of her existence, she managed to convert a life story which had hitherto shown all the elements of a Greek tragedy—disaster leading ineluctably to disaster—into something which ended instead in the classic Christian manner of martyrdom and triumph through death. This transfiguration in the last months of her life, which had the effect of altering the whole balance of her story, was no fortunate accident. The design was hers."[3] What Brant, following Barthes, is elucidating is something ineluctable: a history of the passions. That, above all, is a literary history, and it is the tautologies contained in it that intrigue Brant. When it comes to irony, she is no slouch. It is no accident that Barthes invokes Goethe rather than Austen, nor that Brant's elective affinities are closer to Austen's satiric mode than to Barthes's elegiac one.

Brant's own motto is also larvatus prodeo. *She is too clever not to see the contradictions and tensions in her own argument, but instead of trying to resolve them, she capitalizes on them with a seductive opening gambit. Like Barthes, Brant begins with a tantalizing allusion to personal history. The topics we pursue as scholars reflect our own drives, but Brant (coyly? mercifully?) demurs from discussing these drives, except to remark that while exposing our subjects to the harsh glare of daylight, we mask our own psychic investments in our material. We frame others when we intrude on their intimacy, but we hide our own motives, ambition, jealousies, entanglements, intrigues. Brant points to her mask by alluding to the dark glasses scholars don to disguise their own projections and obsessions. As Barthes re-*

flects: "Identification: the subject painfully identifies himself with some person (or character) who occupies the same position as himself in the amorous structure."[4]

Scholars may don sunglasses, but the good Cambridge dons reduced Mary to an obscure icon, whose very silence fascinates Clare. One does not need to be a psychoanalyst to see what attracted Clare to Mary's portrait. Of the centuries of female erudition that Henry VIII erased, she (Mary, not Clare) is the sole surviving remnant. Clare seizes that saving remnant, portentous as a rune. Rather than speaking for Mary, however, Clare exposes the folly of all those who framed Mary according to their own biases. Her essay itself takes the form of the Loquela, a word that designates the flux of language through which the subject tirelessly rehashes the effects of a wound or the consequences of an action: an emphatic form of the lover's discourse. Brant's, like Jane Austen's before her, is a history without nostalgia. Like the emblem of the cock that supplants the obliterated nunnery famous for learning, her essay mocks rather than crows; it is a mocking reminder of the ruins and debris that pass for history.

Notes

1. Of the innumerable letters I have read for my forthcoming book *Eighteenth-Century Letters and British Culture,* one of the most haunting was a penciled assignation note from John Wilkes, arranging a rendezvous on Westminster Bridge. It was very brief—a command, a time, a place—but seemed to speak volumes.

2. *The Scottish Historical Library* (London, 1736), 56.

3. *The Genuine Letters of Mary Queen of Scots to James Earl of Bothwell,* trans. Edward Simmonds (London, 1726), 48.

4. Walter Goodall, *An Examination of the Letters Said to Be Written by Mary Queen of Scots, to James Earl of Bothwell: Shewing by Intrinsick and Extrinsick Evidence, That They Are Forgeries,* 2 vols. (Edinburgh, 1754), 1:iii.

5. Gilbert Stuart, *The History of Scotland from the Establishment of the Reformation till the Death of Queen Mary,* 2 vols. (London, 1782), 2:384.

6. Michael Lynch, ed., *Mary Stewart: Queen in Three Kingdoms* (New York: Basil Blackwell, 1988), 3.

7. Qtd. in *The Observer,* 5 April 1998.

8. Patrick Collinson, *The English Captivity of Mary Queen of Scots* (Sheffield: Sheffield History Pamphlets, 1987), 4.

9. John Stuart, *A Lost Chapter in the History of Mary Queen of Scots Recovered* (Edinburgh, 1874), 10.

10. Joseph M'Arthur, *The Ruins of Linlithgow, with Selected Notes in Vindication of the Character of Mary, Queen of Scots* (Glasgow, 1798), preface.

11. Stuart, *History,* 1:advertisement.

12. William Tytler, *An Historical and Critical Enquiry into the Evidence Produced by the Earls of*

Murray and Morton, against Mary Queen of Scots (Edinburgh, 1760), v. Hereafter cited in these notes as *Critical Enquiry.*

13. John Whitaker, *Mary Queen of Scots Vindicated,* 3 vols. (London, 1787), 1:vii, ix.

14. The most sensible general account is still Antonia Fraser's *Mary Queen of Scots* (London: Panther Books, 1970); see esp. "Her Privy Letters," 456–83.

15. William Tytler, *An Inquiry, Historical and Critical, into the Evidence against Mary Queen of Scots,* 4th ed., 2 vols. (1760; rpt. London, 1790), 1:35. (This work is an update of his 1760 *Critical Enquiry.*) Hereafter cited in these notes as *Inquiry.*

16. Ibid.

17. Ibid., 1:2.

18. Whitaker, *Mary Queen of Scots,* 1:331.

19. Thomas Carte, *The History of the Revolutions of Portugal, from the Foundation of That Kingdom to the Year 1667* (London, 1740), 170–74.

20. Thomas Carte, *A General History of England,* 4 vols. (London, 1747–55). Hereafter cited in these notes as *History.*

21. Fraser, *Mary Queen of Scots,* 463.

22. Goodall, *Examination,* 1:83.

23. Stuart, *History,* 1:414.

24. Tytler, *Inquiry,* 1:428 (Tytler had got noticeably more squeamish between 1760 and 1794).

25. Tytler, *Critical Enquiry,* 141.

26. Stuart, *History,* 1:385.

27. Whitaker, *Mary Queen of Scots,* 1:315.

28. Stuart, *History,* 1:396.

29. Whitaker, *Mary Queen of Scots,* 2:296.

30. Stuart, *History,* 1:411.

31. Goodall, *Examination,* 1:23.

32. Whitaker, *Mary Queen of Scots,* 3:46; 1:163, 86, 333, 204.

33. Ibid., 1:326, 337.

34. Eliza Haywood, trans., *Mary Stuart, Queen of Scots: Being the Secret History of Her Life, and the Real Causes of All Her Misfortunes* (London, 1725), iii, 1. The title page says this is a translation, but I have not discovered of what.

35. M'Arthur, *Ruins,* 28 (quoting Guthrie).

36. Whitaker, *Mary Queen of Scots,* 1:337–38.

37. Tytler, *Critical Enquiry,* 219–20.

38. *Genuine Letters,* 14.

39. Whitaker, *Mary Queen of Scots,* 2:2, 122; see 3:114.

40. Jane Austen, *The History of England from the Reign of Henry the Fourth to the Death of Charles the First by a Partial, Prejudiced, & Ignorant Historian,* in *The Works of Jane Austen,* ed. R. W. Chapman, rev. ed., 6 vols. (1954; rpt. London: Oxford Univ. Press, 1972), 6:138–49, 146, 12.

41. Another source placed them in a tube in a beer-barrel bung. See John Hungerford Pollen, ed., *Mary Queen of Scots and the Babington Plot* (Edinburgh: Constable, 1922), lxi.

42. Carte, *History,* 3:604. For the significance of the royal female body in an earlier episode of English history, of which eighteenth-century readers would have had some knowledge, see Gerald MacLean's article on Henrietta Maria's letters in this volume.

43. Pollen, *Mary Queen of Scots,* 26.

44. Collinson, *Captivity,* 27.

45. Carte, *History,* 3:608.

46. John Durkan, "The Library of Mary Queen of Scots," in Lynch, ed., *Mary Stewart,* 92.

47. Pollen, *Mary Queen of Scots,* clxxxi.

48. Stuart, *History,* 2:360.

49. See, for example, Whitaker, *Mary Queen of Scots,* 1:31; William Russell, *The History of Modern Europe,* 5 vols. (London, 1779–84), 2:351–61; Stuart, *History,* 2:388.

50. Whitaker, *Mary Queen of Scots,* 3:132. Cf. favorable comparisons between British royalty and the Himalayas in the 1950s.

51. Whitaker, *Mary Queen of Scots,* 1:269, 246.

52. Ironically this recovery of class in discourse coincides with recent feminist work on early modern defamation: see my article "Women, Scandal and the Law," in *Women, Texts and Histories, 1575–1760,* ed. Clare Brant and Diane Purkiss (London: Routledge, 1992); and Laura Gowing, *Domestic Dangers: Women, Words, and Sex in Early Modern England* (Oxford: Clarendon Press, 1996).

53. Carte, *History,* 3:619.

54. Stuart, *History,* 2:386.

55. Austen, *History,* 145. "Anna Bullen" is also satirically exonerated: "It is however but Justice, & my Duty to declare that this amiable Woman was entirely innocent of the Crimes with which she was accused, of which her Beauty, her Elegance, & her Sprightliness were sufficient proofs" (142).

56. Ibid., 149, title page (Austen may have Whitaker in mind: see 145).

57. Haywood, *Mary Stuart,* 30, 3.

58. Ibid., 219, 234 (twice).

59. James Boswell, *Life of Johnson,* ed. George Birbeck Hill, rev. L. F. Powell, 6 vols. (Oxford: Clarendon Press, 1934–58), 2:33–42. Boswell called this episode "one of the most remarkable incidents of Johnson's life" (33).

60. Carte, *History,* 3:702.

Notes to Postscript

1. Roland Barthes, *A Lover's Discourse,* trans. Richard Howard (Harmondsworth: Penguin, 1990), 131, 43.

2. Ibid., 181.

3. Antonia Fraser, *Mary Queen of Scots* (London: Panther Books, 1970), 499–500.

4. Barthes, *Lover's Discourse,* 129.

PART 2

Cultures of Letters

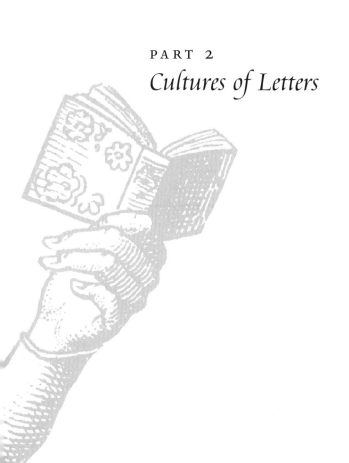

∿ Suppressing the Books of Susan in Emily Dickinson

Martha Nell Smith

Though her relationship with Susan Dickinson proved to be the most literarily generative of all of Emily Dickinson's relationships, and thus was the poet's most fruitful poetic plain, it has been regarded with a kind of critical indifference almost inevitable in a culture with a limited range of story lines for scripting poetic influence and erotic devotions. Indeed, if any man in Dickinson's life—prominent editors Thomas Higginson and Samuel Bowles, her father, her brother, popular minister Charles Wadsworth, or the mysterious "Master"—had received as many writings from her for as long as over five decades, or if the corpus of her writing to any male correspondent represented, as does that to Susan, one of two major archives Dickinson left at her death (the more than eight hundred poems in the "fascicles" constitute the other major archive;[1] there are around five hundred writings to Susan), then study of her relationship with him would have been central to Dickinson studies. However, since Mabel Loomis Todd and Higginson's publication of *Poems by Emily Dickinson* at the end of the last century, books of Susan and Emily Dickinson have been actively suppressed or thought unseemly or even unnecessary.[2] This essay takes the suppression of this highly productive literary liaison as a starting point to interrogate what difference recovering The Book(s) of Susan in Emily Dickinson makes, not only for reading Dickinson's poetic project but also for critical/theoretical understandings of literary history and the profound and lasting effects of the circulation, transmission, and reception of literatures.

In contrast to the "undiscovered public knowledge" available in the Susan corpus—"knowledge that exists 'like scattered pieces of a puzzle' in scholarly books and articles, but remains unknown because its 'logically related parts . . . have never become known'"[3] and then narrated and transmitted in easily intelligible forms—the mysteries (or conscious lack of knowledge) generated by the "Master" letters, indeterminate documents that may or may not be addressed to one or several real male (or cross-dressed female) persons, have been and continue to be widely circulated. Though the writings to Emily Dickinson's most frequently addressed correspondent, Susan, lie dispersed throughout six volumes of poems and letters edited by Thomas H. Johnson and eight edited by Martha Dickinson Bianchi (most with Alfred Leete Hampson),[4] *The Master Letters of Emily Dickinson* have been produced in a Book all their own and are the three epistolary pieces (out of more than one thousand letters certainly sent) that have been most widely promoted in criticism and biography of the last half century.[5] Stories of romantic thralldom with men or of relationships with a male mentor are proliferatively familiar and so more easily and readily scripted than that of a lifelong passion for another woman who, though unprofessional, was a committed writer and Emily's mentor. Because both corpora (to Susan and to "Master") are mysterious (though in very different ways), a hermeneutics of speculation surrounds each—speculation about the identity of the writings to Susan (How should such highly metaphorical, passionate writings to another woman be counted in the Dickinson canon? Can they be regarded as documents of lesbian history?) and speculation about the identity of the "Master" addressee (Who provoked Dickinson to write "'Chillon' is not funny"? Whom does her speaker address in a playfully pouty way as "it"? Who was "He"?). Though no one knows whether the "Master letters" were sent to any real person, and though no fair copies of the documents exist and their state as drafts raises ontological questions, critics have overwhelmingly interpreted them as if knowledge exists about them that in fact does not—i.e., with the assumption that their identity as letters intended for posting is unassailable. Since their outing in 1955 on the heels of the first lesbian study of Dickinson in 1951, these three writings have been pored over, as if they will explain the work and life of the poet.[6] Yet these drafts will finally not tell much about Emily Dickinson except that she enjoyed passionate writing and labored over her prose, reworking it for particular effect. However, acquaintance with these three items is not necessary to know those facts about Dickinson the writer, since the passion and care of both her poetry and prose are readily evident in random samplings of her work.

What are unique and informative about these "Master" drafts, and pertinent for evaluating their role in suppressing the knowledge scattered across various editions containing portions of the writings to Susan, are their preservation and reception: showing Dickinson's pages-long revising strategies in order to make scriptures that appear to be spontaneous pleadings, the "Master letters" (especially A 828 and A 829; *ML* 21–46)[7] are the most extensive surviving records from stages in a process, the products of which were routinely regarded as refuse and treated accordingly (i.e., most of the records from this point in Dickinson's revising process were disposed of); yet as compelling as the records are, and even after being collected into a book of their own, they have almost never been interpreted as writerly stagings of emotional outbursts. Instead of being read as the lengthiest of Dickinson's surviving prose drafts, with the cancellation of lines and whole blocks of texts showing a writer consciously honing her craft, the "Master letters" have been interpreted literally, as unselfconscious discourses of unrequited female longing for an unobtainable male. Read, then, as uncontrollable pinings, these items have been used and reused for the last four decades to achieve the same end as the goal of their original presentation: to suppress and repress Dickinson's passionate writings to other women. Repeatedly, these three documents are put into service as proof of Dickinson's heterosexual desire to counter a decades-long discourse of desire of one woman for another that survives in hundreds and hundreds of documents from Emily to Susan Dickinson and that spans all of Emily Dickinson's adulthood. Working to limit female authority and to valorize a tired, reductive heterosexual love plot that subjugates women when read literally, the "Master letters" expand and deepen understandings of Emily Dickinson the writer when read literarily. Much "more attention should be paid to the structure of the letters, including the direct use of ideas, wordings, and imagery from both *Aurora Leigh* and *David Copperfield*," as well as from *Jane Eyre, Sonnets from the Portuguese, Kavanagh,* and *Wuthering Heights*,[8] and Dickinson's direct reference to Byron's 1815 monologue "Prisoner of Chillon" (A 828; *ML* 37) has not been scrutinized for its literary allusiveness to a character (modeled on a real person) who finds liberation in a bird's song (often a metaphor for poetry). Instead, these letters have been read as examples of a distinctively feminine epistolarity in which women's writing is writing from and of the heart and is in fact motivated by emotion, not literary objectives. This commonplace story line overtakes Dickinson's actual record, so that the draft nature of these documents is almost never remarked, while a parade of male candidates for addressee dominates critical and popular discussions alike.

Though the "Master letters" have been stalked to derive information about Emily Dickinson's desires, and in that pursuit of her erotic interest have produced only mysteries, recognition of the collective inability to see them as "drafts" and their subsequent reception tell much, making plain the cultural obsessions that conventionally render women helpless when in love. Within this convention of reading, knowledge that can be produced by recognizing the "draft" nature of these writings is eschewed while conjectures about what cannot be known, the love object of these scriptures, multiply. Twentieth-century critical practices compulsively repeat, then, centuries-old novelistic love plots, plots that perpetuate critical fictions, narrating much of the vast body of scholarship generated by her work and life, and that likewise commandeer fictional responses to Dickinson. For example, two novels published during the past two years, one a mystery novel about Dickinson scholars and the other a fictional account of Emily's young adulthood, both climax with the identification of "Master."[9] Thus the same story, with variations enough to resell the tale, is told over and over and applauded time and again. By contrast, telling the story of her love for her sister-in-law Susan Huntington Gilbert Dickinson renders women taking some control of their love plot and will not fit comfortably into any known story line. Relatively unprepared to imagine a story of literary mentorship between women in love, critics, biographers, and fiction writers alike have by and large left it a tale untold. Thus the near-hegemonic prevalence of conscriptive heterosexual story lines render inscrutable the imaginary explosion from one woman lover to another beloved woman embedded in Emily Dickinson's "Susan correspondence," an explosion comparable to the poetic and epistolary correspondences of Elizabeth Barrett and Robert Browning.

Like the Brownings, Susan and Emily Dickinson were deeply committed to literature. For Emily, "Poetry and Love . . . coeval come" (H 364; P 1247);[10] for Susan, poetry is "sermon . . . hope . . . solace . . . life."[11] For four decades, they exchanged literary materials, both written by themselves and written by others and printed in periodicals and books. Susan made scrapbooks and kept commonplace books of literatures she prized, and, sending Emily's poems to the local *Springfield Republican* and to Civil War journals, Susan even acted as agent for her beloved friend's work. When "Safe in Their Alabaster Chambers" was printed in the *Republican* as "The Sleeping," Susan enthusiastically wrote, *"Has Girl read Republican?* It takes as long to start our Fleet as the Burnside" (H B94), comparing the fact of obtaining the wider circulation of the poem afforded by its printing to a Civil War general's lengthy siege and eventual capture of Roanoke Island.[12] Susan's use of a war metaphor and Dickinson's famous practice of withholding her poems from the world of mechanical reproduction suggest that correspondence with the literary industry of capital and print was a struggle. Emily Dickinson did not depend on print distribution, however, but circulated her writings by hand to at least ninety-nine correspondents, both by sending poems out with her letters through the postal service and by delivering writings through selected couriers (friends, servants, children). During her lifetime, her writings were not preserved by the few instances of their translation into print in newspapers, Civil War journals, and Helen Hunt Jackson's anthology of numerous anonymous authors in the No Name Series, but by her personal means of storage for dissemination as gifts.[13]

By the time of her death in 1886, Dickinson already had quite a reputation as a writer (everyone who knew her knew she was a poet) and her sister Lavinia resolved to have her poems published conventionally in printed volumes. But they had been left in bundles and loose leaves and scraps in her room, and as letters and messages to friends around the neighborhood and across the country. To make a book of her poetry for the commodified realm of print required an editor, and Lavinia knew she was not up to the task. As everyone knew that Emily Dickinson was a writer, so almost everyone knew that her most trusted audience, the person most intimately acquainted with her work, was Susan Dickinson. So Lavinia turned, reflexively, to Susan and asked that she edit Emily's poems, that she usher the poems from the culture of gift exchange to that of professionalized distribution. After rounds of disappointment and disagreements among family members (all of which might be described as being over who owned the poetry and who should determine how it should be shared with the world), the task of editing Emily Dickinson's writings, or at least those that Lavinia claimed as her property, eventually fell to acclaimed editor Higginson and to a young Amherst woman with failed literary aspirations of her own, Loomis Todd.[14]

For the first six and the last fifty years (1890–96; 1945–present) of Dickinson's appearance in print volumes, which Loomis Todd's books inaugurated, two major forces, one cultural (already discussed in part) and one personal, have conspired to downplay Susan's importance for Emily's poetic process. The cultural reason consists of the fact that for late-nineteenth-century audiences the poetess was a cultural icon and a stereotype in the minds of readers. Late-twentieth-century audiences by and large have amnesia about this stereotype of the woman who could only write from the heart and whose story line has served as a powerful complement to the standard heterosexual love plot of women helplessly in love—the Poetess often robed herself in white, was reclusive, and harbored some "secret sorrow" quietly as she wrote poems at home.[15] The personal reason for minimizing the importance of Dickinson's primary correspondent is that one of Dickinson's editors from 1890–96, Loomis Todd, was the mistress of Susan's husband, Emily's brother Austin, and her daughter, Millicent Todd Bingham, resumed editing Dickinson's works in 1945. Bingham had considerable influence with the editor of the variorum of Dickinson's poems, Thomas H. Johnson; and Richard B. Sewall, author of the most widely circulated biography of Dickinson, wrote at the behest of Bingham, who wanted "'the whole story' of her mother's involvement [with the Dickinsons] told—but told in the setting of the larger story of Emily Dickinson."[16] Not surprisingly, the story told by the "other woman" about Dickinson's relationships is predictably biased and seeks to discount the importance of the *"wife forgotten"* (H L20; *L* 93);[17] hence, editions and biographical accounts by Loomis Todd, Bingham, and those over whom they had editorial sway are markedly partial in their persistent elision of Susan's crucial role in Emily's literary productions.

Even *The Single Hound: Poems of a Lifetime,* edited in 1914 by Susan's daughter, Emily's niece Martha Dickinson Bianchi—and offered as a memorial to the love of these "Dear, dead Women," Susan and Emily—nevertheless begins to emphasize Dickinson's separateness and thus simultaneously suppresses, even while it promotes the importance of their relationship for Emily's poetry, the story of these women's highly productive, intensely erotic literary liaison. Bianchi, who would later talk of her

Aunt Emily's tragic pining after an unobtainable male lover, but who in the preface to *The Single Hound* sneered at those who taught her aunt "as a rare strange being; a weird recluse, eating her heart out in morbid and unhappy longing, or a victim of unsatisfied passion," still used words like "peculiar" to characterize Emily Dickinson's genius.[18] Thus, for the quarter century that she edited her aunt's work, Bianchi emphasized, both proudly and guardedly, the lifelong intimacy between her mother and her aunt. Bianchi's ambivalence confused relationships of pieces of information to one another and thereby obscured the scope of Susan's profound involvement with Emily's writing.

Nevertheless, in Bianchi's work of producing Emily Dickinson for public consumption are imprints of Susan's influence—illustrations, for instance, abound, as do humorous anecdotes, as if Susan's critiques of the Higginson and Loomis Todd volumes and her declarations in letters to editors had been taken to heart and, at least for a time, then to editorial hand.[19] By her own account in an 1890 letter to Higginson, Susan describes how she had imagined a volume of Emily's writings with "many bits of her prose—passages from early letters quite surpassing the correspondence of Gunderodi[e] with Bettine—quaint bits to my children &c &c. Of course I should have forestalled criticism by only printing them." In a March 1891 letter to William Hayes Ward, editor of the *Independent,* she elaborates her vision for such a volume that would also include Emily's "illustrations," "showing her witty humorous side, which has all been left out of" the 1890 *Poems.*[20] Susan describes a much more holistic volume, one much more closely aligned with the culture of gift exchange in which she and Emily had worked, than the epitome of the late-nineteenth-century poetry book for sale produced by Higginson and Todd. Susan's "Book of Emily" would have been filled with drawings and jokes as well as profound lyrics, and her outline for the production shows that she would not have divided the poems into the conventional categories of "Life," "Love," "Time and Eternity," and "Nature" but would have emphasized poetry's integration with quotidian experience, Emily's intellectual prowess, and her philosophical interrogations of the spiritual, corporeal, emotional, and mental realms. Yet Higginson had discouraged production of such a volume, telling Susan that it would be "un-presentable."[21] Her critiques of the printed volumes he made with Mabel Loomis Todd and descriptions of how she would have managed preparing a production performance of

Emily's writings for "Auction" to the world are (*P* 709), for late-twentieth-century readers immured in mechanical and high-tech images of print and screen, avenues into the nineteenth-century manuscript culture of literary exchange in which Susan and Emily were constant participants, a manuscript world that Higginson thought ancillary to real bookmaking.

Among Susan's papers are fascicles of favorite poems that both she and her sister Martha copied out sometime in the 1850s. Rooted in a culture where modes of literary exchange frequently included sending consolation poems and making fascicles of favorite poems, as well as commonplace books, and scrapbooks of treasured literary pieces, Dickinson's fascicle assembly of her own poems (there were forty handmade manuscript books found after her death) and distribution of her own poems in epistolary contexts are, then, anything but eccentric. Both Emily and Susan were careful to distinguish between the often synonymously used terms "publish" and "print." When Emily guesses that Higginson may have seen "A narrow Fellow in / the Grass" (Set 6c; *P* 986) in the *Republican,* she does not say, "I had told you I did not *publish*"; she says, "I had told you I did not *print*" (BPL Higg 52; *L* 265). Susan is equally precise in writing editor Ward, "I shall not be annoyed if you decide not to publish at all. I should have said *printed*" (H Lowell Autograph; Smith 11–15). The distinction these two women writers draw between the terms is, as is Susan's description of what her volume of Emily's writings would have featured, a sign of the literary culture in which their works were so deeply embedded, a literary culture of vital manuscript exchange in which even printed works were recirculated in holograph form. This manuscript culture that Emily and Susan knew so well and in which each practiced as writers is one that late-twentieth-century literary history tends to have forgotten.[22] Had Susan produced a volume modeled on the practices of this hand-to-hand culture for the world at large, Dickinson's readers would have had a much broader sense of the range of Emily's writings from the beginning, would have had a much stronger sense of the manuscript culture in which Emily Dickinson's poetic project was far from an aberration, and would have had a much clearer understanding of the scope and objectives of that project. Instead of remaking Emily's writings to fit the contours, categories, and poetic forms driven by the machine of the printed book,[23] Susan's volume would have been oriented and shaped by those hand-fashioned modes of literary exchange that constituted one form of "publishing" and circulating works in nineteenth-century parlor culture, a form practically lost to twentieth-century readers, in that it is quickly relegated as "private" by anachronistic (and in that overly rigid) demarcations between the "public" and "private" spheres.

The textual body, Dickinson's manuscripts, is a powerful witness to Susan's entanglements in Emily's compositional and distribution practices and to the fact that their ambitions for poetry, for literature, were mutual and were not driven by systems of commodification but by intellectual, emotional, and spiritual goals to achieve connection. Sending another writings in one's casual script (as Emily does to Susan), in the handwriting more similar to one's private notes for developing expression, is an act that speaks trust, familiarity, routine. Sometimes placing those writings on less formal stationery—scraps of paper lacking gilt edges or elegant embossments to impress—likewise signals the intimacy of comfortable quotidian exchange, a correspondence not bounded by and to special occasions, an everyday writing habit taking as its subject any element of the everyday, from the monumental death of a beloved to the presumably negligible nuisance of indigestion. These expressions to and about Susan uttered in pencil, ink, on elegant stationery and on the backs of envelopes were powerful enough to drive Susan herself to destroy those "too personal and adulatory ever to be printed,"[24] and to provoke someone else to scissor half of a sheet out of one of Emily's early, four-page letters to Austin, to erase several lines out of another, and to ink over every line of "One Sister have I in the house" (*F* 2; *P* 14).

Public and private forces have worked in concert to leave untold stories about what it means that so many poems were sent to a single contemporary and about what might motivate readers (including the addressee herself) to feel justified in suppressing writings to that primary audience of Dickinson. In determining what information is important to note, editors making printed volumes for public distribution must adopt principles of selection; following the conventions of typographical bookmaking, editors first working with the Dickinson documents were more focused on relaying the linguistic elements of her writings and the stories embedded therein than on the stories spelled by the material elements of the manuscripts, of the poems as they were embodied by Emily Dickinson. As the first century of reading Dickinson progressed and editors such as Johnson and R. W. Franklin began to grapple more and more with those material elements, the amount of information to be gleaned, sorted, and evaluated proved to be astounding, and principles of selection again prevailed. Also, by that point a particular reception of Susan had been set, and so this extraordinary body—"so many mss. of Emily's" sent to Susan[25]—and its many characteristics, especially physical aspects that relay information about the nature of this relationship, tended to confound, to be regarded as accidental or occasional or unique to the correspondence to Susan and so not crucially relevant to Emily's poetic project as a whole. Though that reception diminishing Susan as participatory primary audience for Emily's writing was by the mid-twentieth century a public one and has influenced Dickinson's editors, its origins are private, rooted in a mistress's desire to undermine the importance of the wife. The failure to interpret these stories conveyed through the distinctive nature of the writings to Susan and then through physical handlings of them has not simply been a matter of editorial priorities to translate Emily Dickinson's writings most intelligibly to a mass market but has also been the result of that early conscious effort to remove Susan's presence from the body of writings assembled under the author "Emily Dickinson."

When posthumous editors moved the circulation of Dickinson's writings from manuscript distribution in her correspondences to circulation in printed books, a notion of "public" and "private" began to prevail in interpretations of her poetic project that made it easy to lose sight of her objectives. In this, "public" is equated with print and aligned with the definite, and "private" equated with manuscript and aligned with the provisional. This sharp division between spheres assumes that Dickinson and her cohort did not regard their parlor and epistolary exchanges as what might be called the "public sphere" of salon culture, a public sphere constituted by private people influencing society, but as privatized discourse of family and friends enclosed within the space of the patriarchal family.[26] What this assumption overlooks is the geography of the Dickinson houses (both their situation to the town and the architecture of their floor plans) and the relationship of their inhabitants to Amherst society and to the institutions of education and the state. The Dickinsons were very public figures—Edward Dickinson represented Massachusetts's Tenth Congressional

District for one term, and his leadership proved crucial for bringing the railroad to Amherst. Both the Homestead, Edward Dickinson's house in which his daughter Emily lived for most of her life, and the Evergreens, Austin and Susan Dickinson's house next door, are located on Main Street, close to Amherst's town center, and both have ample front parlors well suited not simply for entertaining an intimate circle of friends but also for hosting receptions extended to a more general public. In fact, the graduation reception for Amherst College, established by Emily Dickinson's grandfather, was an annual event hosted by the Dickinsons for decades (first in the Homestead and then in the Evergreens), and the Evergreens especially became a cultural center where citizens greeted visiting luminaries. When Emily and Susan Dickinson circulated their writings in this parlor culture, they did not operate under a twentieth-century assumption that the work would be privatized, for these systems of distribution reached influential editors (Bowles of the *Republican,* J. G. Holland, who founded *Scribner's;* Richard Salter Storrs, who edited the Civil War journal *Drum Beat;* and Higginson, prominent editor and contributor to the *Atlantic Monthly*) and created access to lawmakers, statesmen (Judge Otis P. Lord, for example), and philosophers (Ralph Waldo Emerson, for example).

Yet in evaluating her poetic objectives, interpretive frameworks have not accounted for the public outreach of the Dickinson households. That critical fact and the lack of a cultural model for Susan and Emily Dickinson's intimacy obscure the relationships among the following set of facts, available in part since 1914 and almost in full since 1955–58 (when Johnson published the *Poems* and *Letters*): "I am not suited dear Emily with the second verse—It is remarkable as the chain lightening [*sic*] that blinds us hot nights in the Southern sky but it does not go with the ghostly shimmer of the first verse as well as the other one," Susan wrote to her beloved friend and sister-in-law circa 1861; in this, Susan responds to a version of "Safe in Their Alabaster Chambers," one that featured a whole other second stanza than the two-stanza poem she had already seen; among the ten lyrics known to be printed during the poet's lifetime, "Safe in Their Alabaster Chambers" offers the only example of Emily Dickinson responding directly to another reader's advice; at the behest of Susan, Dickinson revised this poem several times; as readers can see from the account rendered in "Emily Dickinson Writing a Poem,"[27] she labored over its composition, searching for an appropriate second stanza, and in the process wrote four different verses for possible coupling with the striking first[28]—these facts are especially important since "Emily Dickinson" is perhaps most well known for her isolation, for purportedly writing in complete solitude.

Until the 1990s, critics and biographers have been virtually silent on what this exchange between the two women means, for these facts have been "privatized," rendered as relevant to biography perhaps but not contributing in any significant way to public knowledge about Dickinson's compositional strategies. Both of the women were writers, yet neither was what one would call a professional writer. Both were readers, yet neither was what one would call a professional reader, a critic, an expert. If this were Wordsworth and Coleridge, or Hawthorne and Melville, or Elizabeth Barrett and Robert Browning, interpreters would with certainty declare this a literary liaison of significance for public understanding and discourse about "Emily Dickinson." Yet most have balked, hesitated, and some have shrugged, saying this is the exception (of Dickinson reaching out to another concerning the writing of a poem) that proves the rule (that reaching out was not her habit). However, the ease with which Emily approaches Sue and with which Sue delivers her response suggests that this exchange was a habit of their relationship, that this kind of give-and-take between them was the rule. Indeed, reading through their correspondence and seeing the number of "drafts" that Emily shared with Susan, one can see that such consultations were routine.

Turning to an example frequently (and accurately) remarked to document Dickinson's resistance to "expert," professional, publicly acclaimed advice helps clarify interpretation of the exchange with Sue. Suppose readers insert Higginson—a professional man of letters and widely published essayist, well-known agitator for women's rights, abolitionist, and correspondent of Dickinson's for almost twenty-five years—into the position of first-person singular speaking, "I am not suited—dear Emily." When one imagines Higginson as speaker, the relationship connoted by the exchange is easily read as one of poet consulting a trusted audience, a mentor of notable *public* standing. The many drafts of poems forwarded to Sue over the entire course of Emily's decades-long writing career make visible Sue's role as consultant, collaborator, confidante. The most extensive single example of her contributions, Emily and Susan Dickinson's exchange over the writing of "Safe in Their Alabaster Chambers," indicates that Sue critiqued the text while Dickinson was in the process of writing, that the effects of Sue's responses to reading the poem are evident in its various incarnations. Gushing with enthusiasm when she writes to Emily about its printing in the *Republican,* likely responsible for its printing in the newspaper read by the Dickinson households, and willing to spend time and energy writing back and forth about the poem's identity, it is clear that Sue was a vital participant in its composition and transmission. Had the same exchange occurred between Dickinson and Higginson, readers would have approached these facts with anything but the critical indifference with which they have in fact usually been handled. Had the public figure Higginson been the player instead of Sue, this exchange would have been at the center of Dickinson studies.

Important for reading and understanding Susan and Emily's exchange and the critical responses (or lack thereof) to the situation are that structures of "public" and "private" prime audiences to receive Higginson as authoritative, legitimate critic and Susan as amateur. Also confusing the picture is the fact that their passionate relationship throughout adulthood until Emily's death resists paradigms for standardizing emotional alliances. Although their relationship has strong elements of romantic friendship and also might be called prototypically lesbian, as well as mutually mentoring, and although their relationship might even be considered an alternative kind of "marriage," their dynamic devotion does not fit comfortably into any standard category—lover or sister or mentor or best friend or neighbor or companion or spouse—though it has strong elements of each.

Dickinson herself characterized their relationship in literary terms—comparing her love for Susan to Dante's love for Beatrice, Swift's for Stella, and Mirabeau's for Sophie de Ruffey (H B95; *L* 393), and comparing her tutelage with Susan to one with Shakespeare (*L* 757). Clearly, she valued Sue's opinions about writing and reading, and both women shared an affective theory of poetry. Of "Safe in Their Alabaster Chambers," Sue wrote that the first verse is so compelling that "I always go to the fire and get warm after thinking of it, but I never *can* again" (H B74c);[29] a few years later, Higginson paraphrased Emily's critical commentary, echoing Sue's—"If I read a book [and] it makes my whole body so cold no fire ever can warm me I know *that* is poetry" (*L* 342a).

As is already clear, a shared passion in their relationship was writing, and in this correspondence readers can see the astonishing range of writings sent from Emily to Susan over a lifetime—from a note joking about flatulence to poems interrogating the role of romantic love in women's lives and women's circumstance in nineteenth-century America, to letter-poems posing questions of faith and doubt, to poems spoofing Charles Dickens's sentimental characterization of "Little Nell" and others on her father's strict rules, to emotionally wrenching letter-poems on the death of Susan and Austin's youngest child, Gib, at the tender age of eight. Dickinson's poetry flourished in the writing to Susan, and her hybrid genre, the letter-poem, seems to have originated in their exchanges; the writings showcase changes in style and experimentations with punctuation, lineation, drawings, and with mixing media via layouts (e.g., attaching illustrations from novels and standard textbooks like the *New England Primer* to her poems to make "cartoons"[30]) and even calligraphic orthography, and repeatedly display Dickinson's vivacious sense of humor and her highly self-conscious textual play as well as her devoted affections.

The surviving documents of their decades of eroticized spiritual, emotional, and physical discourse tells a story of a highly charged, emotional relationship. Their relationship was a key component of Emily Dickinson's Poetry Workshop, and signs of their mutual passion for literature as readers and writers abound. From the beginning to the end of their correspondence, there are frequent allusions that attest to their voraciousness as readers, corroborated by the vast holdings of both household libraries, especially the Evergreens. There are also linguistic and material allusions to their mutual writing endeavors: from one of the earliest letters (April 1852), readers learn that Emily wants to get Susan's journal bound; a letter of but a couple of months later (11 June 1852) has two holes on each third of the folds similar to some of those made in the fascicles, as if the missive was at some point prepared for binding into a handmade book; Emily at one point christens herself and Sue "Combined Girl" for their artistic affinities (H B178, P 302); a mid-1860s letter to Sue from Samuel Bowles, publisher of the *Republican* and dear family friend, remarks, "Speaking of writing, do you & Emily give us some gems for the '*Springfield Musket*,' & then come to the Fair."[31]

In her December 1890 letter to Higginson, Susan underscores their relationship's literary, intellectual nature, as well as the intensity of their emotional engagement, when she compares her relationship with Emily and the lifetime of writing exchanged between them to a relationship that was written up in *Goethe's Correspondence with a Child* (incorporated into the volume at his request)—the intense dynamic of poet Karoline von Gunderode's correspondence with writer Bettina von Arnim, whose *Gunderode* Margaret Fuller translated into English. Susan proceeds to speak with quiet but unassailable authority about his and Loomis Todd's editing of Emily's poems. Making clear that she is thoroughly acquainted with Emily's poetic corpus, Susan approves of most of the titles used in the 1890 *Poems* and, in a 4 January 1891 letter, corrects "a blunder (of the printer I suppose)," "afar" to "ajar" in "I know some lonely Houses / off the Road" (*F* 13; *P* 289). Higginson took Susan's suggestion and in subsequent editions the word was changed.

Though the writings of her beloved friend had moved from the realm of gift exchange to that of commodities bought and sold, from a world where Emily's "Mine" was Susan's "your own" (H B158, *L* 908, *P* 1599) and "Copyright" mutual (H B144, *L* 909) to a province where "Publication—is the Auction" (*F* 37; *P* 704), law prevails, and copyright is mandated by courts, Susan generously continues her participation in its presentation and circulation. In commodification's geography of being, poetry is not so much "my sermon—my hope—my solace—my life," as it was to Susan, but is "my property." Authors in the realm of literary trade are often celebrities, as was the Poetess in the late nineteenth century. "Property" and "celebrity" are far from the spiritual, emotional, erotic, and intellectual concerns demonstrated by both Emily and Susan in their poetic praxes, but they are clearly elements of nineteenth-century literary life that they had thought about: numerous poems to Susan reflect on fame, that "fickle food / Upon a shifting plate" (H ST8c; *P* 1659), and Susan's awareness of authors being "on stage" is apparent from the metaphor she chooses to thank Higginson "for her as well as for myself for the perfect way you have led her before the curtain—but for that, her verses would have waited a long time for the recognition your name and fame have won for them" (December 1890 letter). In the world of literary "Auction," audience desires and expectations begin to shape publishers' notions of how authors are, even of what authors look like, and imaginative tendencies begin to function as stereotypes. Just as the image of long hair, blue jeans, and lots of sex and drugs still lurks around the performance of any rock 'n' roller today, so the composite (stereotypical) biography of the poetess lurked in the minds of all of a nineteenth-century poetess's readers (including herself). In 1890 audiences were prepared to receive this mourning figure, and publishers knew that such a solitary singer was marketable. Emily Dickinson's life had enough elements that the biographer of the author "Emily Dickinson" could be told to conform to this image, and a version of the Poetess is exactly what Loomis Todd, who never met the poet face-to-face, and Higginson, who only met her twice and for whom she clearly "posed," delivered to contextualize *Poems by Emily Dickinson*.[32]

Between Dickinson's death and the first production of a printed volume of her work four years later, Susan Dickinson began to work on her "Book of Emily." As Dickinson's primary audience, Susan determined that including writings that were "rather more full, and varied" (December 1890 letter) than the conventional presentation by Loomis Todd and Higginson was in order. Rather than separating the poems from their original contexts and dividing them into the predictable subjects that audiences expected, Susan wanted to showcase Emily's emotional attachments, particularly the bond between them and the literature it generated (comparable to that celebrated by Goethe), highlight her humor and her work in multimedia (adding drawings, engravings, and other cutouts to her own words). Yet forty manuscript books and scores of poems on loose sheets had been found after Dickinson's death, and her sister Lavinia had wanted poems from that trove incorporated into a printed volume and turned to Susan to accomplish the task. Susan struggled with how to make a book from those fascicles, reading through the astonishing production of her dearest friend and marking individual lyrics with initials (*D, F, L, N, P, S, W*) and "*X's*" in order to categorize them, not only in deference to Vinnie's wishes but also bowing to Higginson's market judgment that the kind of diversified volume she had first imagined was "un-presentable." In other words, she tried to make *their* "Book of Emily" but could not because it went against her better judgment, informed not by the market but by decades of her creative collaboration with Emily. Conflicted, distracted, and grieved by the loss of Emily and her husband's flagrant affair with Mabel, Susan moved slowly, and Vinnie grew impatient and demanded that the fascicle poems be returned so that another editor, one who could get the job done more quickly, could work on the project. Though she was to work on designs for her "Book of Emily" for the rest of her life,[33] Susan returned the fascicle poems, knowing that they would be given to Loomis Todd, her husband's mistress, to be edited for a printed volume.

At that very early point in the first-century transmission of Emily Dickinson's writings to the reading public, personal and cultural forces converged to suppress Susan's crucial role as audience for Emily's poetry. Wanting for rather obvious reasons to suppress that Emily Dickinson's primary audience was in fact the "wife forgotten" who completed the triangle of Mabel and her lover Emily's brother Austin, Loomis Todd was more than happy to play up the image of the solitary woman writer in her editorial productions. In a letter to her parents, Loomis Todd flatly declared her awareness that Amherst stories of Emily's life were very much "like a book,"[34] and for reasons that were not entirely professional, her iterations of the life of the poet conformed to audience expectations that deemphasized the writer's audience. She refused Higginson's recommendation that Susan's obituary of Emily, which emphasized that she kept her own company but was "not disappointed with the world" (*Republican,* 18 May 1886), serve as the introduction to the 1890 *Poems,* and instead used a three-paragraph introduction by Higginson that proclaimed that Emily was "a recluse by temperament and habit."[35] Not surprisingly, when Loomis Todd produced *The Letters of Emily Dickinson* (1894), Dickinson's primary correspondent of several decades is not even mentioned, nor are any of the hundreds of letters to her reproduced, though Susan's sister Martha, to whom Emily sent a handful of letters, is. The machine of the book introducing "Emily Dickinson" to the world has, then, plowed under the relationship that was at the center of her literary production.

From the distance of a century, and after study of Dickinson and her works has become an industry, readers cannot help but approach this relationship with the assumption that Emily was the writer and Sue the reader, always. Yet Sue wrote essays, reviews, stories, journals, poems, letters, and memorials (many of which were published) constantly throughout her life and produced commonplace books and scrapbooks of her own publications (review essays and poems) in the *Springfield Republican,* as well as of admired figures such as Queen Victoria, and of favorite poems, essays, and stories of other writers, including Emily. Recovering the reciprocal relationship of these two writers, one of whom has become a literary celebrity, reveals much about the histories of literary production, reproduction, and exchange. "Emily Dickinson" has been produced beneath the shadow of an illusion of ahistoricity, yet contextualizing her work with that of her mentor takes readers inside the parlors of Emily's home, the Homestead, and Susan's, the Evergreens, reminding us that the Dickinsons were deeply concerned with key issues of their day such as abolition and women's rights and enjoyed a rich literary and cultural life of converse with Emerson, landscape architect Frederick Olmsted, Harriet Beecher Stowe, and abolitionist Wendell Phillips. One of Susan's most poignant recollections is of the graduation of Elizabeth Blackwell, the first woman doctor in the United States, which Susan witnessed. Writing about that event because "the picture and sketch of Dr. Blackwell in the Sunday Republican . . . so stirred my own that 'forth I must print them,'" Susan used the occasion to muse upon the fear of intellectual women ("of course women deplored her"), something both she and Emily knew all too well.[36]

Because they have been contextualized by the machinery of book publication rather than by the nineteenth-century parlor world of literary circulation, Emily Dickinson's literary habits have usually been seen as eccentric, the result of "private," insular praxes. The machine of the book taxonomizes presentation of writings by genre—the letter and poem—rather than according to their original presentation as love letters, in scrapbooks, for commonplace books, for handmade poetry volumes. That she did not publish her poems in the conventional way via printed books, but rather circulated and "published" them in her letters as well as in the forty manuscript books or handmade fascicles discovered after her death, has disqualified them as publication, for the information lies in pieces scattered throughout printed volumes, overlaid with bibliographic information that makes the pieces appear disconnected rather than as parts of a story crucial to Emily Dickinson's poetic project. Yet investigating her correspondence with Susan Dickinson, and doing so in the context of Susan's writing practices and the volumes she had planned to produce of Emily's writings, reveals how deeply embedded both of their writing practices are within nineteenth-century cultural exchanges of the love letter, an occasion for poetic connection, and of manuscript volumes of favorite poems. Study of their correspondence also reveals how the two equated poetic union, or linguistic coition, with erotic union, how false our distinction can be between textual study and biography, and how, for them, in the words of Emily, "Poetry and Love . . . coeval come" (P 1247).

Postscript by Clare Brant

The Poetics of Scraps and Other Epistolary Materials
The sister-in-law is an unsung relationship for women, between women. It is both a matter of accident—your sibling chose this person, not you—and election—you may be obliged to be polite, but you are still free to like or dislike. These choices are recip-rocal, like correspondence. Sisters-in-law come in at the cusp of an old joke, that God gave you your family but thank heaven you can choose your friends. Warm re-lations between sisters-in-law show that family cohesion depends on individual wills; cool ones remind grown-up women that sisterhood can be a chore. Martha Nell Smith's essay argues persuasively that correspondence is a good temperature-taker, and that critics have occluded the relationship between Emily and Susan Dickinson in order to impose their own agendas: first, to let pass the mistress-editor's desire to silence the wife-correspondent, and second, to play detective in a romantic mystery that makes Dickinson's "Master" a person rather than a figure of allegory, a Dark Gentleman to partner Shakespeare's Dark Lady. Frustrating the orthodoxy that Dickinson's most important writing should be read off texts of repression (the "Master" letters), Martha Nell Smith does not like other critics crash into a seclud-ed bedroom, but walks around the parlor and out to Susan Dickinson's house next door. This rescues Emily Dickinson from critics who want to tie her to a heterosexu-al imperative, and skirts thoughtfully round the Charybdis alternative of making her a closet lesbian.

Historicizing domestic space, and especially the scene of writing, seems crucial here: too often we imagine a letter writer to be solitary because we want letters to enclose secrets and truths, or desires which the writer entertains in preference to ac-tual company. The feminine and the private thus service epistolarity. Martha Nell Smith argues that Sue is a significant advisor to Emily—more significant than the usual suspects rounded up for identification with the Master—because the two women correspond consciously and constantly about literature. Emily Dickinson has enough faith in herself as a writer to show poems to her sister-in-law, alter them, and chat about those alterations informally; short and scrappy letters show a busy writer confident enough to dispense with agonizing and justifying. But this kind of letter is more difficult to read as literature, however much it enacts a literary rela-tionship. If the deletions and substitutions of poetic drafts show repression at work, letters that discuss alterations to poems are like an analysand's conscious engage-ment with unconscious material, a state of mind in which (like diaries?) the first-person voice is knowing about unknowing. Biographers and editors fighting over who knows the writer best prefer to see an addressee as the point of focus; perhaps

*the true handmaid (or dark gentleman) is the form of letters—a medium not of con-
fession but of work-in-progress.*

    *Following the gendered presentation of the Dickinsons' exchanges, what Martha
Nell Smith's essay set me thinking most about was their informality, their scrappi-
ness in a material sense. Smith suggests that Emily and Sue's feminine culture of
gift exchange is suppressed by an editorializing tied to the machine-made book.
"Scrap" needs a gloss here: when I apologize for a scrappy letter, as I often do, I mean
one that is a bit disheveled. "Scrap" to a nineteenth-century woman would have
meant a remnant for which there might be a further use, like pieces of material saved
for quilting. (Compare Elaine Showalter's valorization of this as a metaphor for
women's writing.) The scrap is both a leftover from one process (like bits of iron remaining after casting, piled up into the proverbial scrap heap, or discarded pieces of
food), but it also has the potential to become not-waste, to be transformed into something worthy of preserving. Hence the invention of the scrapbook: extracts from
newspapers or magazines, photographs, printed images of all kinds could be kept
alongside manuscript fragments such as autographs or copies of poems. Like the
commonplace book (which is anything but to its compiler), the scrapbook is an irony,
a collection composed by hand that mimics a book, and an invention that appears
not coincidentally in the early nineteenth century when the mechanization of print
is speeding up. Martha Nell Smith presents the conversion of the Dickinsons' manuscripts into published editions as a story of mangling, deceit, and loss; the machine
of the book destroys an artisanal culture in which women feature as equal, generous, and creative. The handmade and the homemade are plowed under (her phrase)
by the mass-produced.*

    *I sympathize with this nostalgia, all the more because Smith uses it to service a
sharp exposé of sexual bias in how Emily is represented (and Susan is not) as a
writer and a letter writer. But one should not forget that editing family correspondence gave many nineteenth-century women an entry into print culture, and when
Elizabeth Barrett Browning asked, where are our literary grandmothers, one answer
should have been, in attics, in letters, being unbundled by diligent female descen-
dants. If some had mixed intentions, many labored to good effect. Although we rely
on editors to get the texts right for readers of printed versions, it would be a pity if
epistolary manuscripts were always to take precedence over printed texts—first because it means more power to biographers, editors, and historians, and less to literary critics, who I think have done more interesting things with letters; and second
because it plays host to technophobia. Martha Nell Smith's technophile promise of
color reproductions of letters is thus very welcome; it also invites cultural contextualizing regardless of academic discipline. For example, a nineteenth-century predilec-
tion for writing in violet ink should be connected to related Victorian partialities for*

violets (in soaps, corsages, china, greeting-card sentimentalities), for violet in choco-
lates and desserts, for the scent of heliotrope, even a partiality for purple prose.
The materiality of letters is a double story, of evolution and how we perceive
that evolution. I would like to offer two examples. The first concerns e-mail and its
symbolic apparatus of images of an older epistolary technology: an icon of an envelope, a dustbin, and a mailbox. I find the mailbox logical but alien, American rather
than homely. My post is delivered through my front door, so an equivalent icon evok-
ing an older site of postal arrival would show a front door with a letter box (which
is not a box but a decorative iron flap, usually with a large German shepherd behind
it eager to get her teeth into the letters, preferably with the postman's hand still attached.) New epistolary technology promotes itself as evolutionary precisely by being modestly nostalgic: more imaginative icons showing, say, Pony Express outrid-
ers, or Inca runners carrying quipos or strings of coded knots (quite an apt image
for http//:), would overstretch the memory.
My second example concerns the postcard. Plain postcards evolved in Austria
and Germany in the 1870s; picture postcards spread across Europe in the 1880s and
'90s, and were taken up in England in 1894, whence began what collectors like to
call its heyday, until about 1915. The postcard's invention widened the practice of
letter writing even as it condensed it; rather like e-mail, it was seen as a less literary but more energetic kind of letter writing. The postcard has subsequently had attractions for critics, novelists, and poets (Derrida, Carrie Fisher, Craig Raine), although for all postmodernism's multimedia affinities they seem to take it up for its
neat scriptive space, its portability, its articulation of displacements. I refer here (do
other writers too?) to a standard postcard with an image on one side and the other
side divided in two, half reserved for address, the other half enticingly blank. This
simultaneously brings together and divides the handwritten part from the mass-produced part. They are on different sides, like heads and tails of a coin. We think of
the script as personal, though not exactly private—most people write something with
the possibility in mind that it may be read by others. (Those friends who send me
postcards from art galleries usually put them in an envelope, as if the high culture
of art leans to privacy—or vice versa?) The mass-produced image, usually now a
photograph and typically a topographical scene, we individuate through the act of
selection, or ascription—this image for this person, which has echoes of gift giving:
I chose this one for you. Early postcards, however, had different configurations of
their writing space: many had a white border, or a little white rectangle, on the front
of the card, below or alongside the image, with the reverse reserved wholly for the
address. So the handwritten and the mass-produced are contingent on the same side.
This is a surprise to a modern eye, for it seems to connect the labor of professional
photography with the effort of writing: both are communications, though the image

dominates, prophetically. Some early cards have on their reverse a message. You may
write your communication now in this space, *as if writers had to be taught
how to reposition the handmade. That "now" is curious, too: postcards are an un-
celebrated part of modernism, and "now" suggests a modernist preference for the
present tense. I wonder if the opposite is postmodernism's nostalgia, or whether letters are a genre we will always connect with the handmade, even as our experience
of them becomes more mechanical.*

*Discussing the work of art in the age of mechanical reproduction, Walter
Benjamin said there is no tactile equivalent to optical contemplation. Those of us
who work with letters know there is—it comes from not forgetting the handmade
dimension of letters, the metonymy of "hand" to link the writer's body to script and
vice versa, the passage of the letter through other hands, the pleasure of handling
letters when opening and reading them. From scholarly editors who meticulously
record details of postmarks, to e-mail icons of envelopes and mailboxes, mechanical
versions of letters preserve traces of their origins. We seem to desire those to be handmade: for example, given the technological history of letter writing, it would be more
logical to have an icon of a typewriter to represent the material (dis)continuities of
e-mail. Perhaps future critics writing on e-mails will use a machine whose nostalgic
icons include the personal computer; either way, epistolary materialities, even of
scrappy letters, survive the technological changes that re-present them.*

Notes

1. The forty handmade fascicles have been available in facsimile for the past two decades;
see R. W. Franklin, ed., *The Manuscript Books of Emily Dickinson* (Cambridge MA: Belknap Press
of Harvard University Press, 1981). References to this edition will use *F* and the fascicle number assigned by Franklin.

2. See Mabel Loomis Todd and T. W. Higginson, eds., *Poems by Emily Dickinson* (Boston:
Roberts Brothers, 1890); T. W. Higginson and Mabel Loomis Todd, eds., *Poems by Emily
Dickinson*, 2d ser. (Boston: Roberts Brothers, 1891); Mabel Loomis Todd, ed., *Poems by Emily
Dickinson*, 3d ser. (Boston: Roberts Brothers, 1896). In her edition of the letters, the earliest to
be printed, Loomis Todd does not include a single letter to Susan, Emily's most frequently ad-
dressed correspondent, and set a century of ghosting Susan's influence in motion; see Mabel
Loomis Todd, ed., *Letters of Emily Dickinson* (Boston: Roberts Brothers, 1894).

3. Harold Love, *Scribal Publication in Seventeenth-Century England* (Oxford: Clarendon Press,
1993), 9; Love quotes Don R. Swanson, "Undiscovered Public Knowledge," *Library Quarterly*
56 (1986): 116.

4. Ellen Louise Hart and I have edited a volume collecting hundreds of Emily's writings to
Susan, in *Open Me Carefully: Emily Dickinson's Intimate Letters to Susan Huntington Gilbert* (Ashfield
MA: Paris Press, 1998); while even a facsimile presentation of the "Master" letters with diplomatic transcriptions, introduction, and notes makes a thin book of but forty-eight pages, our
selection of writings to Susan Dickinson is consciously restrained to make a three-hundred-

page book. Presentation of all of Emily's writings to Susan as Franklin presents the "Master" letters would be seven hundred or so pages long, but all of the information, including color photographic facsimiles (instead of in black-and-white photography's shades of gray) and assembled in a easily and thoroughly searchable form, will be available in *Emily Dickinson's Correspondences*, ed. Martha Nell Smith, Ellen Louise Hart, and Marta Werner (online publication; Chadwyck-Healey, 1999).

5. R. W. Franklin, ed., *The Master Letters of Emily Dickinson*, (Amherst MA: Amherst College Press, 1986); references to this edition will use the initials *ML* and the page number. Though there is no evidence that these drafts were sent via the postal service or any other courier, this facsimile presentation includes an envelope with the letters enclosed, as if they had been mailed, and thus emphasizes a particular interpretation of the writings' identity.

6. In 1951 Rebecca Patterson shocked the Dickinson world by publishing a book arguing that Kate Anthon was loved passionately by Emily, as was Susan. Four years later Millicent Todd Bingham reacted and avidly began to "correct" any such wayward notion, encouraging readers to search for Emily Dickinson's male lover by circulating the "Master" documents as mysterious, "real" love letters. See Patterson, *The Riddle of Emily Dickinson* (Boston: Houghton Mifflin Co., 1951); Bingham, *Emily Dickinson's Home: Letters of Edward Dickinson and His Family* (New York: Harper Brothers Publishers, 1955). Nearly simultaneously, Bingham also published a volume purporting to disclose that Judge Otis P. Lord was Dickinson's mystery lover. See Bingham, *Emily Dickinson: A Revelation* (New York: Harper Brothers, 1955).

For a much more extensive analysis of the "Master" letters than is appropriate for this essay, see Martha Nell Smith, "All Men Say 'What' to Me: Sexual Identity and Problems of Literary Creativity," in *Rowing in Eden: Rereading Emily Dickinson* (Austin: Univ. of Texas Press, 1992), 97–127.

7. Emily Dickinson Papers at Amherst College Library will be referred to within the text by the initial "A" followed by the library catalog number.

8. Susan Howe, *My Emily Dickinson* (Berkeley: North Atlantic Books, 1985), 24–25. To the affiliations Howe notes between Dickinson's heightened rhetoric and that of Charles Dickens and Elizabeth Barrett Browning, Barton St. Armand also notes connections to the Brontës, Robert Browning, and Longfellow in *Emily Dickinson and Her Culture: The Soul's Society* (New York: Cambridge Univ. Press, 1984), 83.

9. Joanne Dobson, *Quieter Than Sleep: A Modern Mystery of Emily Dickinson* (New York: Doubleday, 1997); Judith Farr, *I Never Came to You in White: A Novel* (Boston: Houghton Mifflin, 1996).

10. Emily Dickinson Papers at the Houghton Library, Harvard University, will be indicated by the initial "H" followed by the library catalog letter and/or number. Also referred to when quoting poems will be Thomas H. Johnson, *The Poems of Emily Dickinson* (Cambridge MA: Belknap Press of Harvard University Press, 1955); references to this edition will use the initial *P* followed by the poem number assigned by Johnson.

11. Susan Dickinson, letter to Curtis Hidden Page, 1900. Brown University, Papers of Susan H. Dickinson, Martha Dickinson Bianchi Collection, John Hay Library.

12. This manuscript is available in "Writings by Susan Dickinson," ed. Martha Nell Smith, at <http://jefferson.village.virginia.edu/dickinson/susan/> and in "Emily Dickinson Writing a Poem," ed. Martha Nell Smith, at <http://jefferson.village.virginia.edu/dickinson/safe/hb94.html>.

13. Dickinson printed ten, perhaps a few more, poems during her lifetime. See Karen Dandurand, "Another Dickinson Poem Published in Her Lifetime," *American Literature* 54 (1982): 434–37, and "New Dickinson Civil War Publications," *American Literature* 56 (1984): 17–27.

14. Of Loomis Todd's disappointments in her own literary failures, Richard Sewall remarks, "a major frustration of a life sprinkled with minor successes was her failure to achieve the first-rate literary success—as a novelist—she had always dreamed of" (*The Life of Emily Dickinson* [New York: Farrar, Straus, Giroux, 1974], 172).

15. Cheryl Walker, "A Composite Biography" and "Tradition and in Individual Talent," in *The Nightingale's Burden: Women Poets and American Culture before 1900* (Bloomington: Indiana Univ. Press, 1982), 67–116.

16. Sewall, *Life of Emily Dickinson*, xiv.

17. References to printings in Thomas H. Johnson and Theodora Ward, eds., *The Letters of Emily Dickinson*, will be indicated by L and the number assigned to a particular letter by Johnson and Ward.

18. Martha Dickinson Bianchi, ed., *The Single Hound: Poems of a Lifetime* (Boston: Little, Brown, & Co., 1914), v–vi.

19. As Bianchi edited more volumes with Alfred Leete Hampson, who professionalized her presentations of Emily Dickinson, the illustrations that might be considered "quaint bits to my children" disappeared from her production performances of her aunt's work.

20. See <http://jefferson.village.virginia.edu/dickinson/susan/tward4.html>.

21. Letter of December 1890 quoted in Millicent Todd Bingham, *Ancestors' Brocades: The Literary Debut of Emily Dickinson* (New York: Harper & Brothers, 1945), 86–87; discussed in Smith, *Rowing in Eden*, 214–17. The March 1891 letter to William Hayes Ward is available in "Writings by Susan Dickinson" (see n. 12 above).

22. Among the most prominent work reconstructing a more clear sense of literary exchange in nineteenth-century America is Cathy Davidson, *Revolution and the Word: The Rise of the Novel in America* (New York: Oxford Univ. Press, 1986), as well as the collection of essays she edited, *Reading in America: Literature and Social History* (Baltimore: Johns Hopkins Univ. Press, 1989). Both of these volumes invaluably expand knowledge about the hand-to-hand circulation of literatures.

23. Readers might consult Jerome McGann's reflections and speculations on "The Book as a Machine of Knowledge," in "The Rationale of Hyper-Text," at <http://www.iath.virginia.edu/public/jjm2f/rationale.html>, and in *TEXT: An Interdisciplinary Annual of Textual Studies* 9 (1996): 11–32.

24. H Lowell Autograph, 14 March 1891, at <http://jefferson.village.virginia.edu/dickinson/susan/tward3.html>.

25. H Lowell Autograph, 23 March 1891, <http://jefferson.village.virginia.edu/dickinson/susan/tward4.html>.

26. These revisionary applications draw on Habermasian postulations. See Jürgen Habermas, *The Structural Transformation of the Public Sphere: An Inquiry into a Category of Bourgeois Society*, trans. Thomas Burger, with Frederick Lawrence (Cambridge MA: MIT Press, 1989), esp. 27–56.

27. See <http://jefferson.village.virginia.edu/dickinson/>.

28. For extensive analysis of the two women working over "Safe in Their Alabaster Chambers," see Smith, "Dickinson's Poetry Workshop," in *Rowing in Eden*, 182–97. Readers

can review all of the surviving documents surrounding this collaborative exchange in "Emily Dickinson Writing a Poem," at <http://jefferson.village.virginia.edu/dickinson/>, the Dickinson Electronic Archives.

29. See <http://jefferson.village.virginia.edu/dickinson/safe/hb74c.html>.

30. For my examination of "The Poet as Cartoonist," see *Comic Power in Emily Dickinson*, coauthored with Suzanne Juhasz and Cristanne Miller (Austin: Univ. of Texas Press, 1993), 63–102; rpt. in *New Century Views of Emily Dickinson*, ed. Judith Farr (Upper Saddle River NJ: Prentice Hall, 1996), 225–39; see also <http://jefferson.village.virginia.edu/dickinson/>.

31. Jay Leyda, *The Years and Hours of Emily Dickinson* (New Haven: Yale Univ. Press, 1960), 2:93. The *Springfield Musket* was a Civil War publication; in his account, Leyda misreads "Market" for "Musket." I would like to thank Karen Dandurand for bringing Leyda's error to my attention and for apprising me of the *Musket*'s existence.

32. See especially Walker, *Nightingale's Burden*, 82–89. The degree to which this literary figure imbued Dickinson's literary culture is poignantly exemplified by her friend J. G. Holland, using the nom de plume Timothy Titcomb, in "No. 15 of his 'Letter to the Joneses,' To Miss Felicia Hemans Jones, Concerning Her Strong Desire to Become an Authoress": "It is not unfrequently true that those whose affections have been unsatisfied at home—whose plans of domestic life have miscarried . . . —turn to the public life for that which has been denied them at home"; see Leyda, *Years and Hours*, 2:81.

33. Susan's outline for making her "Book of Emily" includes emphasizing Dickinson's love of flowers, her affection, her witty and wise sayings ("Facts but not the phosphorescence of learning," for instance), and her giddy lampooning of a popular period piece entitled "The Devil" while entertaining guests by her piano playing in the Evergreens parlor (H Box 9; *Single Hound*, xi). Bianchi clearly followed Susan's plans to make *The Single Hound*, so much so that Susan, though deceased a year earlier, could clearly be called a coeditor (as was Mabel of Bingham's *Bolts of Melody*, produced thirteen years after Loomis Todd's death). To read more about Susan's editorial work and writings, readers can consult "Writings by Susan Dickinson" at <http://jefferson.village.virginia.edu/dickinson/susan/>.

34. Leyda, *Years and Hours*, 2:357.

35. Loomis Todd and Higginson, *Poems*, iv. Though Loomis Todd refused to use the obituary as introduction to the 1890 *Poems*, she mined it but a year later for her introduction to the 1891 *Poems* (see Smith, *Rowing in Eden*, 207–8).

36. Susan's "Memoir of Elizabeth Blackwell" is quoted in full at <http://jefferson.village.virginia.edu/dickinson/susan/>.

∾ Bodies in Pieces, Texts Entwined: Correspondence and Intertextuality in Melville and Hawthorne

Richard Hardack

In Melville's letters, Hawthorne serves as a crucial nexus for Melville's formulation of the boundaries of his own works and even his own body. Hawthorne was not only Melville's role model and projected ideal reader; he was, particularly for a work like *Moby-Dick,* practically his *only* reader. (In fact, one almost suspects that some of Melville's letters gained a wider audience than his novels, and that letter writing appealed to Melville partly though its guarantee of readership.) The extent of Melville's intertextuality with Hawthorne can be explained by the intensity of Melville's desire for Hawthorne's approval. Through their elaborate correspondence—which as far as can be reconstructed saw the exchange of dozens of letters over the three-year period from 1850 to 1852—Melville came to formulate not only his model of male fraternity but also that of textual interdependence. (Unfortunately, whereas Julian Hawthorne subsequently transcribed and preserved many of Melville's letters to Hawthorne, almost none of Hawthorne's letters to Melville have survived, so our reading of the correspondence is necessarily one-sided and partially reconstructed at best.) As Linda S. Kauffman and other critics have recently argued, each epistolary text is a kind of "transcript [of] scraps," combining the fictional and the real, inhabiting an inherently intertextual medium.[1] In other words, in keeping with his conception of creation and transformation in a male transcendental nature, Melville produced texts and letters by *recombining* existing texts and letters. In this essay, I focus on the intertextuality both of letters and of bodies in Hawthorne and Melville, a blurring of borders that stems primarily from the transcendental pantheism Melville repeatedly invokes in his missives to Hawthorne. Melville's correspondence *to* Hawthorne reflects his correspondence *with* Hawthorne, what Melville imagines as their physical and literary merger.

In his letters, Melville first uses Hawthorne as a rhetorical springboard in order to stage the consequences of the beliefs, such as pantheism, by which he is involuntarily compelled, and by which he feels he is being seduced. Melville ultimately projects these notably Emersonian beliefs onto Hawthorne and his texts in order to justify them, yet also profusely apologizes to Hawthorne for holding them. By measuring both his body and his body of work against Hawthorne's, Melville turns abstract and metaphorical comparisons into literal equivalences and exchanges; that is, Melville claims their bodies and letters are literally merged or intertextual. In this essay, I first set up the pattern of Melville's physical intertextuality with Hawthorne, and with male bodies, and then trace the specific influence of Hawthorne in Melville's letters, and finally some ramifications of their correspondence in *Pierre*. My approach also explicates Melville's attempt to use an Emersonian pantheistic doctrine of male merger with other men and the divinity solely through nature—a doctrine that Melville attempts to disavow but perpetually reinscribes—to transcend male individuality, and in fact the male body itself.

In his very pursuit of self-authorship, Melville's intertextuality with Hawthorne's works and body ultimately subverts any stable notion of individual authority, male self-reliance, and physical or textual closure. The letter becomes the perfect means to convey Melville's troubled sense that both individual texts and bodies can only be "read" through circulation and exchange, and are never self-contained, autonomous, or even self-identical. In Melville's imagination, each letter exchanged comes to represent a body circulated through Hawthorne's. The *chain* of letters Melville exchanges with Hawthorne dramatizes his chain of being, one centered around a male fraternity of writers. I wish to argue that Melville could fully formulate his most deeply held philosophical tenets only in the specifically "intertextual" genre of letters. Though Melville deploys catechisms in all his writings—in fact designing almost all of *Mardi* as a kind of staged dialogue of question and answer, call and response—it is only in the active exchange of letters with the author he desires to emulate that he can most fully imagine a consciousness outside his own with which to interact.

Letter writing offers Melville a divine merger with other men in nature, a sacralized epistolary male fraternity—what he calls an "aristocracy of the brain." In a letter of early June 1851, Melville writes to Hawthorne of his expectation of edenic union with his ideal correspondent:

> If ever, my dear Hawthorne, in the eternal times that are to come, you and I shall sit down in Paradise, in some shady little corner by ourselves . . . [perhaps] to smuggle a basket of champagne there . . . we shall then cross our celestial legs in the celestial grass that is forever tropical, and *strike* our glasses and our heads together, till both musically ring in concert. . . . Let us swear that, though now we sweat, yet it is because of the dry heat which is indispensable to the nourishment of the vine which is to bear the grapes that are to give us the champagne hereafter [emphasis added].[2]

In writing to Hawthorne, Melville always imagines a perfect overlap, a physical harmony arising between them: a "tuning" of heads to common pitch, a crossing of each other's legs, a sharing of liquids, a merger in a natural paradise. (Whatever Melville exchanges with or receives from Hawthorne, he essentially hears it through this grapevine.) In the extended postscript to this letter, Melville shares with Hawthorne his feeling of splendor in this same grassy repose: "In reading some of Goethe's sayings . . . I came across this, '*Live in the all.*' . . . what nonsense! . . . This 'all' feeling, though, there is some truth in. You must often have felt it, lying on the grass on a warm summer's day. Your legs seem to send out shoots into the earth. Your hair feels like leaves on your head. This is the *all* feeling."[3] This *All* feeling, merger with other men in a pantheistic nature, the merger of the individual body into the body of All and all other men, is here achieved when the medium of nature is reached through the medium of letter writing, through what we might consider a kind of daisy-chain letter. Melville repeatedly invokes this merger with nature and Hawthorne's particular body as part of his sense of the divine correspondence of all aspects of creation. As Melville adds, "your separate identity is but a wretched one," and the transcendence of that painful individuality is achieved by going postal: through the exchange and admixture of what are at first wretchedly separate letters, texts, and finally bodies and identities. Later that same month, Melville would write to Hawthorne that "men like you and me and some others form a chain of God's posts around the world."[4] These posts are both physical pillars along an Appian Way and, of course, postal way stations of the divinity. This chain of *posts* enacts a circuit for divine correspondences between Melville's and Hawthorne's texts and bodies.

Despite his own repugnance for systems of naturalism, Hawthorne specifically and systematically prompts, or is the locus for, Melville's invocations of pantheism, of bodies whose borders blur with each other and with nature. In letter writing, Melville often expressed what he could or would not directly articulate in his fiction, even through his most pantheistic or intertextual characters like Ishmael and Pierre. His letters become forms of interactive diaries, enacting his sense that any text is a kind of catalytic letter, a message that infuses and becomes part of the recipient. As we will see, Melville even went so far as to send Hawthorne an extensive letter containing a long oral narrative he had transcribed that he wished his friend to use for a story; in his relationship with Hawthorne, then, it would seem, a text of any kind should begin and end with a letter—for example, a story idea and finally a review. (And like Sterne, Melville was, of course, not above penning a review of his own work under a pseudonym if no one else would corroborate it for him.) A book is truly published only as a letter, and fully posted only when one receives a response, a review, or a riposte to complete the circuit: as Melville appeals to Richard Henry Dana, a fellow sea writer, "I almost think, I should hereafter get my M.S.S. neatly & legibly copied by a scrivener—send you that one copy—& deem such a procedure the best publication."[5] Well before Gertrude Stein, Melville had thus already concluded that writing is a kind of copying whose publication turns the manuscript into an epistolary text. He was not primarily recuperating the epistolary tradition of *Clarissa* in constructing his texts through the internal exchange of letters, though he certainly used this device on occasion, but instead suggested that the text itself is externally an intertextual letter.

In his letter of 17 November 1851, Melville again writes to Hawthorne concerning his "pantheistic feelings." He visualizes transcending man's separation from God and from other men, and his own physical separation from Hawthorne: "I speak now of my profoundest sense of being, not of an incidental feeling. Whence came you Hawthorne? By what right do you drink from my flagon of life? And when I put it to my lips—lo, they are yours and not mine. I feel that the Godhead is broken up like the bread at the Supper, and that we are the pieces. Hence this infinite fraternity of feeling."[6] The champagne Melville repeatedly shares with Hawthorne must literally go to both their heads. From this bodily intertextuality comes the intertextuality of Melville's letters to Hawthorne with his own fiction, and of Hawthorne's fiction to Melville's; this intertextuality is itself pantheistic, effacing the borders between bodies, between texts, and finally between bodies and texts as categories. Melville merges his body into the All of nature, and finds that it returns to him with Hawthorne's features, his postmark.

Pantheism is a Neoplatonic doctrine of fragmented or intertextual bodies, for the world or God represents one whole body; and people, fragments of this once-unified text. Ironically, Melville has a fully Emersonian relationship with Hawthorne, one based on transcendental precepts about the divine whole and inconsistent fragments. When Melville writes his own texts and reads Hawthorne's words, he imagines their actual bodies intertwined, even finding Hawthorne's heart beating beneath his own ribs: "So now I can't write what I felt. But I felt pantheistic then—your heart beat in my ribs and mine in yours, and both in God's. . . . But truth is ever incoherent, and when the big hearts *strike* together, the concussion is a little stunning. . . . Ineffable socialities are in me. I would sit down and dine with you and all the gods in old Rome's Pantheon" (emphasis added).[7] On this, as on other occasions, Melville imagines his body and Hawthorne's "striking" together in perfect overlap; he has also crucially moved from striking heads to striking hearts, for Melville a more important index of physical correlation.[8] Their exchange of letters immediately leads to an exchange of bodies; through their correspondence, Melville and Hawthorne transform a once piecemeal text/body into a divine corpus.

Such physical intertextuality immediately causes Melville to lose his sense of physical self-identity, fostering an inability to identify his own hands, and finally his own letters and texts; an "intertextual" pantheism leaves the writer in perpetual self-variance, alienated from any textual or physical sense of closure. Melville soon finds Hawthorne's ribs, his stories and novels, beneath the frameworks of his own texts. Melville again reveals that his writing to Hawthorne has left him incapable of setting final boundaries to his writing or the body that produces it: "Lord, when shall we be done growing? . . . Possibly, if you do answer [this letter], and direct it to Herman Melville, you will missend it—for the very fingers that now guide the pen are not precisely the same that just took it up and put it on this paper. Lord, when shall we be done changing? . . . I should have a papermill established at one end of the house, and so have an endless riband of foolscap rolling in upon my desk; and upon that endless riband I should write a thousand—a million—billion thoughts, all under the form of a letter to you."[9] (The prospect of this endless riband might have worried Hawthorne, for whom Melville had almost come to take on some of the psychological characteristics of a celebrity stalker. Hawthorne at first seemed to tolerate Melville's effusive sentiments, but gradually pulled away from his acolyte's attempts to correspond with and to him.) The proliferation of Melville's letter writing specifically to or for Hawthorne creates a series of disruptions or incursions of other texts and bodies into his own; his body will never be done first growing, and then more ominously changing, while his persona is continually interweaving with Hawthorne's. Even within the confines of his *own* letter, Melville's work has started to self-differ, producing two authors' hands, two pens, before he has even received a response. Melville writes to Hawthorne that as an author he cannot even know his own identity; the hand that guides the pen becomes "intertextual," not bound to one body, book or consciousness. Through the conceit of this endless riband/letter, Melville also produces a self-perpetuating correspondence, an infinite production that would literally transform his body into the intertextual letter to Hawthorne. This radical correspondence ironically subverts the idea of an autonomous male author even while Melville attempts to become one by measuring himself against Hawthorne.

Melville's body becomes a kind of player piano for texts, for an endless, emphatically *authorless,* riband. As Melville pushes the notion further, the writer is ground up by his own mill; writing is a skill that literally costs an arm and a leg to develop. To write a letter is to self-differ, to pick up a pen to dismember one's hand. (In *Mardi,* for example, Taji laments, "My cheek blanches white while I write. I start at the scratch of my pen, my own mad brood of eagles devours me. . . . an iron-mailed hand clenches mine in a vice and prints down every letter in my spite. Fain would I hurl off this Dionysus that rides me. My thoughts crush me. . . . And like many a monarch, I am less to be envied than the veriest hind in the land."[10] The Melvillean writer is endemically situated as a victim of a Dionysian force he cannot control.) Intertextuality possesses, or dispossesses, the writer from his work and body. By the time of *The Confidence-Man,* the operations of this magical paper mill of letter writing, already destabilized in *Pierre,* are wholly given over to the Mephistophelian operations of the printer's devil: there "truth is like a thrashing-machine."[11] The paper mill becomes a thrasher that chops up and recombines the bodies of both writers and texts, from Samoa, Dr. Cuticle, and Ahab to *Pierre* and *The Confidence-Man.* Melville tries to tether his decentered self to Hawthorne, to his influence, but the already precarious process fails entirely once Melville's friendship with Hawthorne wanes.[12] By the time of *The Confidence-Man,* when Hawthorne is largely a memory, Melville further literalizes this debilitating notion of perpetual self-variance, of progressively unfolding inconsistency, until "the difference between this man and that man is not so great as the difference between what the same man be today and what he may be in days to come."[13] These sentiments of self-alienation and self-difference have their roots in Melville's letters to Hawthorne, where his body and his writer's hands begin to differ from themselves. By the writing of *Clarel,* even "Great Pan" himself—Melville's emblem of the divine correspondence of men in nature—is precisely "overawed by sense of change," by his own intertextual nature, which produces not the sum of its parts but an empty cipher.[14]

Still, until late in his writing life Melville believed that letter writing serves as the ultimate fraternal bond, what joins men to other men, most transparently between himself and Hawthorne; but Melville also wrote to Dana, for example, that when he read *Two Years before the Mast* for the first time, he was "while so engaged, as it were, tied and welded to [him] by a sort of Siamese link of affectionate sympathy."[15] These Siamese links and chains bind Melville to his influences and his characters to their literary counterparts, and make them representative through their connection to one another. (Hawthorne's "connecting link" of missing evidence throughout *The House of the Seven Gables,* or the "connecting link" between Moodie and Zenobia in *The Blithedale Romance,* suggests that Melville's dream of pantheistic connection, or at least what he sees as textual linkage, is partly shared with, and partly derived from, Hawthorne;[16] Hawthorne's connections, however, rarely suggest the possibility of transcendence, only of ineluctable pattern.) In another letter to Dana, Melville closes, "believe me fraternally Yours—a sea-brother."[17] The pantheistic mindset pursues a particular type of exclusively male familiarization, for Emerson and Melville a literal project of choosing new male-centered families, a brotherhood whose membership is formalized with a letter's seal.

Writing to Sarah Huyler Morewood, Melville admonishes that *Moby-Dick* is "not a peice [*sic*] of fine feminine Spitalfields silk—but is of the horrible texture of a fabric that should be woven of ships' cables and hausers."[18] Again, in his correspondence Melville reveals the internal correspondence of his writing, its masculine cords and fabrics. Just as he makes a bid to control the process of female reproduction in much of his writing, Melville appropriates weaving as a quintessentially male activity. (In *Moby-Dick,* the amputation of bodies, conducted in the complete absence of women, serves as a surrogate for reproduction, and sailors' weaving an overlay on what would otherwise be the sentimental, female domain of correspondence. Until *Pierre,* Melville's men continue to merge, weave, and connect with each other, but not with women.) These suppositions again remind us of Emerson, who insists that all genuine correspondence must be male: where Emerson the father claims that "I and Waldo were of one mind," he writes to Margaret Fuller, "I on the contrary do constantly aver that you & I are not inhabitants of one thought of the Divine Mind, but of two thoughts."[19] When Melville writes to Hawthorne, he also imagines their bodies and texts commingling as one thread: when he writes to Morewood, he warns her that the fabrics and chains of connection cannot accommodate her.

Each letter thus serves as the primary connecting or corresponding link between men in a divine nature, and by the time of *Pierre,* even between men and women, or at least women to whom one is closely related. Melville's Pierre ultimately stands with Lucy "in *linked correspondence* with the summer lightnings" (*P,* 59; emphasis added). Throughout this text, women serve as the electric links of connection between all forms of natural bodies. Much later, once Pierre has joined Isabel, this lightning, which here represents a feminized pantheism, again charts the links of correspondence: "Strangest feelings, almost supernatural, now stole into Pierre. . . . With the lightning's flash . . . then most ponder upon final causes. . . . all their myriad *links* rattle in the mournful mystery" (*P,* 138; emphasis added). The "physical electricalness of Isabel"—who acts as a human lightning rod throughout the novel—is "one with that Pantheistic master-spell," turning Melville's "chain letters" into chain lightning (*P,* 181).

Through the symbol of lightning, this now dangerously "feminized" pantheism violently fuses bodies and texts. As I shortly note, *Pierre* is structured around, and receives its "connecting links" and electrical connections from, the writing and reception of an increasingly feminized correspondence.

While I do not have space here to discuss fully the gender implications of Melville's epistolary epistemology, I want to mention that in *Pierre* familial interconnections—cords and chains, connecting wires—are again at least partly played out through correspondence. Pierre of course first learns of his half sister's existence only when she sends him a letter, and the entire course of the novel can be traced through the subsequent exchange of missives. "It was while seated solitary in his room one morning," as specifically solitary as Ahab, "solitary as at the pole," that Pierre turns toward "the naked floor, following the seams in it, which as wires, led straight from where he sat to the connecting door, and disappeared beneath it into the chamber of Isabel" (*P*, 348, 381). Under this door, Isabel thereupon immediately delivers to Pierre a letter from Lucy, who protests that "still we are one, Pierre . . . and I hasten to re-tie myself to thee" (*P*, 349). The letter produces what Wai Chee Dimock would call a circuit of identity, but also a breakdown of physical and social boundaries:[20] Melville's body merges into Hawthorne's, Pierre's mother turns into his sister, his lover into his half sister and back again, and his fiancée into his alleged cousin. No middle ground exists between absolute isolation and solitude and complete correspondence and merger. Melville is clearly playing with the conceits of the formulaic epistolary love triangle, but he is also elevating the importance of his alternative notion of letter writing to a matter of life and death. Pierre effectively meets his end in letters, finally attacked by his publisher and his male cousin: "in these hands I feel that I now hold the final poniards that shall stab me. . . . He folded the left-hand letter, and put it beneath his left heel, and stood upon it so; and then opened the right-hand letter . . . and stood upon both" (*P*, 398–99). Once he is no longer merging—connecting or linking—in his correspondence, Pierre quickly engages in a fight to the death. The letter that fails to conjoin bodies leads to their violent fragmentation.

For Melville, all objects in the world ultimately represent bodies and texts, which can be merged and recombined. Even the chains on Melville's ships, for example, are configured as kinds of merged textual bodies; on

Redburn's deck, sailors manufacture "a clumsy sort of twine, called *spun-yarn*. For material, they use odds and ends of old rigging called '*junk,*' the yarn of which are picked to pieces, and then twisted into new combinations, something as most books are manufactured."[21] Books, of course always composed of these spun-*yarns*, are thus combinations of masculinized ropes or ties, the same bonds that weld men to men. Throughout his works, Melville describes his characters as connected by these fibers and tethers, and bearing bodies, like Ishmael's and Queequeg's, that combine. Whole chapters of *Moby-Dick* trace the way men lose track of where their own hands begin and end, as occurs for instance in the sperm cassocks (though as always in Melville, while men seem abstractly to merge and become "intertextual" above the surface, below that surface their actual bodies, like those of the sharks and Ahab, are incessantly disconnected and amputated). Male bodies and texts intertwine and merge, are picked to pieces and then twisted into new combinations of bodies and texts.

Through much of his writing, Melville employs a language of chains and joints, of correspondences, to situate his characters in society. For Melville, all men are enveloped in whale lines, joined by fraternal bonds and literal umbilical cords: monkey ropes, chains, connecting links, cunning analogies, magnets and meridians. These connections are modeled on, parallel with, his fraternal letter writing; they are divine posts connecting the hearts of men. Even the maniacally isolated Ahab feels that Pip "is woven to [him] by cords woven of [his] heart strings."[22] (Such language echoes Emerson's insistence that men are but "magnetized" steel filings: as Emerson writes, "What heart drawings I feel to thee!"[23]) Positing the indissoluble relation of all to all, Melville's pantheism incurs a dissolution of the boundaries of identity, the self's fragmentation through a variety of amputations and its accretion through absolute merger. Each interconnection between men is a kind of inscription; the cords of correspondence, of letter writing, link all men to one another, and turn them into corresponding magnets.

"As with all great genius," Melville wrote to Hawthorne in June 1851, "there is an immense deal of flummery in Goethe, and in proportion to my own contact with him, a monstrous deal of it in me."[24] What this admission tells us is that *all forms of contact* for Melville precipitate intertextuality, which is also a kind of irremediable infection or contamination; each letter is in itself a carrier. As Melville frequently attests with regard to Hawthorne, his admiration for other writers' work transforms his body into theirs, repeatedly and literally merges them together. It is correspondence that turns Melville into the original version of Zelig.

Melville consistently associates texts with the bodies of male authors, including his own. After thanking Hawthorne for "despising the imperfect body, but embracing the soul" of *Moby-Dick*, Melville writes: "The divine magnet is in you, and my magnet responds. Which is the biggest? A foolish question—they are *One*."[25] Like *Moby-Dick*, all letters and authors have bodies that are defined through one another and can, through a divine nature, be endlessly recombined. These bodies both attract and repel Melville, who must situate them against his own without losing himself in them; if Hawthorne and Melville "exchange" lips and ribs through a pantheistic divinity, their masculine bodies must be equivalent in every way. Through these divine posts, chains, or connecting magnets, Melville tries to stabilize his intertextuality, his inability to identify his own hands; they allow Melville to imagine that intertextual bodies or letters perfectly overlap. Instead of a body that is never done changing, perhaps he could have a body that becomes One with the All. As Emerson writes, in the same half-philosophical, half-sexual terms, "It is necessary to suppose that every hose in nature fits every hydrant."[26] Through Melville's perpetual interweaving of textual fibers and body parts, all intellectual contact creates a chain of divine equivalence: spiritual or metaphoric contiguity becomes literal and physical equivalence. Hawthorne's body fits into and becomes an absolute surrogate for Melville's, his rhetoric of connection merges with Melville's, and the figures of his texts—from the Beatrice of "Rappaccini's Daughter" to the late Pan of *The Marble Faun*—become models for Melville's characters. Aside from Melville's phallic comparisons of the size of Hawthorne's divine magnet under the rubric of *Moby-Dick*, Melville tells us that each body is a kind of magnet, exerting a field of gravity or influence on the bodies and texts around it. These bodies and texts must either merge or, as in Pierre—his journal, his novel, his very body—finally be torn to pieces.

Many of Pierre's transcendental ideas of connection are developed from the Emersonian notion that social interaction between men is acceptable only in nature. Emerson, for example, had concluded in his lecture "The Heart" that "man is insular and cannot be touched. Every man is an infinitely repellent orb, and holds his individual being on that condition. In fact, men are continually separating and not nearing by acquaintance. . . . Best amputate."[27] Even the divine magnet that for Melville fixes his body to Hawthorne's would finally not be able to overcome this repulsion of individual parts, which owe allegiance only to themselves. And these "repellent orbs," transparent eyeballs and repulsive individuals, can only separate by acquaintance (that is, see and not be); ironically, where Melville can at least fantasize his body as cathected to Hawthorne's, Emerson primarily configures male bodies as inverted magnets. Like Emerson's infinitely repellent orbs, in Melville the male bodies/texts that fail perfectly to overlap are dismembered.[28] Pierre refutes his merger with Goethe (surrogate for Emerson) in a way that also undoes Melville's merger with Hawthorne; Goethe is, after all, the pantheist Melville explicitly evoked in asking for Hawthorne to merge with him in the All. After here taking a comparative inventory of Goethe's heartless frame, Pierre mock-castrates his body and decides the universe can get on without him "and could still spare a million more of that same identical kidney" (*P*, 342). Where identical parts had brought Melville and Hawthorne together, they drive Pierre and Goethe apart. Melville hopes correspondence and intertextuality can overcome the repulsion of male bodies, but, as exemplified by Pierre, most of his characters instead experience dismemberment as a kind of failed merger—a kind of organ rejection.

Most male American Renaissance writers envision the pantheistic merger of bodies as a feminine attribute, though they can rarely imagine merging with women. Where, for example, men tend to amputate and cut bodies (and texts) throughout Emerson's and Melville's writings—from Emerson's truncated man of "The American Scholar" to Melville's Surgeon Cuticle and Ahab—women are represented as existing nonindividually as "merged" plants. Unlike men, women are virtually never depicted as missing body parts during this period, and this male conception of women as unfragmented and nonamputated reflects a projected fantasy of women as lacking individuation, as always already in correspondence with nature. Male bodies and texts are imagined to have defined and sharp edges, while female bodies and texts are imagined to be fluid and interchangeable. Women's bodies are represented as unmediated forms of nature, parts of a collective, preindividuated, inherently intertextual or boundaryless existence. In the writings of male pantheists, individual women become all women (much as typically occurs in Fellini movies).

Though Melville represents merger as feminine, and soon depicts Pierre as desperately entangled with a specifically feminine merger, he clearly imagines his growing correspondence with Sophia Hawthorne as a route of access to her husband. He writes to Hawthorne, "The side-blow through Mrs. Hawthorne will not do. I am not to be charmed out of my promised pleasure by any visit of that lady's syrenisms. *You,* sir, I hold accountable, & and the visit (in all its original integrity) must be made. What *spend the day,* only with us? . . . you may spend the period of your visit in bed, if you like. . . . Come—no nonsense. If you don't—I will send Constables after you. . . . By the way—should Mrs. Hawthorne for any reason conclude that *she,* for one, can not stay overnight with us—then You must—& the children if you please."[29] Aside from the homoerotic undercurrent of Melville's insistent overnight invitation, the letter is noteworthy in framing correspondence with Sophia as a side-blow, a mis*strike,* in his efforts to contact and physically correspond with her husband. Given the overwrought eagerness of Melville's invitations, one can readily imagine the more reticent, retiring and, decorous Hawthorne precisely trying to stave off at least some of Melville's attentions through this surrogate correspondence with Sophia.

Before closing, I want to give an example of how Melville's "theory" of letters is put into practice in his fiction, how his letters become intertextual guides to his work. Just as Melville's body becomes "intertextual" with Hawthorne's, his texts often become versions of Hawthorne's, particularly when dealing with issues of gender and bodily fragmentation. Much of Melville's configuration of women as botanical and nonindividuated, for example, can be traced directly to Hawthorne as well as Goethe, the two figures he invokes most overtly in relation to pantheism. Written in 1844, Hawthorne's "Rappaccini's Daughter" suggests to Melville an exigent connection between the feminine and a botanical, intertextual pantheism. In Hawthorne's story about a father's fatal love and a daughter's final poisoning, a kind of male parthenogenesis and female "inhumanity" are conjoined. Hawthorne's Beatrice, whose name, character, and symbolic function Melville obsessively recuperates in a variety of ways throughout *Pierre,* remarks that her father "created" the flower with which she is associated: "He is a man fearfully acquainted with the secrets of Nature, and, at the hour when I first drew breath, this plant sprang from the soil, the offspring of his science, of his intellect, while I was but his earthly child."[30] Beatrice's body is then indissociable from, intertextual with, the body of the plant; this "female"-coded intertextuality—the absolute correspondence of human and plant—proceeds from too great an acquaintance with nature, and from a pantheism that "creates" by merging rather than cutting and reassembling bodies. It turns out that male individuality is a sword that dismantles the bearer: Pierre at first dreams that "you lose your sharp individuality, and become delightfully merged in that soft social Pantheism, as it were, that rosy melting of all into one . . . no one draws the sword of his own individuality" (*P*, 286). But the sword of what degenerates from "soft-social" into "corporate pantheism" cuts Pierre's body, like Enceladus's, to pieces by the end of the tale; only female bodies can "correspond" effortlessly by merging into a nature they already represent. Men must finally not merge but be cut apart to correspond.

In *Pierre*, Melville's blatant rewriting of Hawthorne's tale of incest and poisoning, Isabel serves as the nexus for Melville's desire to merge with Hawthorne, his feelings of pantheism, and his anxieties about influence and reproduction. Isabel is dangerous because she expresses the unvoiced undercurrent of Pierre's own desire, wishing she were able to live, or perhaps more precisely merely to exist nonindividually, as a plant. This is precisely Melville's own fantasy throughout his "pantheistic" letters to Hawthorne. When Melville writes that he is coming to the "inmost leaf of the bulb," and that Hawthorne must surely have shared "the *all* feeling"—that is, feelings of pantheism, when, as noted, your "legs seem to send out shoots into the earth [and] your hair feels like leaves upon your head"—he is asking for a feminine merger with Hawthorne in a sacralized nature, one Beatrice and Isabel achieve without effort.[31] To join together in nature is to exist in the mutual transcendence of male individuality, as an undifferentiated plant in a universal garden whose roots are all intertwined. It is a state so threatening to male individuality that, though men endlessly pursue it with one another, Queequeg cannot survive it with Ishmael, and Pierre can only express his desire for it through Isabel. Despite his qualifications, Melville admits to Hawthorne that his feeling of merger or intertextuality represents his profoundest sense of being, not an accidental or temporary feeling.

Melville's profoundest sense of being, then, involves a feminine, botanical merger that he often dissimulates. Isabel has thus in fiction explicitly taken up Melville's epistolary prayer to Hawthorne: "I pray for peace—for motionlessness—for the feeling of myself, as of some plant, reabsorbing life without seeking it, and existing without individual sensation. I feel that there can be no perfect peace in individualness. Therefore, I hope one day to feel myself drank up into the pervading spirit animating all things" (*P*, 146). The intertextuality of letters and bodies is imagined as a feminine "cure" for the extremity of male individualism during the American Renaissance, and it takes the form of a pantheistic merger of all kinds of bodies with one another in nature. With no perfect peace in male individuality, individual texts and individual bodies must merge with one another in nature; being an isolated male body is like being an unsent letter, isolated and unconsummated. Letter writing is imagined as a transcendental act, a way for men to merge with one another through the All or oversoul, creating a whole far greater than its wretched parts. Such physical merger, such longing to transcend individual identity, produces an entire ontology of intertextuality.

It is only when Melville has exhausted intertextual merger with men that he directly turns to women in *Pierre*. But in fact, Melville had configured himself as "feminized" in much of his liaison with Hawthorne. Quoting a (now unavailable) letter from Melville to her husband, Sophia Hawthorne writes that she "enclose[s] a very remarkable quotation from a private letter to Mr. Hawthorne about the House of S.G. but as it is wholly confidential *do not show it*. The fresh, sincere, glowing mind that utters it is in a state of 'fluid consciousness.'" In another letter to Hawthorne, a full copy of which does exist, Melville writes, in "a passing word said to [Hawthorne] over [his] garden gate . . . [,] I thank you for your easy-flowing long letter (received yesterday) which flowed through me, and refreshed all my meadows, as the Housatonic—opposite me—does in reality."[32] Letters thus transcend gates and physical borders and leave the correspondents emphatically fluid and thus intermingled: Melville almost literally receives a blood transfusion, a fluid physical merger with Hawthorne, through their correspondence. Once hard-edged male bodies are doused, pollinated, invigorated, and made permeable through correspondence. In the novel he was immediately about to begin, Melville's self-described states of fluidity come perfectly to match Pierre's "fluidity" in his proximity to Isabel. While voicing Pierre's/Melville's own pantheistic fantasies, Isabel in many ways also becomes a version not just of Hawthorne's characters but of Hawthorne himself. (The extent to which Melville identifies his "sweet man of mosses" with Isabel herself, however, is revealed by the fact that he calls the Hawthorne figure of *Clarel* "Vine," a name definitive not just of his own correspondence, but of Isabel's arboreal hair.)

In Melville's model of human development, babies are inherently "feminine" and "intertextual," and cannot distinguish between the self and the inanimate world; as a child, Isabel starts out wholly undifferentiated from—at one with—nature and all other bodies. To achieve true correspondence is to return to that undifferentiated state where all bodies are the same body. Isabel explains that a beautiful infant in her second home first brought

me to my own mind, as it were; . . . first undid in me the fancy that all people were as stones, trees, cats; first filled me with the sweet idea of humanness. . . . [S]omehow I felt that all good, harmless men and women were human things, placed at cross-purposes, in a world of snakes and lightnings, in a world of horrible and inscrutable inhumanities. . . . [O]ther things I was ignorant of, except the general feeling of my humanness among the inhumanities. . . . They taught me to sew, and work with wool, and spin the wool . . . [,] which partly brought to me the power of being sensible of myself as something human. . . . I thanked—not God, for I had been taught no God—I thanked the bright human summer, and the joyful human sun in the sky. I thanked the human summer and the sun that they had given me the woman, and I would sometimes steal away into the beautiful grass, and worship the kind summer and the sun. (*P*, 150–51)

Isabel becomes partially exiled from the natural world but, after protesting too much about her humanness, incessantly humanizes what is inhuman; she pantheistically worships a "human summer." Isabel claims the infant helps her find humanness distinct from things, plants, and animals, yet continues to call the summer and sun human, to imagine herself a plant, and to be the very conductor of an inhuman lightning: she does not translate nature into art, as men do, but gives it unmediated vent into the world.[33]

The above passages from *Pierre,* and their "family mergers," human summer and human sun, are also clearly inspired by Hawthorne's

"Rappaccini's Daughter." There Beatrice, who as a child is as isolated from society as Isabel is, remarks, "I grew up and blossomed with the plant and was nourished with its breath. It was my sister, and I loved it with a human affection." We here have a sisterhood of correspondence with nature to parallel Melville's fraternity with Hawthorne. Repeatedly described as "another flower, the human sister of those vegetable ones," Beatrice is as close to Isabel's mother, or antecedent, as one can find.[34] Brought up a "savage," without a father, Isabel knows no God, but like Beatrice finds "the guitar was human," and it "learned [her] to play" on it (P, 153–54). Women are not human in Hawthorne's story and in most of Melville's work, for they humanize, become physically "intertextual" with, everything else; they eliminate the distinction between human and inhuman by achieving a radical, total correspondence with nature. Women in fact take Melville's own pantheistic feelings to their logical extreme, treating nature, and finally inanimate objects, with a human affection. Women's bodies merge into the body of the world, for they represent an unmediated nature, an unfragmented text or body, and exist in transcendental male fantasy as unindividuated.

Finally, I also want to propose that letter writing dramatizes Melville's longing for a kind of male parthenogenesis. As in "Rappaccini's Daughter," in *Pierre* the woman so closely allied with nature effectively has no mother at all; in Hawthorne's tale she is parthenogenetically generated, while in Melville's novel she is born of a woman completely effaced from the narrative. The deification of nature, the pantheistic redefinition of boundary between self and nature, produces a feminine merger with the world, and finally an intertextuality of male bodies, but occludes actual reproduction. Melville would ideally reproduce himself and Hawthorne in this same process, through merger and recombination (rather than reproduction) in nature. Bodily intertextuality in Melville ultimately represents a fantasy of male reproduction; where new texts or bodies cannot be produced from nothing, they are created through recombination or intertextuality. This process allows men to reproduce new texts together, to reproduce matter without mother. The self-reliant male writer joins his body and letters to those of other writers, and Melville's epistolary intertextuality with Hawthorne comes to represent his form of literary "reproduction" with his only/ideal reader.

Postscript by Anne L. Bower

In "Bodies in Pieces, Texts Entwined," Richard Hardack's enthusiastic prose creates a palpable sense of Melville's intensely emotional correspondence with Hawthorne. Hardack asserts that letters provided Melville the ideal location in which to "imagine a consciousness outside his own with which to interact." And the essay effectively details how Melville's letters formulate a "blurring of borders" in relationship to Hawthorne, demonstrating Melville's "desire for Hawthorne's approval" and his view of himself and Hawthorne as "merged" both literally and figuratively.

In our unfortunately homophobic and nonepistolary times, we might be convinced by Hardack that the content and style of Melville's letters to Hawthorne were unique to him and his situation. However, I do not think this is quite true. While Hardack highlights and analyzes the extremely corporeal imagery Melville employed and the fierceness of his "need" for Hawthorne, I would like to offer the notion that Melville was frequently enacting within his correspondence cultural patterns common to his time. As a sidebar to Hardack's essay, let me provide here support for the notion that Melville's letters have much in common with those of other mid-nineteenth-century epistolarians and also incorporate images and stylistics drawn from the popular culture of the period.

Nineteenth-century men and women depended on letters in ways we, at the end of the twentieth century, have seldom (if ever) experienced. Yes, we still send thank-you and condolence notes, but extended missives, exchanged via the postal service, are rare. We disparagingly refer to "snail mail" to distinguish old-fashioned letters from our "real" or "usual" means of communicating (phone calls, e-mail, and faxes). But a century and a half ago, letters were the only way, other than oral messages passed along by family and friends, of sending information or expressions of feeling to those at a distance.

Since letters were such an essential part of life, many people developed elaborate and enduring correspondences, with stylistic conventions very different from those we employ in our faxes, e-mails, and telephone conversations. As William Decker makes clear in Epistolary Practices, *discussing letters of the nineteenth century and earlier, "Distances were more formidable, the presence and absence of one person to another possessed fewer gradations than what they assume in a world of beamed simulacra, and separated parties more commonly created elaborate texts of their friendships."[1] Decker effectively shows that even those who lived within just a few miles of each other might devote considerable writing space to their concern with separation and all it symbolized. The content of many letters emphasized the uncertainty, even the impossibility, of maintaining closeness between the correspondents, as well as their sense that physical distance and separation not only repre-*

sented estrangement—in terms of personal friendship, love, spiritual concordance, intellectual interchange, and so on—but also symbolized death itself.

Among the transcendentalists in Hawthorne's circle, interpretations of perceived parallelism between earthly experience and spiritual/intellectual life took on great significance and occupied these writers in their letters, essays, poetry, and fiction. In addition, conventions of the time allowed for these fears and worries to be expressed with greater emotional effusion between letter writers than is commonly found in communications exchanged during the late twentieth century. Using examples from the correspondence of Emerson, Dickinson, Fuller, Thoreau, and others, Decker gives his readers a substantial sense of the vital role expressive, descriptive language played for these writers.

Metonymic uses of body imagery and bold statements of attachment were common in nineteenth-century letters. Thus Emily Dickinson writes to her friend Elizabeth Holland: "I kiss my paper here for you . . . would it were cheeks instead." Writing to the relative of a friend who had died, she puts her condolence in physical terms: "To take the hand of my friend's friend, even apparitionally, is a hallowed pleasure."[2] Dickinson's embodied, impassioned prose, like that which Hardack finds in the correspondence of Melville, links body parts and emotional impulses in ways intended to break down the separation between correspondents—the separateness caused by actual space as well as by the existential condition of individuality. Likewise, we find that Ralph Waldo Emerson and his correspondents, although often concerned with matters abstract and cerebral, frequently make use of language that is imagistically and emotionally laden. Early in their correspondence, Emerson writes to Thomas Carlyle: "I hope you do not measure my love by the tardiness of my messages." Such easy reference to love between same-sex friends was commonplace in the nineteenth century, although much rarer nowadays. Much later in their epistolary relationship, Carlyle writes to Emerson that receiving a letter from him after a long gap in time is like once again seeing him "face to face . . . not a feature . . . changed."[3] Here again, we find the easy association of a body aspect with the text being created. What Decker makes clear is that, although the transcendentalists sought spiritual and enduring meaning in their mental, imaginational communion (with each other, with nature, with some greater power), often their expression of that communion relied upon or referred to body images. With such insight into the epistolary habits of the nineteenth century, we might read Melville's naming of legs, hands, heart, and so on as dramatic instances of a somewhat common rhetorical practice.

For another kind of parallel to Melville's physical imagery, I turn to the less intimate and more troubled correspondence between Whitman and Emerson. Here, too, physical imagery is evident. When Whitman writes his "manifesto" letter to

Emerson in August 1856 (used as an afterword in the 1856 edition of Leaves of Grass), *we can see the same kind of desire for a special, nurturing, mentoring relationship that Melville sought from Hawthorne. Addressing Emerson as "dear Friend and Master," Whitman fills his long oratorical letter with lavishly detailed ideals of creative and intellectual life in a democracy. Typical of Whitman, this long letter uses strong physical images—he designates poetic language as "an American rude tongue," finds the purpose of literature "to be electric, fresh, lusty, to express the full-sized body, male and female," and terms the creation of new American modes of expression the "true heirs, begotten of yourself, blooded with your own blood."[4] While Whitman's sentences do not "embody" Emerson directly or work to form a physical relationship solely between Emerson and Whitman in exactly the same way that Melville uses physical imagery in his letters to Hawthorne, I think we can see in Whitman's letter the same reliance on bodied imagery to form bonds and congruence of thoughts.*

The kind of dramatic and fleshly imagery that shows up in some mid-nineteenth-century letters turns out to have been quite common not only within letters but in the culture at large. In The Art of Democracy, *Jim Cullen reminds us that the religious revival known as the Second Great Awakening, in evangelical preaching and voluminous publication of tracts (printed in large runs and widely distributed), stressed "personal perfectibility" via highly melodramatic presentations. This religious impulse also merged with other reformist energies that were directed at "social perfectibility." The vernacular language of religious tracts and communications produced by reform speakers (abolitionists, temperance workers, suffragists, and others), along with the sensationalistic style of dime novels, had powerful influences on artists of the mid-nineteenth century, Cullen believes, affecting the content and style, for example, of Walt Whitman's 1842 novel* Franklin Evans *as well as his 1855* Leaves of Grass.[5]

Hawthorne and Melville also drew on the material proliferating around them. According to David S. Reynolds, both of these writers found in reformist literature, tracts, and speeches reinforcement for their own distrust of fanatic do-gooders. While they critiqued popular approaches to reform, both writers had an interest in their own era's moral dilemmas and both were influenced by language of the age's reformist publications. Looking at Melville's work, Reynolds concludes that his association with Hawthorne was based in part upon a shared interest in what Reynolds terms "subversive" reform literature, that is, writings that stressed the "grisly, perverse results of vice, such as shattered homes, sadomasochistic violence, eroticism, nightmare visions, and the disillusioning collapse of romantic ideals." Hawthorne's 1852 Blithedale Romance, *for example, demonstrated the "fragmentation and superficiality of modern reform movements" using a dramatic and dark style influenced by popular writing of the time. In* Moby-Dick, *Reynolds finds Melville working with the "ambiguity" of reformist tendencies in the culture. In this novel, he says, "reform content was abandoned but reform images and subversive spirit were retained," releasing "an explosive symbolization" that included use of images commonly used in reformist tracts, such as oceans, whales, and ships.[6]*

At the same time, Cullen reminds us that humorous narratives of the Southwest (along with sensationalist romances, western adventures, and dime novels) were also very popular, with Davy Crockett being a star figure. Biographies of Crockett, a ghostwritten autobiography, and an enduring series of "Crockett Almanacs" were big sellers between 1835 and 1856. This material, like the period's dime novels and crime literature, was full of grotesque imagery. For example, in one almanac, Davy Crockett's uncle gives his bride-to-be two eyeballs he had gouged from an enemy's head. She dries them and wears them as earrings! Cullen contends that this kind of imagery influenced "the horror stories of Edgar Allan Poe and the often bizarre images in some of Herman Melville's work. Even Ralph Waldo Emerson's famous depiction of the artist as a 'transparent eyeball' was an adaptation of the imagery common to a Crockett almanac."[7]

It is easy to forget that the mid-nineteenth century was awash in vivid prose, jammed full of strong images of the body. After all, this is the period in which Harriet Beecher Stowe and Frederick Douglass provided fictional and autobiographical writings that gave their readers both literal and metaphoric uses of blood and bones imagery. I am not contending that these authors or those who penned dime novels, religious tracts, or folk-based humorous narratives were engaging in the kind of intertextuality that Hardack finds within Melville's prose. Rather, I am saying that the existence of such mass and popular culture helped Melville access the corporeal images he needed for his fiction and for the expression, within his letters to Hawthorne, of ideas and feelings.

Hardack's portrayal of Melville's desire for Hawthorne—his mind, heart, body, his mentorship, and his support—is convincing. Melville's letters were a critical part of his artistic expression, and through the correspondence with Hawthorne he discovered or explored imagery and thematics that were important to his fiction. This "trial run" use of letters was also quite usual for other writers of the time. We see that Emerson's letters often contain the germ of material later elaborated in journals and essays; Dickinson writes lines in her letters that are poemlike, or become lines in poems.[8]

What strikes me as particularly useful in Hardack's essay is the way he demonstrates the constancy and depth of Melville's attachment to Hawthorne, as if Hawthorne were some transhuman source of dark energy and material from which Melville was compelled to drink. From their first major association, when Melville wrote *"Hawthorne and His Mosses" just two weeks after meeting Hawthorne, we see the bodied language, the physical images, the desire to break down interpersonal boundaries that Hardack shows us pervaded the lettered and literary relationship. "Already I feel that this Hawthorne has dropped germinous seeds into my soul. He expands and deepens down, the more I contemplate him; and further, and further, shoots his strong New-England roots into the hot soil of my . . . soul."⁹ In this statement, which precedes any substantial correspondence between the two men, we see the very impulses that Hardack elaborates so well.*

The vividly imaged and heavily intertextual letters from Melville to Hawthorne may represent, as Hardack puts it "a fantasy of male reproduction" that "allows men to reproduce new texts altogether, to reproduce matter without mother," but as I hope I have shown, the language and emotional tendencies we find in the letters from Melville to Hawthorne were not entirely unusual; rather, Melville takes to extremes discursive practices we find operating in many elements of his culture. Decker's work helps us to understand the letter-writing norms of Melville's period: "the progressive dematerialization of epistolary media in our own time puts us in a unique position to recognize the place of the body in older correspondence."¹⁰ We can also see that popular culture, with its dark reformist messages and grotesque images, melodrama, and broad-brush humor, had a strong if varied effect on all the writers of the American Renaissance. To understand Melville's intertextual use of the body, especially within his letters to Hawthorne, we need to read the letters within the context of mid-nineteenth-century cultural customs.

Notes

An earlier version of this paper was presented to the Nathaniel Hawthorne Society Panel on Intertextuality, at the Modern Languages Association conference in Toronto, Canada, December 1993: thanks to Frederick Newberry for his help with this panel, and to Wil Verhoeven and Amanda Gilroy for their hospitality and assistance during the conference "Correspondences: Letters and Literary Theory," held at the University of Groningen, The Netherlands, November 1994.

1. See Linda S. Kauffman, *Special Delivery: Epistolary Modes in Modern Fiction* (Chicago: Univ. Chicago Press, 1992), xxii. Kauffman's observation that love letters disseminate "the ideology of romantic love" and thus disguise "relationships of power, politics, and economics" can also be applied to Melville's essentially romantic (and hence literary / economic) adulation of Hawthorne.

Melville belies Emerson's sense, and that of many contemporary critics who draw on Kristevan and Barthesian theories of intertextuality, that such intertextual correspondence must ultimately be impersonal, a function more of the text and discourse than of an author himself. In Melville's case, the traces of specific—and also unidentifiable—multiple authors in one work do not erase his subjectivity, but in fact determine the very scope and nature of that subjectivity.

2. *Correspondence*, ed. Lynn Horth, vol. 14 of *The Writings of Herman Melville* (Evanston IL: Northwestern Univ. Press, 1993), 191; hereafter cited as *Correspondence*. Melville himself repeatedly acknowledges the botanical configuration of his merger and his correspondent, writing for example, in terms consistent with his own pseudonymous "Hawthorne and His Mosses," that "the Hawthorne is a sweet flower; may it flourish in every hedge" (*Correspondence*, 230).

3. Ibid., 193–94.

4. Ibid., 195.

5. Ibid., 160. In a letter to Dana, this invocation of the MSS might bear an oblique nautical pun (HMS) or double correspondence; in *White-Jacket*, for instance, Melville suggests publishing texts from ship cannons.

6. Ibid., 212.

7. Ibid., 212–13. Melville also speaks not just of exchanging bodies, but texts, surrogate body parts. He writes that Hawthorne had "urged" him to complete the story of Agatha, set in the Isles of Shoals, about which Hawthorne expressed uncertainty; Melville thus tries "impertinently . . . [to] restor[e]" to Hawthorne a story that Melville claimed already belonged to him. This offer occasioned a series of exchanges as Melville zealously prompted Hawthorne to edit, critique and possibly finish the story Melville had resumed on his behalf. For the Melville who so desired Hawthorne's validation, pleas for pantheistic intertextuality would finally necessitate the active collaboration Hawthorne actively resisted. Yet as the story at issue so effectively and reflexively would have revealed, the relationship between the two writers was failing: as Agatha waits for a letter from her husband,"her hopes gradually decay in her, so does the post itself & the little box decay. The post rots in the ground at last. . . . At last the post fails." It would be hard not to read this story as at least a partial account of Melville's decaying relationship with the man with whom he had hoped to form "a chain of god's posts" (*Correspondence*, 238–42, 236).

8. Melville routinely castigates figures like Emerson and Goethe for being heartless, too much brain and too little heart; in disturbing ways, Melville herein equates Emerson with God, remarking to Hawthorne that men fear and dislike God because "they rather distrust his heart, and fancy him all brain like a watch" (*Correspondence*, 192). Here, Melville also asserts that "in those men who have fine brains and work them well, the heart extends down to the hams" (ibid.). This description is in perfect accord with Melville's consistent sense that Emerson's (as well as Goethe's) brains and heart are in the wrong place, and that Emerson fancies himself as able to correct the initial flaws of the universe. Melville had several years earlier noted to Duyckinck that "[Emerson's] belly, sir, is in his chest, & his brains descend down into his neck" (ibid., 122). In this schema, only Hawthorne's heart is in the right place (beneath Melville's ribs).

9. Ibid., 213. As Merrell Davis and William Gilman note, this is the only letter to someone outside his family to which Melville signs only his first name. See *The Letters of Herman Melville*, ed. Merrell R. Davis and William H. Gilman (New Haven: Yale Univ. Press, 1960), 143.

Melville wrote effusively to his "dear fellow-mortal" that his "joy-giving and exultation-breeding letter" is more reward for his work than the good goddess had stipulated (*Correspondence*, 199, 212). In *Pierre*, publishers are lured by the promise of the writer's "future popularity," and "certain speculators came to the meadows to survey its waterpower, if any, with a view to start a paper mill expressly for the great author, and so monopolize his stationery dealings" (*Pierre; or, The Ambiguities* [1852; rpt. New York: Signet, 1964], 300; hereafter cited parenthetically, identified by the letter *P*). This recurring image of the paper mill consistently represents some "monopolization" of correspondence and writing. It also again charts the deterioration of Melville's faith and his friendship with Hawthorne: by the time of *Pierre*, the once magical mill and infinite riband become demonic devices of the marketplace; here, Melville's rendering of writing as a transcendental enterprise reaches its crescendo. Writing now functions as a corollary not of merger and correspondence but of amputation, the cutting of cloths as well as bodies in what comes to be called "the metamorphosing mill" (*P*, 282). Both the meat markets and "meat mergers" of *Moby-Dick* are transformed in Pierre's mill, which conflates cloth and skin and finally turns male body parts into infinite texts.

10. *Mardi; and a Voyage Thither* (1849; rpt. New York: Signet, 1964), 306.

11. *The Confidence-Man: His Masquerade* (1857; rpt. New York: Signet, 1954), 127.

12. As Melville eulogizes Hawthorne in "Monody," "To have known him, to have loved him / After loneness long; And then to be estranged in life, / And neither in the wrong." Melville again associates Hawthorne with the vine, lamenting that "glazed now with ice [is] the cloistral vine / That hid the shyest grape." See *Collected Poems of Herman Melville*, ed. Howard Vincent (Chicago: Packard, 1947), 228.

13. Melville, *Confidence-Man*, 229.

14. *Clarel: A Poem and Pilgrimage in the Holy Land* (1876; rpt. New York: Hendricks House, 1960), 4:187.

In this context, we can view Melville's striking relevance for contemporary theory. In *Gender Trouble*, for example, Judith Butler asks what seem like pointedly Melvillean questions regarding the boundaries of individuality: "What can be meant by 'identity,' then, and what grounds the presumption that identities are self-identical, persisting through time as the same, unified and internally coherent?" Such a query echoes Melville's supposition in his letters and in *The Confidence-Man* that the self differs from "itself" not only from day to day, but from moment to moment. See Judith Butler, *Gender Trouble* (New York: Routledge, 1990), 16.

15. *Correspondence*, 160.

16. Nathaniel Hawthorne, *The Blithedale Romance* (New York: Norton, 1958), 107, 116.

17. *Correspondence*, 141.

18. Ibid., 206.

19. *The Journals and Miscellaneous Notebooks of Ralph Waldo Emerson*, ed. William H. Gilman et al., 16 vols. (Cambridge MA: Harvard Univ. Press, 1960–82), 7:358, and *The Letters of Ralph Waldo Emerson*, ed. Ralph L. Rusk, 10 vols. (New York: Columbia Univ. Press, 1939), 2:336–37.

20. Wai Chee Dimock, *Empire for Liberty: Melville and the Poetics of Individualism* (Princeton: Princeton Univ. Press, 1989), 137.

21. Herman Melville, *Redburn: His Voyage* (1849; rpt. Harmondsworth: Penguin, 1976), 173. "Dr. Keehua Roa" echoes this passage in his rather sympathetic introduction to *Symme's Hole*, Ian Wedde's extraordinarily intertextual, Melvillean novel, arguing that Melville was "one of the first to do what postmodern writing now finds familiar: recycle material, make use of existing texts, regard the act of writing as redistribution rather than creation." True to Melville's own play with intertextual ventriloquism and anonymous reviewing, Roa is the novel's author himself in disguise as *Omoo*'s historical personage, Doctor Long Ghost. See the introduction in Ian Wedde, *Symme's Hole* (Auckland: Penguin, 1986), 14.

22. *Moby-Dick; or, The Whale* (1851; rpt. New York: Signet, 1961), 489.

23. Emerson, *Journals and Miscellaneous Notebooks*, 9:67.

24. *Correspondence,* 193–94.

25. Ibid., 213.

26. Emerson, "Natural History of Intellect," in *Journals and Miscellaneous Notebooks,* 12:20.

27. Emerson, "The Heart," in *The Early Lectures of Ralph Waldo Emerson,* ed. Stephen E. Whicher and Robert E. Spiller, 3 vols. (Cambridge MA: Harvard Univ. Press, 1959, 1964), 2:280. Emerson's rhetoric of amputation coincides with his sense that life cannot be confined to individual existence, only the correspondence or connection between particular and universal self: "It is the largest part of a man that is not inventoried. He has many enumerable parts. . . . Nobody has ever yet dispossessed this adhesive self to arrive at any glimpse or guess of the awful Life that lurks under it." This awful lurking Life animates dead matter and independent limbs and leaves the transcendentalist unable to be self-identified. (This idea of an adhesive self is also recuperated in Whitman and Lawrence.) See *Emerson in His Journals,* ed. Joel Porte (Cambridge MA: Harvard Univ. Press, 1982), 350.

28. For a longer discussion of male merger and amputation in the American Renaissance, see my "'Infinitely Repellent Orbs': Visions of the Self in the American Renaissance," in *Languages of Visuality: Crossings between Science, Art, Politics, and Literature,* ed. Beate Allert (Detroit: Wayne State Univ. Press, 1996), 89–110.

29. *Correspondence,* 176–78. Melville repeats the identical phrase in another letter, reflecting his anxiety over enticing Hawthorne's interest: "Walk down one of these mornings and see me. No nonsense; come" (ibid., 187).

30. Hawthorne, "Rappaccini's Daughter," in *Selected Tales and Sketches* (New York: Holt, Rhinehart, and Winston, 1964), 356.

31. *Correspondence,* 193–94. For an insightful assessment of the relationship between Hawthorne's letters and his short fiction, and between Melville's *Pierre* and his later fiction, see Leland S. Person, *Aesthetic Headaches: Women and a Masculine Poetics in Poe, Melville, and Hawthorne* (Athens: Univ. of Georgia Press, 1988).

32. *Correspondence,* 184, 199.

33. Isabel's sinuous sewings and viny connections also thematically situate women in this text as the conductors of correspondence; wondering how Isabel snares Pierre, Mrs. Glendinning concludes with dramatic irony that it was "ay—the sewing!" (*P,* 227). Regendering the ropes and lines of *Moby-Dick,* the feminized chain of associations here fastens the links and threads between characters; it creates, if "once [Pierre] tie[s] the complicating knots about him and Isabel . . . [,] those Cretan labyrinths, to which thy life's cord is leading thee" (*P,* 207).

34. Hawthorne, "Rappaccini's Daughter," 356, 333.

Notes to Postscript

1. William Merrill Decker, *Epistolary Practices: Letter Writing in America before Telecommunications* (Chapel Hill: Univ. of North Carolina Press, 1998), 4.

2. Qtd. in ibid., 40.

3. Qtd. in ibid., 44, 40.

4. Walt Whitman, letter to Ralph Waldo Emerson [August 1856], in *The Norton Anthology of American Literature,* 4th ed., ed. Nina Baym et al. (New York: Norton, 1995), 978–85.

5. Jim Cullen, *The Art of Democracy: A Concise History of Popular Culture in the United States* (New York: Monthly Review Press), 76–77.

6. David S. Reynolds, *Beneath the American Renaissance: The Subversive Imagination in the Age of Emerson and Melville* (New York: Knopf, 1988), 59, 113. Reynolds cites many examples of widely distributed religious and social reformist writings and that featured graphic descriptions of depravity (see esp. 59–66).

7. Cullen, *Art of Democracy*, 74–75.

8. Decker, *Epistolary Practices*, 114, 143.

9. Herman Melville, "Hawthorne and His Mosses," in *Norton Anthology*, ed. Baym et al., 1041.

10. Decker, *Epistolary Practices*, 39.

PART 3

New Epistolary Directions

∾ Dear———: In Search of New (Old) Forms of Critical Address

Anne L. Bower

For years the academic essay's language of debate, argument, and supposedly objective exploration/negotiation has served scholars as an accepted
form for addressing issues, ideas, and each other. When the need arises for
discourse to follow up on aspects of an article we think need further development or questioning, we also have the forums and letters columns in
our journals. The following excerpted policy statement is fairly typical of
those found in many publications, exemplifying the kind of academic exchange we expect: "The editors . . . invite scholars to comment on articles
appearing in current issues. . . . Publication of the comment is not necessarily contingent upon the author's agreement to collaborate, but we encourage an open dialogue among contributors. Our intention is to take advantage of the opportunity for lively debate between authors and readers,
to highlight reader interest in scholarship, and to refine the contributions
and approaches that appear."[1]

While these scholarly frameworks would seem to provide adequate
scope for intellectual adventures, some scholars have found themselves
constrained from full expression by the traditional expectations of essay
style and content within the academic world. Starting from the theoretical position that critical work is inherently subjective, a number of them
have therefore experimented with the *content* of academic publication. In
a number of cases this results in the inclusion of considerable biographical or personal information. Such added content can yield a deeper, clearer sense of the locational and situational contexts within which each critic-
scholar operates. Then, too, some writers find that the personal material

creates a more concrete, realistic, connected, holistic sense of the academic world. The personal approach has now become quite accepted, especially among feminist scholars and in the humanities: I think of such works as Alicia Ostriker's *Writing Like a Woman,* Jane Tompkins's "Me and My Shadow," Diane Freedman's *An Alchemy of Genres,* Susan Howe's *My Emily Dickinson,* and Barbara Christian's "Layered Rhythms: Virginia Woolf and Toni Morrison." The last mentioned piece begins, "I see your face, Toni Morrison," and consistently addresses Morrison as "you."[2]

Some scholars have gone even further, altering the very *form* of their work, as with Julia Kristeva's well-known "Stabat Matar" (where the two-columned presentation instantly lets us know that something unusual is occurring here).[3] And upon occasion, rather than simply *responding* to a novel, an article, a conference presentation, a situation or event, writers move into *corresponding,* turning to the epistolary form. My interest lies with this form of scholarly address—I am drawn to writing that enacts the idea of interacting *with* rather than acting *on* or reacting *to.*[4]

If one judges the standard literary article as too frequently "pseudo-objective, impersonal, and adversarial," as do Diane P. Freedman, Olivia Frey, and Frances Murphy Zauhar (in the introduction to their book *The Intimate Critique: Autobiographical Literary Criticism*),[5] and if one sees the usual shape of such articles as an integral part of the problem, then an epistolary form of academic address could beckon. Actually, taking letters seriously as a form of professional address could lead one to ask, along with Susan Koppelman, why we scholars and critics do not spend more time exchanging true correspondence rather than creating articles. In a letter to a group of friends, Koppelman asks, "[W]hy do you write long essays that are speeches or position papers instead of writing letters to each other?"—asking further if it is "the patriarchy that teaches that discussion of literature has to take that kind of impersonal form, that non-dialogic form, that emotional-after-the-fact form."[6] (I do sometimes wonder, if pressure to publish were reduced, would our ways of exchanging ideas change? Would we read more for pleasure? Exchange ideas less formally? Write more personal letters? Temper scholarly authority with more moments of exchange and inquiry?)

Using the letter form for an article or essay can increase the personal, dialogic, and emotional content of academic writing (clearly, I do not think the presence of emotion is a threat to insight and intellect). A letter text embodies the negotiations of connection: separation and union, here and there, now and then, absence and presence. The shift in form makes these negotiations a more explicit, vital part of critical and theoretical writing. The choice of letter form would also seem to acknowledge the fragmentary and discursive as valid components of discussion, and recognize that distance and absence will never be overcome completely. Although using the epistolary form does not always allow us to say different things than we can within traditional argumentation or via the personal essay, it can signal a definitive shift in attitude toward our material, ourselves, and our readers.

To explore some of the possibilities and complexities of epistolarity criticism, I will first look back to an earlier part of our century—to a book-length study in this form by Virginia Woolf. Then, moving into our own time, I will explore two more books of letters: one by Fay Weldon, the other by Jacques Derrida. Finally, I will look at three shorter essays-as-letters by Gerald MacLean, Gloria Anzaldúa, and Robert Stepto, in each of which the form yields quite different effects.

It seems that until quite recently, only Virginia Woolf dared to publish critical thinking in an epistolary form. Like her earlier *A Room of One's Own* (1929), *Three Guineas,* published in 1938, finds an unusual way to put into effect Woolf's desire to combine the personal and the public.[7] While the text may not at first appear epistolary—lacking dates and headings along with regular salutations and closings—the reader comes to understand that this antiwar treatise is in actuality composed of three long letters.

Woolf struggled with the form of *Three Guineas.* Her December 1935 diary records that she initially imagined it as a series of "articles editors have asked me to write during the past few years—on all sorts of subjects." She liked the idea that such a form would allow her to "wander" and to be in the "position of the one asked." A month later, she pondered calling the book "Answers to Correspondents," and two months further along, was thinking that one letter would be best because "after all separate letters break continuity so." Then in June 1937, she speculated about discontinuing fiction writing: "Were I another person, I would say to myself, please write criticism, biography; *invent a new form* for both" (emphasis added).[8]

Indeed, the form this modernist writer came up with for her critical work was new: an odd amalgam of letters, with their intimacy and urgency, combined with detailed, well-argued, even footnoted exposition.

In *Three Guineas,* Woolf creates an opening situation in which she is responding to a letter from "an educated man" who has inquired about her ideas for ways to avoid war. Positioning herself as a letter writer, Woolf frequently comes back to picturing the actual person to whom she is writing. Such a focus on personal response becomes, in a way, an antiwar strategy: to treat "the other" not as an abstract force, but as a situated, flesh-and-blood human; to picture "the face on the other side of the page—the face that a letter writer always sees."[9] This letter, with its overarching subject of war and its causes, is interrupted by two others—one to a woman who is soliciting funds to support a women's college, and one in response to a solicitation for used clothing for women. The three letters work together to interweave the issues of women's education, economic status, and social and political roles. Near the end of her book, as she declines to join the educated gentleman's society for the prevention of war, she explains that she and other women are better off as "outsiders" to his particular effort: "We can best help you to prevent war not by repeating your words and following your methods, but by finding new words and creating new methods."[10] I see Woolf's use of the letter form as part of that method.

However, in reviews of the book, contemporary critics who reacted positively ignored the work's form, while those who found the book objectionable did so partly on the basis of the form. Q. D. Leavis, for example, judged that the presentation of material showed "a deliberate avoidance of any argument."[11] Perhaps that reaction to the letter form—blind eye or rejection—is part of the reason that epistolary criticism languished until quite recently. From Woolf's time until quite recently, I find an epistolary hiatus. Then, in the 1980s, letter criticism became part of our critical experimentation with voice and form, some postmodern critics capitalizing on letters' special virtues to assert the dialogic side of scholarship and promote revised notions of the scholar's self and audience.

A countrywoman of Woolf's is one of the writers to experiment with a genre-blending book-length use of the letter form. Fay Weldon is known primarily as a novelist. Her *Letters to Alice on First Reading Jane Austen* takes the guise of an epistolary novel, but quickly reveals itself as a cleverly shaped critical text. The epistolary protagonist, *Aunt* Fay, writes to her niece Alice about school, family, writing, and literature, but mostly about Jane Austen's works. Weldon instantly invokes the give-and-take of epistolarity, for the second sentence of the first letter puts forth the situation: "you ask me for advice."[12] (We scholars always want someone to ask us for our insights!) By using the letter form, this novel-criticism blend pretends that the text is one person's response, penned for one other person; this appears to present literary criticism with an appealing level of personalization and humility, since it seems shaped for just one young reader. The very personal letter form also embeds obvious subjectivity within most of the work's generalizations. Jane Austen, the letter-writing Aunt Fay (the advising critic), and the letter-receiving Alice (Fay's niece)—these three individuals emerge as powerful personalities contextualized, each in her own separate community, yet here brought credibly into relationship with the others.

What of that other party to the discussion: what of the external reader? Given the form of *Letters to Alice,* what are the roles implied for and played by you and me, the readers of the book? Objective answers are impossible. My own sense is that the external reader is asked to adopt strategies usually brought to the experience of fiction reading. That is, one becomes, as in reading Samuel Richardson's *Clarissa* or John Barth's *Letters* or Amos Oz's *The Black Box,* a kind of spy on both the internal letter writer and internal letter reader, imagining oneself as either or both, and withholding the kinds of quick critical judgments one might make if Weldon were addressing readers as a scholar speaking to scholars. The "fictional" situation Weldon establishes may allow the external reader greater freedom to "experience" the situatedness of the Aunt and niece and, by extension, the situatedness of Austen too. Finally, Weldon's writerly strategy may work to help the external reader situate herself as well; to think about how she reads Austen and why she reads that work in those particular ways (this could, of course, then extend to a questioning of how one reads other work as well).

The letter form of this work highlights contextualization. Aunt Fay's own physical location, occupation, preoccupations, and prejudices are informally included in her letters, so that we easily see how they shape her reactions to both Jane Austen and to her niece. Austen's context results from the Aunt Fay character's work at providing sociopolitical-historical background on Austen for the niece; Aunt Fay's letters include considerable informative data. Alice's resistance to Austen and to literary study is also contextualized, as Fay refers to her niece's favorite activities and some of her family background. Thus, *Letters to Alice* lodges critical authority in the act of making connections between the critic (Aunt Fay), her audience (the niece), and the object of critical work (in this case, Jane Austen). Using the letter form highlights the distance separating these individuals, but also insists on the possibility of making them more present to each other. As part of the desire for connection, the protagonist seems determined that her addressee will connect to the moral center of literature; will find in Austen and other "capital 'L'" literature "something more"—"intimations of infinity . . . the romance of creation . . . the wonder of love . . . the glory of existence."[13] This moral purpose seems more a part of nineteenth-century criticism than of late-twentieth-century academia. Weldon has set the moral tone right from the book's very start, with a dedication wherein she credits her own mother for "such morality and wisdom as I have," and perhaps has chosen the letter form to somehow permit this focus—an antipostmodern position, if you will. In a similar reaction against the anomie of modern times, Weldon's choice of the letter permits her to underscore physicality. By bringing into Aunt Fay's discourse speculations on the ways we write, including such things as choices of pen versus typewriter or computer, Weldon makes the body and sense of touch part of her discourse. The discussion of how the body writes gives a personal kind of substance to the discourse.

Weldon's use of the letter form produces a special tone—it is productively informal, relative to the traditional essay form. The protagonist's statements sometimes have a realistic tentativeness, as when Fay, doubting that a particular statement will persuade Alice, suggests: "Let's try another way. Let me put to you another notion. Try this." The letter form also permits Weldon to question the legitimacy of factual authority in scholarship. For example, in one letter Aunt Fay firmly proclaims, in anonymously authoritative language, that Jane Austen's contemporaries typically began menstruating quite late—between the ages of eighteen and twenty. Two letters later she discovers her mistake—another source states that menstruation in Austen's day typically began when women were about sixteen. Aunt Fay offhandedly reminds her niece that facts are slippery things.[14] The epistolarity of the form within which Weldon writes accentuates this question of authority, for the "mistaken" data stood uncontested for a number of pages (representing a certain block of time) and was only then undone by Aunt Fay's personal admission.

Letters to Alice, which is, after all, presented as a fiction, participates in the conventions of stable characters and assumes unquestioned faith in language's power to safely refer to a known and shared world "out there." The text manifests a standard chronological timeline and, while not exactly a "page-turner," does have a chartable plot. In contrast, Jacques Derrida's "Envois," a book-length section of *The Post Card,* confronts those conventions strongly.[15]

Derrida explains, in an enigmatic letter on *The Post Card*'s back cover, that he has produced "a satire of epistolary fiction." Simply by placing this letter on the cover of the book, Derrida instantly begins to deconstruct our assumptions about the epistolary form, for such placement elides the privacy of letters and the open casualness of postcards. The letter's content then promises a book "*farci,* stuffed with addresses, postal codes, crypted missives, anonymous letters, all of it confided to so many modes, genres, and tones." Within all those forms, much of the content that follows concerns the acts of writing, reading, and sending letters. Comments are addressed to the protagonist's supposed lover, but because the addressee is so elusive, all statements can also be read as theoretical statements addressed to the external reader(s).

The first letter of the actual text functions as a kind of introduction. In it, Derrida or the Derrida character admits that "as for the 'Envois' themselves, I do not know if their reading is bearable," but quickly goes on to deride the "bad reader" who will predecide what stance to take. In another letter, the epistolary protagonist questions his own writing: "What impels me to write you all this?" While this "you" appears to be the supposed lover of the epistolary satire, "you" could just as well be an imagined critical reader; another critic. At another point, the character becomes involved in a long analysis of the postal system and its implications for all communication. "There is not even the post or the *envoi,* there are *posts* and *envois. . . .* there is postal maneuvering, relays, delay, anticipation, destination, telecommunicating network, the possibility, and therefore the fatal necessity of going astray, etc."[16] Some of Derrida's content seems logical for this satire of an epistolary novel, some seems beyond the limits of that form (as he intends, clearly). Much of the work operates as both love story and psychological insight into (or joke about?) the critical act.

Now, from the seventeenth century on, letter novels have frequently included metacommentary, in the sense that the letter writers dwell on their reading and writing acts; but in Derrida's text, from that first "cover letter" on, metacommentary is a dominant component, often outweighing the narrative aspect of the letters. While the critical material constantly works against the story elements of plot, character, and setting, those fictional components still exist; in fact, their existence, being questioned, becomes central to one's reading. I expect that most readers find themselves oscillating between different reading strategies. There is no comfortable way to read this text. One queries: It is not criticism, it is not fiction, so what is it? Or one wonders: It *is* criticism, it *is* fiction, so what is it? Whatever one decides to call the text, this confusion forces the reader to question the ways he/she reads—how we turn on and off different parts of our psyches and intellects as we encounter those "many modes, genres, and tones." Derrida pushes us to ask, "Who is reading?"

Adopting epistolary address in this quasi-fictional mode, Derrida seems to mock the external reader. Balance occurs, however, for, playing with the convention that the letters in epistolary novels are written by "real" people, Derrida wonders about the authorial identity of any kind of writer: "Who is writing? To whom? . . . I owe it to whatever remains of my honesty to say finally that I do not know."[17] Thus, in this work that is both criticism and fiction, Derrida attempts to deconstruct the concept of scholarly or critical identity, an act previously directed only at authors of fiction, drama, and poetry. He seems to be declaring the "death of the critic," contending that all writerly identity is equally undecidable, equally a construct. Also tenuous is the identity of the addressee, for the "you" written to, the internal reader, may be a fictitious character, the external reader, or perhaps, by implication, a real friend or lover (one or more people!).[18]

In spite and because of these expressed doubts, the desire for connection becomes central to Derrida's text, just as it is in Weldon's. How interesting that this deconstructive scholar, known for dense, abstract, philosophic prose, chooses the most traditional "novel" shape in order to play with ideas of breaking down the separateness of person from person, now from then, the act of engendering from the being (or thing) engendered, signifier from signified. This overarching yearning for connection is exemplified in "Derrida's" letter of 9 September 1977, which includes a statement about the writer's superabundance of mailings: "These are memories that I am sending to you, the essential remaining that I send to you, that I touch you by sending you whatever, even if it is nothing, even if it is without the slightest interest."[19]

Not only the writing act is seen as a desperate attempt at connection; reading too shares that motivation. "I am spending my time rereading you," writes the protagonist.[20] In fiction the letter is the other person, and so to reread the letter is to reread the person. By implication, Derrida is asserting that this is true of theoretical work, too: to reread someone's scholarship can equal rereading the scholar. So, as much as Derrida in other texts and even in this one may theorize away the concepts of person, body, and presence, here he also inscribes the need for, desire for, and illusion of person in all aspects of our lives and work.

Derrida's text, like Woolf's and Weldon's, uses book length to elaborate a complex of critical positions and issues. When the letter form is employed in articles, the epistolary critic usually fine-tunes application of a smaller range of the form's associated traditions and ideologies. A scholar may focus in on the form's link to women's discourse forms, its seeming intimacy, its metonymizing of both absence and presence, its availability to all (almost regardless of educational or technological sophistication), or its association with the personal and the private, to underscore his or her theoretical discussion.

In "Citing the Subject," Gerald MacLean creates five unmailed letters that respond to Jane Tompkins's essay, "Me and My Shadow."[21] Tompkins's nonletter but personal essay calls for the integration of public and private voice, the epistemological valuing of emotion and personal experience, and discourse forms that will inscribe connections, cooperation, "appreciation," and others' voices.[22] By responding to Tompkins's call with letters, MacLean indicates a similar desire for a more community-based scholarship. He also works here to claim personal criticism as a form available to men as well as women.

To his credit, in his introductory letter (placed first, but written last) MacLean queries his own use of the informal epistolary form, wondering if he is not "covering my criticisms of your essay by using an informal style, and insinuating my will by doing what you asked, by seeking to give you pleasure [through the use of the personal]." In the same letter, however, he knowingly questions how much validity and actuality the personal can maintain, given "the problematics of presence."[23]

The five letters explore rhetorical, theoretical, and political problems MacLean finds as he explores uses of the personal within criticism. And while he does include, in the latter part of letter five, details about his own past and present life, the tone of the letters often becomes predominantly didactic and argumentative. At times using the very kind of language and style that Tompkins has decried, MacLean, consciously or unconsciously, forces the reader to question his work with the personal and with the letter form; is this a kind of rhetorical fencing? His discourse makes obvious that letters are no guarantee of true give-and-take, especially when he positions himself to authoritatively ignore certain points made by the person he is addressing. And when he refers to Tompkins in the third person he negates the possibility of intimacy. As Nancy K. Miller puts it, out of frustration at MacLean's patronizing tone, vocabulary, and extensive and very academic footnotes: "'Dear Gerald, . . . Try a letter *to a person.*'"[24]

The fifth and final letter begins with considerable advice to Tompkins on ways to see her anger, her history, her desire for the personal in what to him are more acceptable terms—he feels she should attempt more collective, Marxist-oriented critiques of institutions, for example. Then, in a move that nicely reproduces the way a letter writer sometimes addresses both self and addressee, MacLean appears to face up to his own actions of authority. "So here I am, doing what I was trained to do, telling 'women' what to do, how to think and behave. And I am doing it in that body-less 'objective' language."[25] Are we to read this as a "genuine" self-discovery or, partly because of the weight of his stylistic and linguistic choices, does this become simply a rhetorical wooing of the addressee (and the external reader—particularly the feminist external reader)?

Presumably in order to recuperate Tompkins's respect, MacLean accepts her implicit challenge and moves into autobiographical writing in order to explain his own relationship to authority. While actively exploring the connections among such experiences as growing up in a poverty-stricken, single-parent household, his guilt and pain over the conditions of his mother's death, the violence of his own nature, and his scholarly endeavors, MacLean also strives to show Tompkins (and us) that he, a man, can write the personal.

Yet for MacLean, that section of autobiography must be encapsulated away from the bulk of his critical work. He concludes this letter by explaining that he believes the only way an expression of the personal can benefit anyone beyond the individual writer, for whom its communication may have therapeutic value, is if the writer uses certain kinds of theoretical positioning to perform the collective work of undoing or reforming detrimental social institutions. I do not completely disagree with MacLean's sense that for meaningful social change to occur we have to connect individual experience to "the big picture." My dispute is with *how* we accomplish that task. Accepting the feminist position that the personal is the political, it does not seem necessary that every writer of the personal undertake neo-Marxist or New Historicist theorizing to connect with the socioeconomic situation surrounding his or her discourse. The letter as a form of critical writing can logically and flexibly incorporate narrative, descriptive, or explanatory passages that allow us to understand the letter writer's implied theories about the sociopolitical forces, constraints, and freedoms of her society. For MacLean, the letter is simply a "personal" form of writing; he has no interest in the ideological implications of the form and therefore cannot tap its potential for larger community building or identity-bridging, genre-crossing communication.

It is no real news to state that the adoption of a particular form is a theoretical decision, a rhetorical stance that reflects one's attitude toward oneself as a writer, toward one's readers, toward one's subject and discipline. It is that shift in attitude that some critic-epistolarians seek. The letter becomes a literary "tool" for deconstructing the house of dominant discourse forms, opening up that house to voices previously excluded.

Gloria Anzaldúa's "Speaking in Tongues: A Letter to Third World Women Writers" moves easily between describing social forces and personal actions. Anzaldúa explains that at one point in its creation this piece was a conventional essay; however, she found that this form was "wooden, cold" and did not allow for the "intimacy and immediacy" she desired.[26] Her choice of the letter form indicates a theoretical choice as well, for as a woman of color and a "Third World woman," she resists academia's pressure to "bow down to the sacred bull, form. Put frames and metaframes around the writing. Achieve distance in order to win the coveted title 'literary writer' or 'professional writer.' Above all do not be simple, direct, nor immediate." Anzaldúa fears that too many of her "sister-writers" have been tempted to sell out their beliefs—through conforming in the style and content of their writing (or through simply not communicating at all), but urges that they "not acquiesce." One way she seeks to give them confidence is through the letter form, a form which more than many others can symbolize the message of her content: "You are not alone."[27]

Her letter, addressed to "Dear *mujeres de color,* companions in writing," takes advantage of the letter's informal possibilities to permit a sense of the familiar, with home, food, and body very much part of the discourse. Allowing these personal elements into her text emphasizes the notion of writing as a liberatory act, with writing not conceptualized as a separate, elitist, professional activity, but instead seen as an essential part of daily life, a necessary part of surviving.

Anzaldúa makes it vividly clear that only if she writes in her own voice and in a form that fully allows her thoughts free rein will her own power emerge. Susan Lanser offers this insight about such a conviction: "Despite compelling interrogations of 'voice' as a humanist fiction, for the collectively and personally silenced the term has become a trope of identity and power."[28] Another reason to use one's own voice/style is that writing in what we might call predictable scholarly forms will not free up new insights or solutions for the reader or writer. As Anzaldúa reminds us, if one is to "shock [one]self into new ways of perceiving the world," one must "throw away abstraction and the academic learning, the rules, the map and compass."[29] Obviously no formal device can guarantee the kind of radical creative freedom for which Anzaldúa hopes, but I believe that she effectively models the relevance of that formal epistolary choice.

The writerly freedom Anzaldúa enacts takes place in a specific historical time: the "postcolonial moment." Thus, the interruptions inscribed into "Speaking in Tongues" take on particular significance. That this piece is interrupted and must be written over the course of five days matters. The dates, the extra lines of white space representing time spent not writing, remind us that most women—especially women without professional status, money, or the self-confidence built up through generations of educational achievement or class status—do not have support systems that allow extended writing time: "No long stretches at the typewriter unless you're wealthy or have a patron—you may not even own a typewriter." Or they remind us that writing is part of other activities that also must be attended to—dealings with bureaucracy, household chores, jobs. And, of course, they remind us too that writing is hard work and can't always be accomplished at one go: "Why does writing seem so unnatural for me? I'll do anything to postpone it."[30] As she layers events, conditions, time, and constraints into her letter, Anzaldúa is providing the kind of contextualization that MacLean recommends; however, here the theorizing is not objectified or put at a critical distance; the socioeconomic context is close to home.

By *publishing* her letter to Third World women writers, Anzaldúa necessarily communicates with many who are not encompassed in her salutation. Readers who *are* Third World women writers can take strength from their community with Anzaldúa; they can feel themselves entering the conversation with her. Readers who *are not* Third World women writers will necessarily feel themselves slightly (or largely?) outside of the direct conversation. This formal maneuver quietly and nonconfrontationally positions the reader to recognize his or her own position in society and to think about how that position affects each individual's relationship to reading and writing as parts of the social structure.

Within "Speaking in Tongues," many of the motivations Anzaldúa finds prompting her writing seem to echo the empowering and liberating agentic qualities identified by literary critics as centrally important to the writing protagonists of epistolary fiction: "I write to record what others erase when I speak, to rewrite the stories others have miswritten about me, about you. To become more intimate with myself and you. To discover myself, to preserve myself, to make myself, to achieve autonomy. To dispel the myths that I am a mad prophet or a poor suffering soul. To convince myself that I am worthy and that what I have to say is not a pile of shit. To show that I *can* and that I *will* write, never mind their admonitions to the contrary. And I will write about the unmentionables, never mind the gasp of the censor and the audience."[31] For Anzaldúa, the epistolary essay provides the same space of freedom that epistolary fiction provides many novelists (and their characters).[32]

Robert Stepto has explored the freedom of the letter form very differently from the other critics I have mentioned, although he has not yet published work in this mode. As part of a course at the School of Criticism and Theory during the summer of 1988, Stepto presented a lecture titled "Let Me Tell Your Story: Fraternal Authorship in Narratives of Slavery, Revolt, and Incarceration—Douglass, Montejo, and Wideman." In this presentation he crafted the *form* of his criticism to enter dialogically into readings of Frederick Douglass's "The Heroic Slave," Miguel Barnet's edited version of Esteban Montejo's *Autobiography of a Runaway Slave,* and John Edgar Wideman's *Brothers and Keepers.*[33] Stepto's epistolary form of criticism *participates in* and *connects with,* rather than solely *commenting on,* these three texts.

Two-thirds of Stepto's presentation is given over to epistolary responses that in content and form creatively confront and complement the work of the three authors whose work he investigates. As he explains, his letters aim "to offer brief narratives in a fraternal manner; narratives which both explicate and implicate what I am terming fraternal authorship."[34] Each of Stepto's letters uses a different voice. To Douglass, Stepto writes a letter in the voice of the Reverend Henry Highland Garnet, dated late 1853. To Miguel Barnet he writes in the voice of a Cuban doctor, creating the fiction that Barnet and this doctor shared a flight from New York to Miami around 1959. And to Wideman he writes in his own voice in the present time.[35]

To write a letter in another's voice would seem an evacuation of the personal; after all, Stepto is not present as himself in the three letters he creates. However, in order to create or re-create his letter writers, Stepto must immerse himself in the lives and situations and language of his "characters." He must get personal with the texts he explores in a new way, a way that is traditionally associated more with fiction writing than criticism. I think of Alice Walker's statement about writing *The Color Purple:* "I was sure the characters of my new novel were trying to . . . contact me, to speak *through* me."[36]

To explain a little of what Stepto accomplishes, let me briefly discuss his first letter. Stepto's Garnet, supposedly writing in 1853, praises Frederick Douglass for many achievements, but expresses displeasure with the textual violence within "The Heroic Slave." In fact, "Garnet" hints that Douglass's story plagiarizes Garnet's version of the same narrative.

Two things fascinate me about this fictitious letter. First, that in order to write it, Stepto must immerse himself in the time about which he writes and even study, absorb, and then mimic, to the best of his ability, the prose of a period not his own. Second, he must move out of his own critical mindset and into Garnet's. He must communicate what he imagines would be Garnet's primary objections to Douglass's manipulations of history, objections based on a pragmatic political base within a particular historical moment. Rather than explaining how the Reverend Garnet might have reacted to Douglass's novella or critiquing Douglass from his own 1980s point of view, Stepto enacts a form of fraternal authoring for this exercise. The letter is convincing—one slips into thinking this is an authentic missive from Garnet that Stepto somehow discovered hidden in an attic or folded into an old book. This enactment of "fraternal authoring" becomes a powerful connective exercise; an innovative use of imagination to explore the critical act as well as a particular text. However, I worry that some readers, rather than taking the Garnet letter as a creative path to greater understanding of Douglass from within his own time and situation, might take Stepto's discourse as merely a tour de force—clever, unusual, interesting, stagy—and thereby dismiss it.

All three of Stepto's letters, especially taken collectively, open up issues I find most interesting: questions of critical "colonizing" and ownership, questions about audience (such as, is criticism for critics only?), questions about the exchange of ideas versus the economics of monetary values, and questions about listening—learning, as Stepto puts it in his letter to Edgar Wideman, "to hear someone out."[37] The separation of writer and reader, "natural" to letters, maintains a kind of acknowledgment of the other's subjectivity often eradicated in standard scholarly writing.

It would be naive to suggest that the letter form is some panacea for rhetorical rigidity, scholarly alienation, or the destructive competition often encountered in the academic "game."[38] However, it does seem fair to say that choosing to create letter-style criticism signals a writer's interest in certain issues central to contemporary scholarship and thought. As I hope my brief look at twentieth-century letter form criticism has shown, from Woolf through MacLean and beyond, a scholar publishing in letter form, with multiple audiences and purposes, encounters a number of dilemmas. The letter seems "simple" and "traditional," but with its layers of actual and fictional readers, with its special possibilities for rhetorical complications and manipulations, what purports to be such a personal and direct form of address can never be more than partly personal, partly authentic, partly direct. And there are other difficulties, too.

Both Linda S. Kauffman and Daphne Patai have argued in recent articles against the personal—finding it often solipsistic, self-serving, and/or dull.[39] And, as Nancy K. Miller reminds us, the personal can make its readers feel left out through a "chumminess" of "institutionally authorized personalism," of "privileged selves who get to call each other (and themselves) by their first names in print." Still, when it works, what Miller values is that "the personal in these texts is at odds with the hierarchies of the positional—working more like a relay *between* positions to create critical fluency."[40] For me, it is that "betweenness" that letters underscore.

Letters in critical writing enact the *idea* of personal address, of leaping the distance between correspondents—in the sense of connecting to texts, to concepts, to people. Of course, for every "presence" a letter creates, an "absence" hovers nearby. Every letter delivered, "understood," and responded to initially included the possibility of nondelivery, misunderstanding, and lack of response. Thus, letters as a form of scholarly writing, while offering the writer and reader opportunities for intimacy and engagement, can promise neither. Still, use of the form, at some level, manifests awareness of distance and lack of different kinds of connections, and implies the desire to bridge that distance, to make a connection, to have one's mind changed, to mix up private and public forums, to break boundaries. Criticism in letter form presumably seeks some response, some intimacy with or acknowledgment from an addressee. In part, the letter writer may also be addressing him or herself, attempting thereby to redefine the critical/scholarly self. And in part, the letter writer's address from one particular human to another positions both writer and reader in a world of particulars rather than an abstract world of generalizations. At one or more levels—emotional, psychological, political, intellectual—"lettered" criticism seeks to change the writer, the reader, and the critical act.

Postscript by Gerald MacLean

Anne L. Bower's essay offers a sensitive yet critical treatment of my 1989 foray into gender theory and the strategic possibilities of epistolary form within feminist writing. Reading her essay, I am at once flattered to find myself yoked with Virginia Woolf by a scholar of the epistolary form, and delighted to have the chance to reread and reflect on something I wrote twelve years earlier when the world was quite a different place. No scholar of epistolarity myself, I was taking my leads partly from Derrida's critique of Lacan,[1] but also from Jane Tompkins's important and—as it has rightly proven—paradigmatic call for the personal voice in (feminist) scholarly criticism. To the extent that I have a sense of the responses and reactions my own essay has generated not only in reviews of Linda S. Kauffman's Gender and Theory: Dialogues on Feminist Criticism, *where it appeared, and in Nancy Miller's important manifesto* Getting Personal: Feminist Occasions and Other Autobiographical Acts *(1991), but also in seminars and discussion groups, I am always sad that the contexts of the piece seem to get ignored, since in Kauffman's volume at least, Tompkins's "Me and My Shadow" was positioned as a direct "dialogic response" to Ellen Messer-Davidow's clearing of the air over vexing problems confronting feminist philosophers.*[2]

Nancy Miller's stirring "try a letter to a person," which Bower quotes, presumably favorably, is one of the best moments in Getting Personal *(of course I would think that) precisely because it so emphatically misses the point in the way indignation invariably does. Most of the features of my piece that Bower notices for marking limits to the epistolary are indeed just that, instances where I was staging limits. But Bower's essay is a shrewder and more sophisticated piece, in many ways, than Miller's book. Treating Gloria Anzaldúa's epistolary strategies, she quotes Susan Lanser to remind us that strategic identity, marked as "voice," continues to provide powerful political leverage for disenfranchised groups, despite general agreement over the problematic figure of the self-knowing subject: after all, identity is only ever a rhetorical strategy, available as a trope. I agree. All the same, Bower and I come to epistolarity from different directions and disagree over the potential importance of the "personal" voice. Not surprisingly, we have a different sense of the values of scholarly protocols.*

I reread my essay and did not find the tone to be "didactic" and "argumentative" as Bower says, except insofar as the latter describes voicing disagreement. Where Bower finds "advice to Tompkins," I see myself taking very seriously ideas with which I am only in very partial sympathy, and doing so in tones of formal respect. I thought I did a rather better job of inflecting the epistolary possibilities than Bower gives me credit for. And I still cannot locate in my own prose anything that makes me identify with Miller's charge of "patronizing"—which Bower seems to endorse— but I suspect there to be a disagreement over meaning here. For me, "patronizing," in the contexts of men writing feminist theory, describes that moment in the late seventies and early eighties when—having taken feminist separatism seriously, and having noted the difficulties many women were having being feminists within the academy—some of us (men in the profession) might be said to have patronized feminist scholars by systematically ignoring the problems in the work they were producing, rather than publicly providing antifeminists within the profession with reasons to dismiss their endeavors. I simply cannot find anything, either in tone or argumen-

tative strategy, that is patronizing in my piece; and can only hope Jane Tompkins has never read it so. But authorial intention is little guarantee of anything.

One evident miswriting I would like to correct involves my earlier staging of how the personal (only ever problematically) voices the political. In specific defense of the welfare socialism of 1950s and 1960s Britain, let me disavow "poverty-stricken" as quite what I had hoped to describe or recall living through, at least after moving to England in 1959. I suppose to many, life in a residential trailer, parked on a farm in rural Ontario in the 1950s, sounds pretty crummy. I only recall having a great time, running about the farm and woods without shoes because I did not want them; but I will not trouble you with memories. Having been abandoned by her Canadian husband, my English mother reasonably enough moved herself, my older step-sister, and myself back to Blighty. In Ontario, the trailer had running hot water and central heating. In choosing to live at home on the dole rather than go to work, Margery had to move us into a house with one cold tap, an outside toilet that froze sometimes, inadequate heating, and a roof that leaked. But the state paid for it all—very generous, really. Margery received cash for food, housing, heating allowances, school uniforms, free school meals, free medical care: so long as she stayed at home and was not seen to entertain any male visitors. Surveillance was not that draconian, and Margery claimed she wanted to stay away from men. But folks on our street, many of them also collecting dole payments, kept an eye on things. Through the 1960s, while city council grants paid for most of our neighbors to have domestic improvements—separate bathrooms with hot water, central heating—we remained ineligible because the landlord (Margery's father) refused to contribute toward costs. We were screwed by the family, not the welfare state. We could not afford a car, or holidays, so I did not expect such things. Hard times, perhaps, but "poverty-stricken" is misleading. I may not have found myself living with running hot water until arriving in my freshman rooms at Cambridge, but the city council was paying for me to be there. In my experience, poverty is something that has only really come to Britain since then, as a result (among other things) of the systematic dismantling of the welfare state following Thatcherism.

Finally, having ended my own essay for this volume (mischievously) with the trope of (justifiable) violence, may I end this postscript by noticing what must be a strategic misreading of my earlier argument, one that allows Bower to suggest that I consider "violence" to be the effect or product of something worth calling "nature." This is exactly the opposite of my argument, surely? And I still think that there is a dangerous slide within the case for, and practice of, the personal voice in scholarship whenever it leaves behind the liberating critique of scholarly procedures in favor of autobiographical journalism. I have too much respect for the work of too many scholars who write long footnotes, and for too many analysts, to think otherwise.

Notes

1. "Comment and Reply Policy," *Signs* 22.3 (spring 1997): 792.

2. Alicia Ostriker, *Writing like a Woman* (Ann Arbor: Univ. of Michigan Press, 1983), 363–75; Jane Tompkins, "Me and My Shadow," in *Gender and Theory: Dialogues on Feminist Criticism,* ed. Linda S. Kauffman (Oxford: Basil Blackwell, 1989), 121–39; Susan Howe, *My Emily Dickinson* (Berkeley: North Atlantic Books, 1985); Barbara Christian, "Layered Rhythms: Virginia Woolf and Toni Morrison," *Modern Fiction Studies* 39 (1993): 483–500.

3. Julia Kristeva, "Stabat Matar," in *The Kristeva Reader,* ed. Toril Moi (New York: Columbia Univ. Press, 1986), 160–86.

4. In my book *Epistolary Responses: The Letter in Twentieth-Century American Fiction and Criticism* (Tuscaloosa: Univ. of Alabama Press, 1996), I devoted a chapter to critical writing shaped as letters; that chapter gives numerous examples of such work and elaborates the reasons critics turn to this form. The current essay draws on that chapter and on a talk I gave in 1994 at "Correspondences: Letters and Literary Theory," a conference held at the University of Groningen (The Netherlands).

5. Diane P. Freedman, Olivia Frey, and Frances Murphy Zauhar, eds., *The Intimate Critique: Autobiographical Literary Criticism* (Durham NC: Duke Univ. Press, 1993).

6. Susan Koppelman, "Excerpts from Letters to Friends," in *The Intimate Critique,* 76–77.

7. Virginia Woolf, *Three Guineas,* intro. Hermione Lee (1936; rpt. London: Hogarth Press, 1986).

8. Virginia Woolf, *The Diary of Virginia Woolf,* ed. Anne Olivier Bell, assisted by Andrew McNeillie, 5 vols. (New York: Harcourt Brace Jovanovich, 1982–84), 4:361; 5:3, 18, 91.

9. Woolf, *Three Guineas,* 41.

10. Ibid., 164.

11. Q. D. Leavis, rev. of *Three Guineas,* in *Scrutiny* (September 1938), rpt. in *Virginia Woolf: The Critical Heritage,* ed. Robin Majumder and Allen McLavrin (London: Routledge & Kegan Paul, 1975), 409–19.

12. Fay Weldon, *Letters to Alice on First Reading Jane Austen* (1984; rpt. New York: Tapliner, 1985), 7.

13. Ibid., 7–8.

14. Ibid., 10–11, 28, 49.

15. Jacques Derrida, "Envois," in *The Post Card: From Socrates to Freud and Beyond,* trans. and intro. Alan Bass (Chicago: Univ. of Chicago Press, 1987), 3–256.

16. Ibid., 3, 4, 10, 66.

17. Ibid., 5.

18. Ibid., 5–6.

19. Ibid., 79.

20. Ibid., 50.

21. Gerald M. MacLean, "Citing the Subject," in *Gender and Theory: Dialogues on Feminist Criticism,* ed. Linda S. Kauffman (Oxford: Basil Blackwell, 1989), 140–57.

22. Tompkins, "Me and My Shadow," 121–39.

23. Maclean, "Citing the Subject," 141.

24. Nancy K. Miller, *Getting Personal: Feminist Occasions and Other Autobiographical Acts* (New York: Routledge, 1991), 17.

25. Maclean, "Citing the Subject," 148.

26. Gloria Anzaldúa, "Speaking in Tongues: A Letter to Third World Women Writers," in *This Bridge Called My Back: Writings by Radical Women of Color,* ed. Cherríe Moraga and Gloria Anzaldúa (New York: Kitchen Table: Women of Color Press, 1981), 161–74.

27. Ibid., 167, 169.

28. Susan Sniader Lanser, *Fictions of Authority: Women Writers and Narrative Voice* (Ithaca: Cornell Univ. Press, 1992), 3.

29. Anzaldúa, "Speaking in Tongues," 172, 173.

30. Ibid., 170, 166.

31. Ibid., 169.

32. A number of additional letter articles appear in the same volume in which Anzaldúa's piece appears. Within *This Bridge Called My Back,* some letter articles are *more* personal, such as "Letter to Ma" by Merle Woo, and some are *less* so, such as "An Open Letter to Mary Daly" by Audre Lorde. Besides letters the book also includes other alternatives to the "standard" essay: poems, narratives, interviews, reflections. The only other book I have seen that encompasses such formal diversity is *Words in Our Pockets: The Feminist Writers Guild Handbook on How to Gain Power, Get Published and Get Paid,* ed. Celeste West (Paradise CA: Dustbooks, 1987). For further information on epistolary fiction see my *Epistolary Responses,* Linda S. Kauffman's *Discourses of Desire: Gender, Genre, and Epistolary Fictions* (Ithaca: Cornell Univ. Press, 1986), and her *Special Delivery: Epistolary Modes in Modern Fiction* (Chicago: Univ. of Chicago Press, 1992), as well as Janet Gurkin Altman's *Epistolarity: Approaches to a Form* (Columbus: Ohio State Univ. Press, 1982).

33. Robert Stepto's unpublished lecture entitled "Let Me Tell Your Story: Fraternal Authorship in Narratives of Slavery, Revolt, and Incarceration—Douglass, Montejo, and Wideman," delivered July 1988 at the School of Criticism and Theory, Dartmouth College, used by his permission.

34. Stepto, "Let Me Tell Your Story," 7.

35. Wideman's *Brothers and Keepers* was published in 1984; Barnet published his edition of Esteban Montejo's *Autobiography of a Runaway Slave (Biografía de un Cimarrón)* in 1966 (trans. Jocasta Innes, 1968); and Douglass first published "The Heroic Slave" serially in his own newspaper in 1853 and then in *Autographs for Freedom,* a collection of poetry and prose.

36. Alice Walker, "Writing *The Color Purple,*" in *In Search of Our Mothers' Gardens* (San Diego: Harcourt Brace Jovanovich, 1984), 355–60.

37. Stepto, "Let Me Tell Your Story," 16.

38. I am borrowing the term *game* from Nancy Newton, for like her I believe that the work of the academy is not "merely entertainment or the overseeing of a conventional and inconsequential rite of passage for certain members of society. See her "Mermaids and Minotaurs in Academe: Notes of a Hispanist on Sexuality, Ideology, and Game Playing," *Journal of the Midwest Modern Language Association* 22 (spring 1989): 23–35.

39. Linda S. Kauffman, "The Long Goodbye: Against Personal Testimony, or an Infant Grifter Grows Up," in *American Feminist Thought at Century's End: A Reader,* ed. Linda S. Kauffman (Cambridge MA: Blackwell, 1993), 258–77; Daphne Patai, "Sick and Tired of Scholar's Nouveau Solipsism," *Chronicle of Higher Education,* 23 February 1994, A52.

40. Miller, *Getting Personal,* 25.

Notes to Postscript

1. See Jacques Lacan, "Seminar on 'The Purloined Letter,'" trans. Jeffrey Mehlman, *Yale French Studies* 48 (1972): 38–72, and Derrida's response, "The Purveyor of Truth," *Yale French Studies* 52 (1975): 31–113. Derrida points out that Lacan's analysis of the epistolary subject and (imaginary and unstable) object ignores the position of the narrator who is reporting the scene of writing.

2. But see Mary Poovey's comment: "This is the only critical anthology of any kind with which I am familiar that deserves to be taught as a whole. That the sum of *Gender and Theory* is so much greater than its parts attests . . . to the creative brashness of its editor and the power of her design" ("Recent Studies of Gender," *Modern Philosophy* [May 1991]: 417).

∿ Re-siting the Subject

Gerald MacLean

As the introduction to this volume makes clear, the long eighteenth century, which stretches in England from the Restoration into Romanticism,
elaborated a concept of the letter as a private, sometimes feminine site
where the inner-life achieves self-expression in the search for truth. That
elaboration contributes directly to the early development of the European
novel and continues to engage the interests and presuppositions of feminist theorists and literary historians. Indeed, discussions of epistolarity frequently begin with and restrict themselves to evidence from epistolary
novels.[1] I hope to illustrate that in order to conceive new epistolary directions we might think about some old ones while interrogating that carto-
graphical concept metaphor "direction." Certainly in the case of the epistolary mode, the textual trace of the discoverable past—the "letter" itself,
we might say—is invariably caught and suspended while traveling from
here to there, directed between different sites.

My aim is to complicate a bit what might have been taken for granted
about the origins and progress, the nature, range, and purpose, of epistolary discourse. In seeking to describe some "new epistolary directions," I
shall explore evidence from two pre-eighteenth-century sites: central
Anatolia between the sixth and second millennia B.C. (from the Neolithic
to Hittite eras), and England during the revolutionary decade of the 1640s.
Epistolary evidence left behind at the first of these sites suggests a lengthy
period of early stability and development during which various generic
and structural features gradually emerged that would still be recognized
today in any discussion of the letter. In addition to variable forms of address, these features include the constitutive trace of the third-person read-

er, the person neither writing nor addressed, the reader who is supposed
to be not-there. Evidence from the second site, the archive of letters published during the years immediately preceding the appearance of the novel in England, shows the letter becoming one of the most common of public genres and, in achieving this status, articulating twin humanist crises of
authenticity and identity.

Any historical investigation into the discursive and generic features of
the epistolary mode is immediately bedeviled by a bewildering variety of
evidence, on the one hand, and on the other, by the insurmountable diffi-
culty of framing the right questions.[2] What, after all, is *not* a letter?

> Letters of thanks, letters from banks,
> Letters of joy from girl and boy,
> Receipted bills and invitations
> To inspect new stock or to visit relations,
> And applications for situations,
> And timid lovers' declarations,
> And gossip, gossip from all the nations.[3]

Whatever else they may be, letters are not and never can be an entirely
private exchange involving only two people. Letters may contain or reveal
secrets, but they can never themselves be secrets.

Letters are inscriptions directed from a first person or persons to a second person or group of persons, but as matters of discourse they invariably entail—directly, implicitly, or by way of exclusion—the position of a
third person, singular or plural.[4]

Letters lay claims to ownership and authenticity: to material objects or
particular experiences, to eyewitness knowledge about events or newly revealed truths, to specific rights to do something or go somewhere.

Letters require places. More precisely, what is required are the spaces
separating the places between which the letter travels. Letters are directed
from here to there, across a space in between, the abode of the never entirely absent other.

One question, then, might be not so much *who*, as *where* is the subject
of the letter? Are they not always in danger of being somewhere else, in
transit, on the road?

In these respects, letters—like identities and possessions—have little
meaningful existence outside the predication and signification of the third-

person other or others to whom they simultaneously are and are not addressed. Letters may insist on the identity of the first-person who writes, and on the specificity of the second person or persons addressed; but this insistence only makes sense in light of an absent and excluded third.

Above all, letters make claims about the named writer who is always somewhere else and, in this respect, may be supposed to be historically coterminous with the advent of writing itself, of private property, and, if we trust the evidence, the emergence of settlement and trade. Indeed, letters crucially link the desire to own and the need to signify ownership in the form of inscription with that historical moment when people first started to build settlements in addition to living in caves.

Site 1: *Before the Letter*

The earliest letters were not so much written as they were printed; hence they were reproducible. Among the artifacts excavated by James Mellaart during the 1960s at Çatalhöyük in central Anatolia, perhaps the oldest constructed town in the world, are a number of stamp seals that have been dated from the first half of the sixth millennium B.C. These stamp seals, "made of baked-clay or stone and decorated with geometric figures, provide the earliest evidence for claims of ownership in the Neolithic Age," and are associated with the origins of trade between neighboring settlements.[5] For the best part of four thousand years, Anatolian stamp seals continued to be produced according to type. They remained much the same in form and function, producing geometric designs that informed second and third parties that an object belonged to or originated with a specific and named first party.

Whether the site of that first party was an individual, a family, clan, tribe, or trading group remains obscure until the early second millennium B.C, when stamp seals start showing up in graves, suggesting, if inconclusively, that a specific person's signature was being produced. Although some of these Early Bronze Age stamp seals were made of metal, the biggest change was when the geometric motifs became smaller and finer in detail as the faces of the stamp seals become convex.[6]

It might reasonably be objected that the marks made by stamp seals are not really letters but something else. But the fact that they exist belongs in this chronological survey, I think, because they provide an important and originary link between the written claim of a personal identity, and private property and commerce. And that link provides a first step in the emergence of the letter. What happens next, in Anatolia at least, is the slow but steady arrival, from roughly 2500 B.C. onward, of Assyrian merchants who brought with them a new language together with the cuneiform script, and the cylinder seal: "thus began written history in Anatolia."[7] With the aid of these instruments, the Assyrian merchants had established, by 1950 B.C., a highly sophisticated trading system of markets, centered on Kültepe near modern Kayseri, that extended west beyond Konya, north toward Sivas, and east beyond Diyarbakir. Their success depended on acquiring and maintaining security for their markets and for the safe passage of goods on specific routes across the vast Anatolian landmass. Trade requires roads and letters. Records of merchant's rights took the form of letters written in cuneiform on rectangular clay tablets that were then encased in clay envelopes. Examples have been found "in large numbers, but chiefly at Kültepe."[8] Although letters of permission and safe conduct are addressed by a local ruler to the merchant in question, this group of letters necessarily involved third parties to whom they were implicitly addressed—anyone who might have wanted to interfere in the promised right of passage.

If it be objected that the Anatolian stamp seals continuously produced from 6000 B.C. onward are no sure evidence of an activity worthy of being called letter writing, many of the Kültepe tablets—receipts, taxation agreements, contracts, debt agreements, promissory notes—are indisputably epistolary, "the day-to-day business correspondence" of Assyrian merchants "with their capital city."[9] The names of women sometimes appear in letters of agreement, but only when they own property: in one typical instance "Hanuala and his wife Burka are sureties" for a loan of goods and cash between two merchants.[10] But in addition to letters from local rulers guaranteeing merchants the security of trade routes and numerous "receipted bills and invitations / To inspect new stock," the tablets discovered at Kültepe also include one remarkable letter that puts the epistolary mode once again firmly at the scene of what, in the West, we have traditionally considered to be a further stage in the advance of civilization: military empire building.

Written in cuneiform Hittite, it begins formally with the writer's name, his parentage, title, and a command that the letter be read aloud: "Anitta, son of Pithana, King of Kussara. Speak this: It was pleasing to the Weather-god of Heaven. And, since it was pleasing to the Weather-god, the King of Nesa fell captive to the King of Kussara. The King of Kussara came down out of the town with a great host and took the town of Nesa by storm during the night. He seized the King of Nesa but did no harm to any of the inhabitants of Nesa, treating them like mothers and fathers."[11] The letter continues with a list of the other towns and kings that Anitta subdued in his campaign to become the most powerful human authority in central Anatolia. Experts cannot be sure, but it seems generally agreed that the events described—Anitta's divinely ordained conquest—predate the script in which the letter is composed. Since Anitta transferred his residence from Kussara to Nesa, it can be presumed that the letter was initially addressed to the recently subjugated people of Nesa, though no one is yet certain where either of these towns was located.[12] In any case, the clay tablet announces itself to be a transcript of a now lost commemorative pillar, so at best the text is secondhand, an out-of-date transcription. And let us not forget that it is also, in no small measure, a letter of thanks to the mysterious storm god of the Hittites: in the service of the right gods, seizing land and property can sound like holy war. An imperial address in the form of a letter from an emperor to his or her subjects is entirely public, political, and hence religious (ideological), since the authenticity of the writer's claim to be who he says he is, the ruler, is legitimated through a precise relationship with the divine or Absolute Subject.[13]

Site 2: Under the Letter

> And gossip, gossip from all the nations.
> —W. H. Auden

At site 1, letters regulated the desire to own and the need to signify ownership throughout a period of emergent trade and settlement. Letters functioned discursively, constituting individuals as subjects and installing them within the new forms of public relationship attendant upon the ownership of mobile property, commercial exchange, and, eventually, colonization and imperialism. Letters were instruments of power that constructed, disciplined, and circulated a variety of subjects. Letters redefined their instrumentality at specific moments in the development of productive relations.

What remains constant, right through into the developed form of the imperial letter of state, is a variable rhetorical structure of address centered on the writer's desire and authority to claim ownership, a claim that is never private.

If, by definition, many of these structural features of epistolary address remain constant between sites 1 and 2, the evidence at site 2 nevertheless reveals some significant differences in the discursive functioning of letters. In glancing at some examples, I shall focus primarily on printed documents from the 1640s that call themselves "letters" on their title pages, but will try not to lose sight of other contemporary instances of epistolarity.

As a generic field, the printed letter of the English revolutionary decades has been curiously understudied.[14] Indeed, the use of printed letters in early modern English culture more generally often remains obscure even to specialists. This neglect is probably as much due to the seeming ubiquity of letters as to the form's heterogeneity. Many letters survive from the English seventeenth century that were never intended for publication; some of these have been edited, but in general the archive of private correspondence in this period has been as little studied as that of the printed letter, despite the availability of some useful scholarly editions.[15] Social, political, economic, and literary historians have variously cited evidence from manuscript and printed letters, but in much the same way that they have used other documentary sources, without respect for generic specificity. A generic history of the seventeenth-century letter remains to be written.

Of the letters printed during the civil war era, one key form has been identified: the intercepted letter. Nigel Smith has argued that we must pay special attention to generic detail if we are to understand the relation between literature and the English Revolution, confining himself to one illuminating formal proposition about the letter: "Secrecy became a key element in the construction of different cultural identities: parliamentarian 'secrecy' looks different to royalist 'secrecy.' Lois Potter's emphasis on the obsession with secrecy in royalist literature is but half the story. Both 'sides,' for instance, published in newsbooks the intercepted letters of the enemy."[16] Already by the early 1640s, certainly, epistolary discourse had developed strategies of address geared to revelation, to making state secrets public, to exposing the formerly unknowable. Yet in a sense, too, this is only half the story, since many such letters appeared as separate publications, outside the immediate partisan context of newsbooks, and we know that at least some of them were fake—publishing the enemy's secret could involve all kinds of misinformation and ventriloquism.

In its simplest form, publishing intercepted letters provided an obvious means not simply of revealing enemy secrets but of exposing to public view the motives and characters of those who held them. While purporting to reveal secrets, intercepted letters helped define opposing sides in the civil war by characterizing the enemy in their own voices. By 1643, the practice of publishing intercepted letters had become so common that the letters themselves sometimes anticipated being intercepted. One letter "intercepted at Sea" from a royalist exile writing from France begins with hopes that it "may meet no interception."[17] Letters sometimes were expected to be read by someone else.

Evidently, even in its simplest form, the belief that intercepted letters reveal the enemy's secret requires a general, secularized theory of the epistolary subject not restricted to intercepted letters, and not in evidence at site 1, where we saw Anittas's claim to imperial sovereignty predicated upon the trope of the divine, the Absolute Subject. Rather, at site 2 we find fully developed the humanist notion that letters necessarily threaten to reveal their writers, that letters cannot help but risk exposing writers as they truly are, without disguise. In this secular form, epistolarity performs the truth of the body, having appropriated the function of the Absolute Subject into its own circuitry. In 1691 the stationers Thomas Sawbridge and Matthew Gillyflower outlined a theory of epistolary truth that we will find was already in place fifty years previously. The primary claim to ownership signified by letter writing was a claim over one's own identity, a claim predicated on a body inscribed with the subject's design. Their preface to *Cabala, Sive Scrinia Sacra: Mysteries of State and Government, in Letters of Illustrious Persons, and Great Ministers of State* advertises how the letters in their volume reveal designs formerly hidden by undressing those illustrious persons who wrote them: "A Collection not so much of Letters, as of Keys, to open unto you the Mysteries of Government, and the Management of Publick Transactions, in the late Reigns of the greatest Princes in *Europe;* whose principal Minsters of State and their Negotiations, are here Presented Naked; and their Consultations, Designs, and Policies, as they were Contrived, are here exposed to publick view and observation, without any the least Bias or false Gloss, and with more Truth and Sincerity than *Annals* usually declare to Posterity."[18] The notion that letters, once "exposed to publick view and observation," must necessarily thereby reveal their writers stripped naked, exposing their secrets, rests on an entirely imaginary metaphoric relation between the writer's body and the text. But no trace of such a recognition of metaphoricity appears within the epistolary discourse. The relation between writerly body and epistolary text is assumed to be transparent, both self-authenticating and natural—for which read, ideology at its strongest.

Letters demanded loyalty. Besides revealing their writers to public view, letters constructed imaginary relations involving personal commitments to public causes. During the early years of the civil wars, letters frequently helped sort people into enemy camps. Sometimes letters were written to build alliances, to demand allegiance to a cause and loyalty to its leader. In his *History of the Rebellion and Civil Wars in England,* Clarendon tells "a pleasant story" from August 1642, when the king, camped in Nottingham, was desperately trying to raise funds for his army. Agents were sent with letters, "all written with the King's hand," to two local grandees, begging money. Both managed to refuse, but Lord Dencourt's response "administered some mirth" among members of the royal court. After reading the king's letter, Dencourt "replied that 'he was not such a fool as to believe it; that he had received letters both from this King and from his father'; and hastily ran out of the room, and returned with half a dozen letters in his hand, saying, that 'those were all the King's letters, and that they always begin with *Right trusty and well-beloved,* and that the King's name was ever at the top; but this letter began with *Dencourt,* and ended with *your loving friend C. R.,* which,' he said, 'he was sure could not be the King's hand.'"[19] Although we can easily understand why Dencourt might have wanted to deny the authenticity of the king's letter in order to avoid the request for funds, there's no reason to suppose that he was being disingenuous in his beliefs about epistolary discourse. For Dencourt, the letter is a site of truth where interpretation can be authenticated by the forms of address, signature, and handwriting. He assumes that he knows the king's secret because of his direct access to the knowledge only letters can guarantee. In Clarendon's anecdote, at least, the joke turns upon Dencourt's entirely imaginary relation with the king, a fantasy that leaves out of account the agency of the royal secretary normally employed to write the king's letters for him. The problem of authenticity posed by epistolary form cannot help but involve such imaginary subject positions. In a time of civil war, however, when letters were written and circulated in order to help people decide which side they were to be on, the consequences of such identifications were far from imaginary.[20]

Printed letters were much less ambiguous in the way they demanded loyalty from their readers than those that circulated by the hands of agents. In February 1642, the mayor of London, Isaac Pennington, published in his own name a circular letter requiring that "the Minister of every Parish Church, shall tomorrow publish this [letter] unto his Parishioners, and effectually move them freely to advance some good somme" toward the cost of the parliamentary army under the earl of Essex.[21] For the most part, however, printed letters were designed to construct an enemy. In their simplest form, they might indeed reveal the enemy's secret plans. *A True Copie of a Letter of Speciall Consequence from Roterdam in Holland,* published by Henry Overton on 20 February 1643, warns Londoners that the queen has ships full of arms and ammunition ready and waiting to set sail for England to do battle with freedom-loving supporters of the parliamentary cause.[22] Printed letters constructed the enemy by arousing fear and martial enmity. "P. A."'s *A Letter of Advice to the Londoners to Forewarn Them of Their Neere Approching Miseries, and to Rouze Them (If It Be Possible) Out of Their Senselesse Security* appeared the next day.[23]

Letters also described the enemy. Yet even when printed letters unambiguously gave the enemy a personal name, they operated imaginary relations no less complex than those bedeviling Lord Dencourt. Indeed, the mediation of printing could not help but complicate the material signification of the authentic. On the evidence of such examples from George Thomason's collection of printed documents, begun in 1640 but becoming nearly comprehensive only the next year, most separately published letters—such as those mentioned above—seem to have been produced by a London press that was largely hostile to the king's cause. Intercepted letters commonly revealed conspiracies against parliamentary forces and sympathizers.[24] Although Parliament did not exactly control the press in the early 1640s, many of the letters published then seem to operate within a general attempt to reveal the treachery lurking at the heart of the royal court. Regarding the growing parliamentary hostility to the king and his supporters during December 1640, Clarendon reports how Commons policy entailed a regime that depended on naming and not naming the bad guys. He writes of a campaign to make "as many men apprehend themselves obnoxious to the House as had been in any trust or employment in the kingdom."[25]

Right from the start, printed letters participated in this campaign, naming and ventriloquizing the most reviled of the king's ministers, thereby seeming to authenticate their obnoxious position. The small handful of separately published letters collected by Thomason in 1640 and 1641 includes letters of resignation purporting to be by those ministers of state actually named in Commons debates during December 1640. These letters give the name of the enemy a supposedly personal, if not exactly inner, voice and serve as a warning to anyone hostile to Parliament.

Letters give the enemy a name and a voice revelatory of the opposition's secrets. On the 18th of December 1640, William Laud, Archbishop of Canterbury, was impeached by Parliament and confined to the Tower; there he remained until his trial and execution in January 1645. Interest in the epistolary sign of the much reviled archprelate was such that, by June 1641, Thomason had collected no fewer than three letters purporting to be by him. *A Letter Sent by William Lawd Archbishop of Canterburie. With Divers Manuscripts to the University of Oxford. Which Letter, in Respect It Hath Relation to This Present Parliament, Is Here Inserted* was "Printed in the Yeare, 1641," but the "Answer" from the university orator is internally dated "1640."[26] Although hardly a scandalous document, the *Letter* certainly names and attributes a personal voice to a proclaimed enemy of Parliament. But its relation to the present parliament is, at best, perhaps little more than the need to broadcast the voice of an enemy. Laud briefly declaims against sectarianism in expressive terms: "But in what estate *Ecclesiaticall* businesses are all men may see, there is more then one *Fountaine* of these evills. But there is but one fury of those, who not enduring sound *Doctrine,* which St. *Hilary* observed, desire a corrupt *Doctrine,* among whom, thus stung with the Summer-flye, how bad a thing it is to live amongst them."[27] The "Relation to the present Parliament" that made this letter worthy of publication may indeed lie here, in revealing the hostility of the named enemy. Hardly a secret, but only once we have agreed that Laud is an enemy.

Letters of resignation, including forged ones, could anticipate victory by imagining an enemy already admitting defeat. Such was the importance of revealing the defeated enemy subject, and such was the perceived power of epistolary discourse for achieving this purpose, that two distinct versions of Laud's letter of resignation from his chancellorship of the University Oxford appeared, one "true," the other "fictitious."[28] The genuine article, *The True Copie,* loudly announces that it has been "Published by Occasion of a Base Libell and Forgery that runs under this Title."[29] Yet the fake copy is peculiarly temperate in its representation of the imprisoned prelate's inner life; again, there is not much of a secret here. Rather than overt character assassination, *The Copie of a Letter*[30] performs its libel by an act of robbery, by stealing the right of the name to own itself. Unlike contemporary satires that vilified Laud by representing the obscene interiority of his imagination,[31] *The Copie* more soberly ventriloquizes the voice of the enemy expressing resignation in defeat. Before giving up the chancellorship, the fake Laud is imagined welcoming death as a release from his current condition: "my life is now burthensome unto mee, my mind attended with sad, and grievous thoughts, my soule continually vexed with anxiety & trouble, groaning under the heavey burthen of a displeased *Parliament;* my name disperst, and grossely abused by the multiplicity of Libellous Pamphlets, and my self bard from any wonted accesse to the best of Princes."[32] There are no such personal effusions in *The True Copie;* nor any such admission of the greater authority of Parliament. Indeed, since the authentic Laud nowhere directly addresses Parliament by name, one purpose of the forgery may be nothing more than to construct the voice of the enemy, naming the victor, in defeat. This entirely fictitious expression of resignation neatly contains the enemy's name just as the Tower immures Laud's person: "Laud" is no longer a threat. Epistolary libel steals the defeated enemy's name in order to ventriloquize the imaginary experience of that theft, of the name at once dispersed by printed libels and impotently locked up in the anxieties of being barred from access to power. In June 1641 the war of words demanded that the defeated enemy answer back as such.

But letters were often not what they claimed to be. *A True Copie of a Letter Found in the Kings Army* appeared in late February 1643, passing itself off as if "Delivered to the House by a very welwiller to that great and Honourable Councell concerning matters of moment," so its purported alliances are clear.[33] Here, supposedly, is some insider information about what the supporters of the enemy king are currently thinking. But the scenario of a "welwiller" to Parliament intercepting and printing such a letter is entirely fictitious. With a few minor alterations, this work reprints a "letter" printed back in May 1641, just at the time when the Commons was going after Laud and Finch. This earlier version, *A Coppy of a Letter Found in the Privy Lodgeings at Whitehall*,[34] also declares origins in the royal camp, but leaves open the strategic situation of its printing. The text of the letter is an entirely formal document, offering indirect advice to the king at a time when Charles was known to read what the London press produced. The letter argues that the king must act soon to preserve his majesty and the royal interest; in particular, he should give up certain ministers of state before they are named by the Commons, since if he waits until then, he would then appear to be obeying a lower authority. Without the support of the people, in all events, the king will not be able to preserve certain of his ministers, and indeed the history of English monarchy proves that often the best way for a king "to preserve this power" is "to give it away." The reigns of Henry III, John, and Edward II are cited to prove that "when the Princes have let it [power] goe, the people come and put it in their hands againe, that they may play on, as in Queen *Elizabeth*."[35] Close to the throne, a highly learned letter writer appears to be advising the king that his best interest lies in acting now to anticipate the rebellious will by carefully abandoning some of his supporters before the whole lot are named as malignants by the Commons. What can the status of this advice be when it is reissued by the agency of that imaginary figure of the "welwiller" to Parliament?

Evidence of epistolary activity during the 1640s, including but extending well beyond the letters published in newsbooks,[36] raises questions of authenticity and its public representation. Letters conducted political debates by assuming a variety of voices and positions.[37] Not only did forgery often take the stage but the categories of the personal and private within humanist discourse also generally were clearly in the process of epistolary reconstruction into public and political terms, by means of which war could be conceived and conducted. One of the greatest of the press-managed scandals of the civil war era occurred during the summer of 1645; it involved the capture and publication of the king's personal letters following the defeat of the royalist army at the battle of Naseby. So thorough was the rout of royalist forces that the king's cabinet containing his letters of state was captured, and the contents were in print by 14 July under the title *The King's Cabinet Opened*.[38] Here, selections from Charles's letters on matters of state, many of them directed to the queen, Henrietta Maria, are transcribed with commentary by Henry Parker to show the king to have been plotting with the Catholic French to subvert English, protestant liberties.[39] But royalist apologists were very quickly on the scene to express horror that the royal word had been published, often going on to correct the interpretations of the republican commentators.[40] Within days, one of the king's supporters indignantly attacked their publication in *Some Observations,* insisting that the letters had been misquoted and misinterpreted.[41]

Publishing letters intercepted between kings and queens was felt to violate simultaneously royal prerogative, the privacy of marriage, and humanist principles of honesty and decorum. His letters in print, the king stands naked, his secrets revealed. In one especially indignant royalist defense, this very same epistolary logic, when applied to the mysterious royal body, causes the king to suffer his greatest humiliation from his epistolary undressing. For it is as a mere man that the king has a wife and marital secrets. *A Key to the Kings Cabinet* offers an extended historical parallel to Philip of Macedon, whose letters were found during his civil war with the Athenians; none of them were of any interest except one to his wife, which expounded not only his love for her but also the whole scheme of his plans against the Athenians. "Yet, nothwithstanding all this . . . [t]he whole Assembly rose in some disorder: cryed out, that, that Letter should by no means be opened; but understanding that it was addressed to *Olympias* the Queene, without any the least violation offered to the Sacred Seale, to *Her* they sent it: Protesting that it was a *barbarous* and *unmanly* thing, to betray the secrets between *Man* and *Wife,* unto the whole World, although the knowledge thereof would prove never so beneficiall and advantageious unto them that did it. . . . So did these Turbulent *Athenians* yet, preferre their *Honesty* before their *Profit;* and as great as their *Hostility* was, yet, their *Humanity* still, was greater."[42] Publishing letters from a king to the queen reveals him naked, stripped of office and in defeat. With his marital secrets revealed, he is rendered less than a king, even less than a man. Nevertheless, as the historical parallel makes clear, the defeat of a king means more than robbing a man of his secrets, since such knowledge might prove ever so "beneficiall" and "advantageious" to the robbers.

While the furor over the publication of *The King's Cabinet* continued, printed letters from abroad provided a positively global context for the success of the parliamentary army at Naseby. Letters were part of an emergent public network of international information that resituated the king's defeat within world events. Newsbooks regularly printed letters from abroad, but at this time were testifying that the enemies of protestant reform were in defeat everywhere. In central and eastern Europe, the Thirty Years' War was grinding to a halt, with the Habsburgs smashed. Reflecting on events in the Mediterranean, the writer of *The Scottish Dove* speculated: "who knowes, but that the *Turke* shall in these times be Gods instrument, to destroy the *Pope*? and then God will trouble him and from heaven consume him by the fire of his indignation."[43] The hope that the Turk and the Pope would defeat each other was not uncommon. For 12 August, *The True Informer* reports Turkish landings on Crete with excitement: "We cannot but have great expectations, of these remarkable concussions and combustions in divers parts of this world, but in an especiall manner of those risen between the two great opposites of Jesus Christ the Turke and the Pope."[44] For many Protestant English nationalists, the weeks following the defeat of the king and the royalist army at Naseby were godly times when signs everywhere attested to the impending overthrow of worldly tyrants.

That is to say, letters proclaimed one enemy in defeat, only to name another one. Letters from abroad reporting news of the Turkish siege of Crete began appearing in newsbooks during the first week of August alongside debates concerning the defeated king's letters. Ottoman plans against Malta quickly proved a blind for the attack on Crete, the last stronghold of the Venetian Republic, which finally came on 2 August and was destined to last over twenty years. Letters appearing to be from the Ottoman Sultan kept English readers up to date. On 7 August *Newes from the Great Turke* printed what purports to be a letter from Sultan Ibrahim, here called "Brain," proclaiming an ancient claim on and present grievance against the island of Malta.[45] On 8 August another letter from Ibrahim appeared, this one "sent unto the Prince of Transilvania. Containing many impious, and unheard of Blasphemies, against our Saviour Christ; and fearefull threatnings against all Christendome." One enemy may be defeated, but another arises to take his place: "I will moreover plant my owne Religion effectually therein, and destroy for ever thy Crucified God: whose wrath I feare not, and he cannot afoord you any succour to free you from my hands. I will besides this couple thy Sacred Priests to Plowes: and make Dogs, and the wild beasts to sucke the breasts of women. Thou shalt doe well and wisely to leave the Religion thou hast; For, otherwise, I will have you all burnt."[46] The terrible Turk's obscene threats are followed by commentary that incites English protestants to fear the westward expansion of the Turkish armies, encouraging them to take up arms and defend Christianity lest history relate that the English did nothing to save their religion.[47] The next day, 9 August, *The True Informer* reprinted the text of Sultan Ibrahim's letter with a report on the success of the Venetian fleet against the Turks.[48] On 11 August, at least three separate works appeared dealing with fall out from the publication of the king's letters.[49] The need to construct a national enemy continued during that week, when rumors started circulating that Turkish pirates had actually landed on English shores. "It is reported," claimed *The Scottish Dove* for 8–15 August, "and from credible hands, that some *Turkish* Pyrats have come into Cornwall, and taken away about 240 of the Cornish men, women, and children."[50] For the rest of the month, newsbooks printed letters from abroad that seemed to find the Turkish threat everywhere.

Even those letters printed during the first decade of the English civil war do a great deal more cultural and political work than I can hope to detail or summarize here. But I trust I have made it clear that such evidence as I have presented calls for a more fully historicized account of epistolarity than we are likely to get from critical approaches developed from and for the elucidation of epistolary novels.

Ironically, among the origins of the English novel remaining most underexplored is the printed epistolary discourse of the civil war era. Printed letters of the time will clearly provide crucial evidence for the view that epistolarity marks a site where feminized privacy gets imagined, as we saw in the defense of the king's violated claim to marital secrecy. But they also suggest a great deal about the public nature of epistolary discourse, the absent presence of other readers, and problems of authenticity and identity beyond those I have noted and described above.[51] Whether published separately or in newsbooks, printed letters are by nature public documents, and thus while they constitute only part of the evidence, they give it a public slant. As such they cannot be used to prove that there were not other letters that remained private, successfully exchanging their secrets only between the writer and designated reader. By definition of their success, such letters keep their secrets. But the possibility of interception remains a necessary fiction, constituting their imaginary horizon of privacy. As Elizabeth Heckendorn Cook has shown using different materials, the evidence of actual letters in print and in manuscript suggests that a highly sophisticated epistolary discourse was in place within English print culture long before Richardson.[52]

After the Letter

I began thinking about this essay and the public nature of epistolary writing, about the trace of the third-person reader, while looking at one of the Kültepe letters in the Museum of the Ancient Orient in Istanbul. The clay tablet, I recall being informed by the printed guide (in English), was found in an envelope of clay; tablet and envelope are both inscribed in what I was told is Hittite cuneiform. From the transcriptions provided of the texts on the tablet and the envelope, it looks, to my untrained eye, as if the letter contained within says nothing not already announced on the envelope.

With this special case in mind, I later tried to write about the third reader outside the primary field of epistolary address. The phone rang. It was a friend, a successful London literary agent familiar with the scenes behind the posthumous publication of letters to and from literary giants of recent years, who also has what she would call a "healthy mistrust" of all things Derridean. After outlining my thoughts about the trace of the third reader at the site of the not-there, some person or persons beyond the writer and addressee, she immediately said this was all "nonsense" except for famous people. The letters she writes to her absent partner, she insisted, are entirely personal because neither of them are or are likely to become famous; if he were to show them to anyone else, she would feel justified in killing him. I think she proved us both right.

Postscript by Nancy Armstrong

The Case of the King's Cabinet Opened

"Re-siting the Subject" invites its readers to think twice about what is perhaps our most basic assumption concerning the writing of letters—namely, that they allow a

transaction between one individual and another whereby both can enjoy the privi-leges of privacy. Indeed, feminist critics—myself included—have made a rather big deal of epistolary fiction for just this reason, that here a distinctively feminine sub-ject first found a vehicle for cultural expression. Having re-sited the subject along with MacLean, I, for one, am more than willing to insist that letters are now and always have been—at least since the Neolithic Age—purloined letters. They are writ-ten as if they were going to be intercepted. Always present in the mind's eye of the letter writer is a third party who leaves the mark of such awareness on the letter. I am quite taken with the grandiosity of this claim: if one thing remains constant about literate human beings (a redundancy of sorts in the register in which we are both writing) from primal slime to the present day, it is this curious cultural prac-tice and presumed deep human need to perform a kind of writing that only appears to be private but might in fact also be subject to scrutiny at any moment by an un-known third person. In seventeenth-century England, next to the worst thing in the world for Charles I—and cause of great jubilation on the part of his enemies—was apparently the capture of the letters he wrote to his Catholic wife, no sweetheart of the English people she. To modern readers, the king's practice of keeping a letter book at the Battle of Naseby might appear tantamount to leaving one's keys in the car in a particularly bad neighborhood, but that practice peculiar to early modern letter-writing is beside the point. What interests me here is both the seizure of those letters and MacLean's restaging of that apparent violation of privacy to dramatize the omnipresence of the third party to letter writing in seventeenth-century England.

MacLean has in fact restaged the notorious scene on the scaffold—the moment at the opening of Discipline and Punish *when the element of reversibility sudden-ly infiltrated and destabilized the early modern distribution of power—as some-thing like the rape of the king's cabinet. As Foucault so memorably described it, the execution of Damiens illustrated the possible transfer of political power from the king, there by surrogate in his executioner, to the prisoner spectacularly splayed and dismembered before the crowd, whom we imagine for the first time to feel the thrill of identification rather than difference between themselves and the prisoner subject-ed to power. The seizure of the king's cabinet provides the mise-en-scène of this same transfer of power in terms utterly suitable for English culture. The same reversibili-ty sets in as the Parliamentarians seize the cabinet containing the intimate corre-spondence between Royal husband and wife, pry open that box, and put the king's innards on public display, much to his detriment. In the English spectacle, paradox-ically, the transfer of power fits the Foucauldian paradigm even better, to my mind, than does the execution of Damiens. In the case of the king's cabinet, the act of opening and displaying its insides to the outside world evacuates the monarch's body*

*of power and transfers that power to the nameless, faceless observers of this specta-
cle. In an instant, Charles I—hardly your ordinary individual—becomes a subject
in the double sense (a subject in excess of writing who is subjected to writing) that
marks modern man. Sorry, Mac, I cannot help myself. Your example is too well chosen to dramatize epistemic change just where you would assert continuity.*

*I must confess—for the benefit of the third person or two who will actually read
our exchange—that I have already appropriated this instance of the early modern
violation of modern privacy and begun to run with it, using it, that is, not only to
displace Foucault's scene on the scaffold but also to draw a contrast between this
form of violence done to Charles I and Clarissa's haute literary rape. Indeed, I am
by now well on my way to puzzling out why Lovelace's violation of her "cabinet"
reveals nothing of Clarissa that the reader did not already know, while he is transformed on the spot into the representative of a class unfit to rule. Only the om-
nipresent and timeless third party can make sense of such a situation as this, where
power drains out of ruling-class masculinity without really empowering those who
had been subject to it. As opposed to the seizure of an early modern letter box, in
other words, this modern example is no two-way exchange. With the seizure of
Clarissa's cabinet, power clearly passes out of both parties to the whole spectacle
and into the position of the implied reader, who can at once enjoy Lovelace's inter-
ceptions of Clarissa's letters and deplore his somatization of that act. How stupid
to think he would master Clarissa by seizing her body, when he had already captured her letters! Is it not for such stupidity that we find it impossible to forgive him?*

*My point in thus pursuing this third party into the modern period is to acknowl-
edge that, yes, both MacLean and I are right. He has convinced me there are three
parties to every letter and such triangulation is essential to a structural definition of
the letter, if not to that of the human itself. I am, however, equally convinced that
this third party of his is also the marker of difference, if not progress, between one
historical epoch and another.*

Notes

My thanks to the editors of this volume and to Brie Burkeman, Alison Landsberg, Donna
Landry, Joad Raymond, and Jodi Wyett for illuminating suggestions that I have done my best
to address.

1. But on "the major contemporary trend in epistolary studies," see the discussion of re-
cent work by Janet Gurkin Altman, Nicola J. Watson, Susan Lanser, Mary Favret, and Elizabeth
Heckendorn Cook in the introduction to this volume; and see Ruth Perry, *Women, Letters, and
the Novel* (New York: AMS, 1990). My own thinking also owes something to Jacques Derrida's
The Post Card: From Socrates to Freud and Beyond, trans. and intro. Alan Bass (Chicago: Univ. of
Chicago Press, 1987); Linda S. Kauffman's *Discourses of Desire: Gender, Genre, and Epistolary*

Fictions (Ithaca: Cornell Univ. Press, 1986) and *Special Delivery: Epistolary Modes in Modern Fiction* (Chicago: Univ. of Chicago Press, 1992), 81–130; and Annabel M. Patterson's chapter on the familiar epistle in early modern discourse, "Letters to Friends: The Self in Familiar Form," chap. 5 of her *Censorship and Interpretation: The Conditions of Writing and Reading in Early Modern England* (Madison: Univ. of Wisconsin Press, 1984), 211–40.

2. See Ralph Cohen, "History and Genre," *NLH* 17 (1986): 203–17, for a defense of genre in historical hermeneutics.

3. W. H. Auden, "Night Mail," in *Collected Shorter Poems, 1927–1957* (New York: Random House, 1964), 84.

4. In her essay in this volume, Anne L. Bower usefully writes of the "external reader." Often, the inside / outside metaphor accurately captures epistolary situations. Once displaced, however, the field of the (epistolary) third person opens onto language, grammar, writing, transportation, communication, etc. What might a letter be in a world of only two people?

5. I. Temiszsoy et al., *The Anatolian Civilizations Museum* (Ankara: Anatolian Civilizations Museum, n.d. [c. 1987]), 20.

6. Ibid., 47.

7. Ibid., 65; and see Johannes Lehmann, *The Hittites: People of a Thousand Gods*, trans. J. Maxwell Brownjohn (London: Collins, 1977), 176–78. More generally, see Nimet Özgüç, *The Anatolian Group of Cylinder Seal Impressions from Kültepe* (Ankara: Türk Tarih Kurumu Basimevi, 1965); Sedat Alp, *Zylinder- und Stempelsiegel aus Karahöyük bei Konya* (Ankara: Türk Tarih Kurumu Basimevi, 1968); and Louis L. Orlin, *Assyrian Colonies in Cappadocia* (The Hague: Mouton, 1970).

8. Oliver R. Gurney, *The Hittites* (London: Penguin, 1952), 19.

9. Ibid., 18.

10. Cited in Lehmann, *Hittites,* 177.

11. Ibid., 184.

12. See the discussion in Gurney, *Hittites,* 19–20, 170.

13. See Louis Althusser, "Ideology and Ideological State Apparatuses (Notes towards an Investigation)," in *Lenin and Philosophy and Other Essays,* trans. Ben Brewster (New York: Monthly Review Press, 1971), 127–86.

14. But see Patterson's useful discussion of Renaissance and seventeenth-century epistolary theory in "Letters to Friends." For the U.S. context, I am grateful to Alison Landsberg for drawing my attention to Michael Warner's *The Letters of the Republic: Publication and the Public Sphere in Eighteenth-Century America* (Cambridge MA: Harvard Univ. Press, 1990), which argues that during "the colonial period by far the most popular genres for political debate were the epistolary pamphlet and the dialogue" (40).

15. Of special interest here, the letters of two seventeenth-century Englishwomen have long been available in scholarly editions: see Marjorie Hope Nicolson, ed., *Conway Letters: The Correspondence of Anne, Viscountess Conway, Henry More, and Their Friends, 1642–1684* (New Haven: Yale Univ. Press, 1930), and G. C. Moore Smith, ed., *The Letters of Dorothy Osborne to William Temple* (Oxford: Clarendon Press, 1928).

16. Nigel Smith, *Literature and Revolution in England, 1640–1660* (New Haven: Yale Univ. Press, 1994), 24; Smith cites Lois Potter, *Secret Rites and Secret Writing: Royalist Literature, 1641–1660* (Cambridge: Cambridge Univ. Press, 1989).

17. *A Letter Sent by Mr. Henry Jarmin, Now Resident in Paris, to Mr. William Murrey, of His Majesties Bed-Chamber: As It Was Intercepted at Sea by Captaine James Morgan, Captaine of the Good Ship, Called the Mary-Rose of Bristoll. Wherein Is Expressed the Full and Reall Intentions of the Said Mr. Jarmin, and the Other English Fugitives in France, against the Proceedings of the Honourable, the High Court of Parliament Here in England, 26 Jan.* 1643 (London: printed for James Jobson), 3; LT E.86(12). Shelfmarks for early printed works cited from the Thomason collection in the British Library appear hereafter as "LT," followed by the relevant number.

18. *Cabala, Sive Scrinia Sacra: Mysteries of State and Government, in Letters of Illustrious Persons, and Great Ministers of State,* "The 3rd Edition, with Large Additions," (London: printed for Thomas Sawbridge, Matthew Gillyflower, Richard Bentley, Matthew Wootton, and George Conniers, 1691), sig. A2r.

19. Edward Hyde, Earl of Clarendon, *The History of the Rebellion and Civil Wars in England,* ed. W. Dunn Macray, 6 vols. (Oxford: Clarendon Press, 1888), 4: paragraph 60.

20. See Joyce Lee Malcolm, *Caesar's Due: Loyalty and King Charles, 1642–1646* (London: Royal Historical Society, 1983).

21. Pennington, untitled broadside, "Februar[y]. 18. 1642," LT 669.f.5(125).

22. *A True Copie of a Letter of Speciall Consequence from Roterdam in Holland, Subscribed by Severall Credible Hands; and Sent to a Citizen of Good Note in London: Being Very Considerable to Be Taken Notice of by All the Well Affected throughout the Whole Kingdome; but Especially by the Citie of London* (London: printed for Henry Overton, 1643), broadside; LT 669.f.6(110). See also *The Queens Letter from Holland: Directed to the Kings Most Excellent Majesty. Brought to the Parliament, and Delivered to the Custodie of Henry Elsing,* [18 February 1643] (London: printed for I. Underhill, n.d.), LT E.90(2).

23. "P. A.," *A Letter of Advice to the Londoners to Forewarn Them of Their Neere Approching Miseries, and to Rouze Them (If It Be Possible) Out of Their Senselesse Security* (n.p., n.d.), broadside, LT 669.f.6(113).

24. Two examples from February 1643: *A Letter of Dangerous Consequence, from Sergeant Major Ogle, to Sir Nicholas Crisp at Oxford. As It Was Intercepted by Colonell Goodwin of the Parliaments Forces,* 27 Feb. 1642 [i.e., 1643] (London: printed for Edward Husbands), LT E.91(3); and, the next day, *A Letter Intercepted at a Court-Guard of the City of London: Wherein Is Discovered a Most Desperate and Bloody Act to Be Performed on Divers Good Ministers and Their Congregations, on the Fifth of March Next,* 28 Feb. 1642 [i.e., 1643] (London: printed for Edward Husbands), LT E.91(12).

25. Clarendon (Edward Hyde), *History of the Rebellion,* 3:14.

26. *A Letter Sent by William Lawd Archbishop of Canterburie. With Divers Manuscripts to the University of Oxford. Which Letter, in Respect It Hath Relation to This Present Parliament, Is Here Inserted. Together, with the Answer Which the University Sent Him, Wherein Is Specified Their Integrity, As He Is Their Chancellor. The Tenor Whereof Ensues* (n.p., 1641), LT E.158(8).

27. Ibid., 1.

28. See George Fortescue, *Catalogue of the Pamphlets, Books, Newspapers, and Manuscripts Relating to the Civil War, the Commonwealth, and Restoration, Collected by George Thomason, 1641–1661,* 2 vols. (London: British Museum, 1908), 1:16.

29. *The True Copie of a Letter Sent from the Most High Reverend William Lord Arch-Bishop of Canterbury to the University of Oxford, When He Resign'd His Office of Chancellour. Published by Occasion of a Base Libell and Forgery That Runs under This Title. And Also the Answer of the University to the Said Letter* (Oxford: printed by Leonard Lichfield, 1641), LT E.167(1).

30. *The Copie of a Letter Sent from William Laud Archbishop of Canterbury the 28. of June 1641. Unto the Universitie of Oxford: Specifying, His Willingnesse to Resigne His Chancellorship, and Withall Deploring His Sad Estate Now in the Time of His Imprisonment* (n.p., 1641), LT E.164(1); the title page design suggests that it was printed by the University of Oxford.

31. See, for instance, the satirical engraving "'The Trance and Vision of Archbishop Laud'" (n.p., n.d.), reproduced in Richard Ollard, *This War without an Enemy: A History of the English Civil Wars* (New York: Atheneum, 1976), 95; and see the anti-Laudian satires listed in Fortescue, *Catalogue*, 1:617–18.

32. *Copie of a Letter*, 1.

33. *A True Copie of a Letter Found in the Kings Army, and Delivered to the House by a Very Welwiller to That Great and Honourable Councell Concerning Matters of Moment* (London, 1643), LT E.90(29).

34. *A Coppy of a Letter Found in the Privy Lodgeings at Whitehall* (n.p., 1641), LT E.163(4).

35. Ibid., 10.

36. See Joad Raymond, ed., *Making the News: An Anthology of the Newsbooks of Revolutionary England, 1641–1660* (Moreton-in-the-Marsh, U.K.: Windrush Press, 1993), and the same author's *The Invention of the Newspaper: English Newsbooks, 1641–1649* (Oxford: Clarendon Press, 1996).

37. See, for instance, *A Letter Written to a Friend, Declaring His Opinion, Being Such Tenents, As Are Contrary to the Doctrine of the Church of England* (n.p., 1642), LT E.91(22); *Neutrality Is Malignancy: Asserted in a Letter from an Eminent Person in the Army, to His Friend at Westminster* (1648), LT E.427(14). See the account in Warner, *Letters of the Republic*.

38. *The Kings Cabinet Opened; or, Certain Packets of Secret Letters & Papers, Written with the Kings Own Hand, and Taken in His Cabinet at Nasby-Field, June 14. 1645. by Victorious Sr. Thomas Fairfax; Wherein Many Mysteries of State, Tending to the Justification of That Cause, for Which Sir Thomas Fairfax Joyned Battell That Memorable Day Are Clearly Laid Open; Together, with Some Annotations Thereupon. Published by Speciall Order of the Parliament* (London: printed for Robert Bostock, 1645), LT E.292(27). Thomason identifies the annotator as Henry Parker.

39. Outcry at the treachery revealed by the king's letters included *Three Speeches Spoken at a Common-Hall, Thursday the 3 of July, 1645. by Mr. Lisle, Mr. Tate, Mr. Brown, Members of the House of Commons: Containing Many Observations upon the Kings Letters, Found in His Own Cabinet at Nasby Fight, and Sent to the Parliament by Sir Thomas Fairfax, and Read at a Common-Hall* (London, 1645), LT E.292(29).

40. Satiric verses by Martin Lluelyn, the king's physician, entitled *A Satyr, Occasioned by the Author's Survey of a Scandalous Pamphlet Intituled, The King's Cabinet Opened* (Oxford: Leonard Lichfield, 1645) appeared in early August (LT E.296[1]).

41. "[I]t might seem a vaine thing, to declare a private mans Opinion, concerning the intercepted Letters of the King, since the Preface saies, *He must be a papist, the worst of men, or a Jesuit, the falsest of Papists,* that would defend them.

Well! Let it find beliefe as it will, He is neither *Papist* nor *Jesuit* that dares say, If there be not forgery in some part of the King's Letters, (for a word or two varied, or omitted, may make a new matter) yet the inferences on them, are neither perspicuous, nor modest" (*Some Observations Upon Occasion of the Publishing Their Majesties Letters* [Oxford: Leonard Lichfield, 1645], LTE.296[2], 1).

42. *A Key to the Kings Cabinet; or Animadversions upon the Three Printed Speeches, of Mr. Lisle,*

Mr. Tate, and Mr. Browne, Spoken at a Common-Hall in London, 3. July, 1645: Detecting the Malice and Falshood of Their Blasphemous Observations Made upon the King and Queenes Letters (Oxford: Leonard Lichfield, 1645), LT E.297(10), 2.

43. *The Scottish Dove Sent Out, and Returning* 95 (8–15 Aug. 1645), LT E.296(26), 751.

44. *The True Informer* 17 (9–16 August, 1645), LT E.296(29), 132.

45. *Newes from the Great Turke. A Blasphemous Manifestation of the Grand Siegnior of Constantinople, against the Christians; of His Entrance into Christendome, and the Particulars of His Great Armie. As It Was Sent to a Merchant of Note in London. As Also What Forces Are Preparing against Him by the Venetians, and Other Christian Princes, viz. the Duke of Florence, and Duke of Parma; the Great Master of Malta. All Faithfully Translated Out of the Italian and French Copies. Published by Authoritie; That All Christains May Take Notice of the Great Pride and Horrid Blasphemy of the Turkes* (London: printed for Jo. Handcock, 1645), LT E.295(6).

46. *The Great Turkes Letter, Sent unto the Prince of Transilvania. Containing Many Impious, and Unheard of Blasphemies, against Our Saviour Christ; and Fearefull Threatnings against All Christendome. Translated Out of the French Copy Printed in Paris. And Re-printed Here According to Order* (London: printed by T. Forcet, 1645), LT E.296(3), 3–4.

47. "Let us then die like Christians, Let us spend our lives for the defence of his cause that dyed for us. God will direct our hands in the day of battell, and will make our Armies to prosper" (ibid., 4).

48. *True Informer* 16 (2–9 August, 1645), LT E.296(8).

49. *Mercurius Anti-Britannicus; or, Part of the King's Cabinet Vindicated from the Aspersions of an Impotent Libeller, Who Commonly Calls Himselfe Mercurius Britanicus*, LT E.296(9); *Mercurius Britanicus, His Apologie to All Well-Affected People. Together with an Humble Addresse to the High Court of Parliament* (London: printed for R. W., 1645), LT E.296(10); *A Letter, in Which the Arguments of the Annotator, and Three Other Speeches, upon Their Majestie's Letters Published at London, Are Examined and Answered* (n.p., 1645), LT E.296(15).

50. *Scottish Dove* 95 (8–15 Aug. 1645): 751. The rumor quickly circulated. In *Mercurius Britanicus* 93 (11–18 August, 1645), LT E.296(34), Marchamont Needham defended himself from attacks regarding his position on the controversy over *The King's Cabinet*, then turned to the news from Cornwall: "Divers *Turkes* came on shore lately in *Cornwall*, carrying away many Inhabitants of both *Sexes*, of the Gentry also and others. If they continue routing thereabout, 'tis ten to one, but *George Digby* will send them a *Commission* to seize our *Merchants* Ships. And why not to them, as well as the *Dunkerkers?*"

51. For more on the public nature of epistolarity, see Cook, *Epistolary Bodies*, 5–29.

52. N. H. Keeble offers another interesting epistolary direction at this time, arguing that non-Conformist communities remained united after the restoration of the Anglican Church in 1660 by following the biblical example of copying and circulating letters to the faithful from important ministers: "By their letters they maintained a sense of community and fellowship despite being forcibly separated" (*The Literary Culture of Nonconformity in Later Seventeenth-Century England* [Athens: University of Georgia Press, 1987], 78; see also 79–80).

∾ Not a Love Story: Retrospective and Prospective Epistolary Directions

Linda S. Kauffman

In memoriam Kathy Acker 1944–1997

When I began writing about love letters in 1978, I was preoccupied with heroines obsessed with romantic love. In *Discourses of Desire* (1986), I was startled to discover that, in works ranging from Ovid's *Heroides* to *Clarissa* to *The Three Marias: New Portuguese Letters,* the heroines eventually find more satisfaction in *writing* about love than in love itself.[1] In the immortal words of Mariane, the nun seduced by a French chevalier in *Letters of a Portuguese Nun,* written in French in 1669, "I realized the whole terrible power of my love only when I exerted all my efforts to rid myself of it. I discovered that it was not so much you as my own passion to which I was attached; it was remarkable how I suffered while struggling with it even after you had become despicable to me through your wretched behavior."[2] Then, I saw the nun as a victim. Today, I marvel at the venomous economy of these words. The letter "murders to dissect"; it is not a love story.

Mariane remains a haunting presence in the imagination of both writers and theorists, as I discovered in writing *Special Delivery: Epistolary Modes in Modern Fiction* (1992). There, I show how both Jacques Derrida in *The Post Card: From Socrates to Freud and Beyond* and Roland Barthes in *A Lover's Discourse: Fragments* skillfully mimic the passion, disorder, and delirium of

---

Segments of this essay originally appeared in a different form in Linda S. Kauffman, *Bad Girls and Sick Boys: Fantasies in Contemporary Art and Culture* (Berkeley: University of California Press, 1998); reprinted with permission of the University of California Press.

the *Letters of a Portuguese Nun*. (Students of French literature readily recognize the allusions, for to write "à la Portugaise" became a veritable code
for a certain style of writing-to-the-moment, at the height of intensity and
anguish.[3]) Were I to rewrite *Special Delivery*, I would stress more emphatically that *The Post Card* should be read as an original contribution to fiction in general, the letter novel in particular.

But *Special Delivery* also demonstrates that while Derrida and Barthes
were reaccentuating this traditional figure of femininity, women novelists
had become obsessed with global politics, rather than romantic love. Doris
Lessing's *The Golden Notebook,* which is indebted to epistolary technique,
chronicles the cataclysms of the twentieth century; Alice Walker's *The Color
Purple* depicts transglobal racism and misogyny; Margaret Atwood's *The
Handmaid's Tale*'s dystopia draws from repressive regimes ranging from
Nazi Germany to the fundamentalist theocracy in Iran.

Even today, I cannot stop thinking about *The Handmaid's Tale,* because
more than a decade after publication, it is still eerily prophetic, for the fundamentalist coup Atwood describes is ostensibly organized to protect
women from persecution and pornography. Atwood warns that censoring
pornography does not free women; it only provides a rationale to repress
them further. Every time politicians and charismatic leaders promise to
protect women from "harm," women end up worse off than before. In the
1980s, working in alliance with the New Right and the Meese Commission
on Pornography, Andrea Dworkin and Catharine MacKinnon helped turn
the prosecution of pornography in the United States into a *civil rights* violation, rather than a criminal matter. Central to their argument is "the
viewpoint of harm": if you portray any image that I find "harmful," I can
sue you on the grounds that the image has violated my *civil* rights. For the
first time in American history, then, censorship is presented as *furthering*
civil rights.[4] Congress is considering passage of a Pornography Victims'
Compensation Bill, based on the MacKinnon-Dworkin viewpoint of harm.
Similarly repressive measures have popped up all over the country: legisla-
tors tried to ban discussion of abortion on the Internet in 1996, and
Washington State considered passing a bill in 1991 that prohibited people
under the age of 18 from having sex, which included "heavy petting." The
fine: $5,000 and a year in jail—unless the guilty couple decided to marry!
It is hard to say whether we have *regressed* to the eighteenth-century world
of Samuel Richardson's *Clarissa,* or whether Margaret Atwood's dystopic

predictions of a right-wing fundamentalist takeover have already come true.

Indeed, in Washington, D.C., where I live, Louis Farrakhan led a "Million Man" March in the fall of 1996 to empower black men to reaffirm their God-given roles as manly men. In the fall of 1997, nearly the same number of mostly white men descended on the Mall with the same mission. Led by a football coach, these "Promise Keepers" confessed their sins, renounced adultery and pornography, and rededicated themselves to dominance in the domestic household.

As I look back on twenty years of research on love letters, I now realize that what I really wanted to do was to expose the pernicious effects of the ideology of romantic love. The antiporn crusade is sometimes called "the redemptive sex project" because it assumes that sex only has value if related to love. That is why I have borrowed my title from Bonnie Klein's 1983 film *Not a Love Story,* a pseudodocumentary that shows the shocked reaction of feminists as they tour the sex shops and strip joints on Forty-second Street in New York City. Klein's point is that sex *should* be above love, even if this film is *not.* Frankly, I sincerely hope that "the redemptive sex project" *fails.* Seeing that women are the ones who have been most enslaved by that ideology, they may have the most to gain by endorsing an anti-aesthetic that defies it.

The Epistolary Anti-Aesthetic

A number of contemporary writers working with epistolary conventions seem to agree. Robert Coover's *Spanking the Maid* (1982) is a sort of writer's diary; every page is inscribed with revisions and corrections. Coover uses spanking as a metaphor for the travails of writing. John Hawkes's *Virginie: Her Two Lives* (1981), a meditation on the Marquis de Sade, similarly deploys epistolarity to explore the erotics of writing. As with Coover, the sexual activity and the written description of it follow hard on one another. The topic of both novels is the obsessive-compulsive nature of literary composition, with its unremitting discipline, punishment, and endlessly deferred gratification. D. M. Thomas's *The White Hotel* (1981), which includes diaries, love letters, and letters to and from Freud, is a study of the creative process and attendant repressions. Set against the background of the Holocaust, it is an extended meditation on *Beyond the*

Pleasure Principle. It is a case study about Freudian case studies, as is Avodah Offit's *Virtual Love* (1994), which consists of the e-mail correspondence of two psychiatrists engaged in dialogue about their patients' symptoms and their own repressed desires. Space does not permit me to discuss all these writers in depth; instead, I shall focus on Kathy Acker, who is representative of the tendencies in recent epistolary fiction that I want to discuss. All these writers stage the production of writing as an experiment in psychoanalytic transference. All are in the process of inventing an anti-aesthetic that has four major motifs:

1. Critiques of mimesis. These writers subvert the notion that the aim of art is to hold the mirror up to nature. Instead, they highlight the experimental, partial, and—like all epistolary novels—the fragmentary aspects of artistic production. The texts are supremely self-referential exercises about writing's frustrations.

2. The ironic awareness that no anti-aesthetic is wholly transgressive or even *new.* Indeed, the notion of an anti-aesthetic has ancient generic roots, dating back to Menippean satire, as Mikhail Bakhtin has shown. Carnival's roots in pre-Christian Greece and Rome subsequently became associated with pre-Lenten celebrations—a brief moment when the lords of misrule sanctioned pleasure and carnality. The carnivalesque revels in the grossness and carnality of the lower body and glorifies lust over love, anarchy over social propriety, the physical over the rational intellect. Far from exalting the True, the Good, and the Beautiful, the anti-aesthetic substitutes the ugly, the perverse, the antiromantic—a welcome antidote to the ideology of romantic love.

3. Dissolution of dichotomies dividing high/low culture, theory, and practice. While this is characteristic of postmodernism, these writers see postmodernism as an oppositional politics rather than a mere pastiche of parodic moments. There are two different "postmodernisms": one preserves the humanist tradition by turning postmodernism into a mere style; the other deconstructs traditions, critiques origins, questions rather than exploits cultural codes to expose social, sexual, and political affiliations.[5] These writers are in the latter camp.

4. Finally, the anti-aesthetic cannot be defined solely in relation to a single medium, epistolary or otherwise. Instead, it is defined in relation to the logical operations of a set of cultural terms.[6] As a result, the nature of

criticism has changed as well as the nature of epistolary production. A new model of interactivity is emerging—and with it, a new model of subjectivity.

Kathy Acker's Experimental Fiction

Kathy Acker is emerging as one of the leading voices of her generation, despite the fact that she stubbornly avoided the mainstream. She lived on the margins of society in San Francisco and New York City, where she worked in a sex show. All her work focuses on the sadomasochism of everyday life—the raw obscenity of poverty and power relations in contemporary America. As a theorist of epistolarity, I find her particularly important because she so thoroughly debunks the vestigial stereotype of the genteel lady letter writer. Her narrative experiments advance the anti-aesthetic aims outlined above: she explores the interpenetration of mind and body, high and low culture, art and politics. Postmodernism is not a style, but a politics: a means of exposing social and political dogmas.

The paradox Acker confronts is how to reconcile the need for love with a critique of romance's ideology. In *Don Quixote* (1986), which is full of letters, poems, essays, and tales, she traces the evolution of romance from Amadis of Gaul to modern romance. Courtly love—already outdated by 1615—gives way to such debased versions as Harlequin romances, which celebrate feminine masochism and portray love as the sole source of fulfillment for women. By transforming Quixote into a woman driven by sexual and emotional need, Acker's Quixote is immediately launched into the messy physical world of sex and reproduction. The novel commences with her abortion, an operation that in one stroke drives her mad and plants the insane idea for her quest. Her act of supreme idealism is to make the decision to love: "By loving another person, she would right every manner of political, social, and individual wrong: she would put herself in those situations so perilous the glory of her name would resound."[7] Acker's characteristic technique is precisely this kind of mock-naiveté, for love seldom rights political, social, or even individual wrongs. Acker shows how men and literature have conspired to convince women that love is their sole raison d'être. By choosing Cervantes, Acker highlights the fact that since its invention, the novel has been a self-conscious, ironic, and antimimetic genre. In a culture hooked on romance, how can one reconcile the damaging effects of the ideology of romantic love with the desperate yearn-

ing for love? Is that ideology by definition *quixotic?* Are romance and imagination refuges or traps?

Like many epistolary heroines before her, Acker's Quixote is a love
junkie. While one of Acker's voices in the novel is that of the paranoid social observer, another is the infant who simply wants, who is desperate for
some—*any*—emotional connection. In this regard, she is a direct descen-
dent of Mariane in *Letters of a Portuguese Nun.* Acker's prose elevates presocial, primal emotions. Her novels have been called a cri de coeur[8]—although her language is more a scream than a cry.

In all of Acker's novels, the experience of reading is a vertiginous as-
sault. *Great Expectations* (1982), written in imitation of Dickens but with
many epistolary allusions, accentuates the themes of feminine masochism,
unrequited love, and the abjection of orphanhood. She divides the novel
into three sections: "Plagiarism," "The Beginnings of Romance," and "The
End." But by beginning with "Plagiarism," Acker highlights Bakhtin's notion of the novel as a dialogic enterprise, in dialogue with all literature.
Since epistolarity by definition stages the production of writing, Acker exploits that trait by portraying writing as psychoanalytic transference. In all
her fiction, she does not so much write "about" literature as "to" literature, weaving many masterpieces into her novels: Catullus, Sade, Proust,
the Brontës, Dickens, Faulkner, Gertrude Stein, William Burroughs, Jorge
Luis Borges, Julia Kristeva, Hélène Cixous, Luce Irigaray. While "plagia-
rizing" Dickens's classic, her title mocks the "great expectations" readers
bring to the act of reading—the desire for unity, plot, resolution, and closure. The plagiarized text is overwhelmed by the preoccupations she im-
poses upon it.[9] Her collage-novels are like action painting; you drop in and
out whenever and wherever you wish. My very use of an analogy from
painting reinforces the point I made earlier about one distinguishing characteristic of the anti-aesthetic: it cannot be defined in relation to a single
medium.

Acker is like the French performance artist, Orlan, who stages plastic
surgery operations in art galleries. Acker does to the written page what
Orlan does to her face: she cuts it up and reassembles it to highlight the
arbitrariness of the construction, and to show how it is *fabricated.* Her
Quixote's final words: "'Make Me up'" (*DQ,* 207). As Robert Siegle notes,
Acker discovers that "if identity is painfully etched, then pain recalls the
moment of inscription and the noncultural memory of flesh before the

cut of the pen."[10] Acker says the same thing about the art of tatoo when she relates the word to the word *taboo:* "Tattooing . . . [is] art that's on your flesh. . . . Julia Kristeva has written a book, *Powers of Horror,* about . . . [how] art comes from a gesture of power turned against itself. She calls it 'ejection': when you take that emotion and turn it *in* on itself—which is what tattooing does."[11] Since one of the conventions of epistolarity is the physical signs of bodily suffering (tears, blood, etc.) on the page, Acker's insight is particularly astute. The theme of abjection ties Acker's novels to Julia Kristeva's work, for tattooing is one means of dismantling the mind/body split, of elevating a "low" art to the level of "high" art, and of accentuating the relationship between power and emotion. Just as epistolary heroines strive to document tangible signs of the body's suffering (tears, blood, etc.) on the letter, tattooing is a means of imprinting on the body what has been repressed by the culture.

In all her novels, Acker includes mock-essays that combine literary criticism and critical theory. In addition to Kristeva, she is particularly indebted to Hélène Cixous's and Luce Irigaray's ideas about *écriture féminine.* She critiques the phallocentric view of woman as either a sexual commodity or a mere void: "If I wasn't loved, I couldn't fit into this marketplace or world of total devaluation" (*DQ,* 115).[12] Cixous's "The Laugh of the Medusa" calls for "the invention of a *new insurgent* writing" that "will return to the body," that "will tear her away from the superegoized structure in which she has always occupied the place reserved for the guilty," and that will enable the writer "to forge for herself the anti-logos weapon."[13]

Acker's insurgent writing puts into practice Cixous's theories. She advances the aims of a new anti-aesthetic by rejecting the high modernist values of aesthetic autonomy, objectivity, beauty, and wholeness. Her work consists of holes, not wholes; and she uses that word in the vulgar sense to refer literally to her vagina and metaphorically to her all-consuming need for love: "Endless hole I am an endless hole I can't bear this" (*DQ,* 158). In *Great Expectations,* similarly, her narrator, like Dickens's Pip, realizes that "all my life is endings. Not endings . . . but holes. For instance, when my mother died, the 'I' I had always known dropped out. All my history went away."[14] The final words are an epistolary address to "Dear mother,"—the comma poignantly highlighting the fact that writing never ceases because desire never ceases.

However much Acker cannibalizes literature, she always distills some fundamental kernel from the original text, as here, where she captures the loneliness and lack so central in all of Dickens's work. Her letters cut through conventional clichés and decorum, right to the heart of want and desire. (In Dickens's *Great Expectations,* Miss Havisham inhabits Satis House, residence of voracious, insatiable obsessions and needs.) My favorite Acker title is *Hannibal Lecter, My Father;* Hannibal Lecter was the serial killer and cannibal in Jonathan Demme's film *The Silence of the Lambs.* Acker's fiction is about emotional vampirism. All her novels contain myriad letters: unwritten, unmailed letters, letters to politicians, letters to boyfriends who spurn her—like the following:

Dear Peter,
I think your new girl friend stinks. . . . She's only pretty because she's wearing a mask. You're hooked on . . . sex cause when you were young you were fat and no girl wanted to fuck you. . . . Your new girlfriend is insane and she's poisoning you.
    Love,
    Rosa,
P.S. I'm only telling you this for your own good. (*GE,* 25)

Written in the tone of a bright (if somewhat maniacal) undergraduate, Acker's mock-naiveté is apparent when Rosa, the epistolary heroine of her *Great Expectations,* addresses letters to famous authors, the living as well as the dead. To Susan Sontag she writes: "Dear Susan Sontag, / Would you please read my books and make me famous? . . . I understand you're very literate, Susan Sontag" (*GE,* 27, 28). As in Dickens's novel, Acker's heroine desires wealth, status, and fame. Like so many epistolary novelists before her, she also blurs the lines between fiction and reality by including morsels of information that seem to be about her "real life"; she writes to Sylvère Lotringer, as she might write to a lover; Lotringer introduced her to critical theory and published her work in *Semiotext(e):* "Dear Sylvère. . . . / Remember what we do together when I'm unparanoid enough to see you" (*GE,*27, 28).

She writes to David Antin, the American language poet known for his attempts to blur the boundaries between discourse, the artist, and the audience. Like Acker, Antin wants to mime "live" voices; he creates "field situations" and evokes collective celebration through ritual. His aim is to transform the passive reader/spectator into an active one. Acker's heroine in *Great Expectations* writes to him:

Dear David. . . .

I used to hate you because you didn't love me. . . . I should have stopped making demands that you not be the closet female-hating sadist you are. . . . [Y]ou're telling me you're as poor as me when you know I have to [perform] in porn films . . . so I can pay Peter . . . his goddamn rent. (*GE*, 28–29)

An interesting update on the venomous economy of the *Letters of a Portuguese Nun!* Recent epistolary fiction seizes the latent aggression in classic texts, and makes it manifest, active, in-your-face. Here, the epistle is tangibly connected to the messy material business of food, shelter, survival. This passage is a good example of how the True, the Good, and the Beautiful have been supplanted by the ugly, the perverse, and the antiromantic, for Acker writes with a primal aggressive energy.

Although Acker has been attacked for being pornographic, her work reminds us of the etymological meaning of *pornographos:* the writing of, on, about, or by prostitutes and their patrons—not just scenes of sex, in other words, but scenes of everyday life, specifically the "lowlife" of America's disenfranchised and dispossessed. Acker herself worked in the sex industry in New York City, in the very strip joints that shocked the bourgeois, antiporn feminists in Bonnie Klein's *Not a Love Story*. Her "hands-on" experience exposes their pious hypocrisy.

Indeed, in *Don Quixote* she attacks Andrea Dworkin. The whole point of Cervantes's parody is that words are not deeds, but both Dworkin and MacKinnon assume that words *are* deeds, as MacKinnon's ironically titled *Only Words* indicates.[15] Just as Cervantes satirizes the pedants, Acker is horrified by the way scholarship reinforces institutional interests. Imitating Quixote's mad logic, she lumps all the "evil enchanters" together: the media, the academy, leftists, liberals, Andrea Dworkin have all contributed to the Stalinist stifling of creativity in the art world. Acker's Don goes to America to find out how politics work. To her horror, she discovers that the citizens have been indoctrinated by the great American myths, "for economic and political war or control now is taking place at the level of language or myth" (*DQ*, 177). The mercantile interests of America are protected by "dogs" like Richard Nixon, Jimmy Carter, and Henry Kissinger—manipulators of the military-industrial complex who promote destruction and death. International finance has become a highly successful war strategy (*DQ*, 73). She concludes a letter to Nixon by saying: "Please accept my apology that my left hand isn't forming these letters correctly. I wasn't sent to Oxford or anywhere, so what I do to write is cut crosses into the insides of my wrists. I write in fever" (*DQ*, 106–7). What does it take, Acker asks, to get the attention of the world's leaders—letters written in our own blood? She reminds us of the obsessional quality of epistolary writing, the tears that are used to validate the sincerity of feeling, the authenticity of pain.

Acker zanily juxtaposes high culture and low, serious world problems and petty academic squabbles. She rails against starvation in Biafra, AIDS in Haiti. Who are the evil enchanters of this world? Andrea Dworkin, the *Times Literary Supplement,* and Ronald Reagan control the nexus of government and culture (*DQ*, 101). The U.S.A. is run by the media and the "dogs'" greed. The novel is a map of the blood-lust of politicians and the disturbed political psyche.

We are obviously a long way from the sappy sentimentalism of *The Man of La Mancha.* Don Quixote has been transformed from impossible dreamer into conspiracy theorist, a paranoiac trapped in the nightmare America created. Acker implicitly compares past inquisitions and present censorship campaigns. Cervantes, after all, was no stranger to repression; *Don Quixote* was conceived in prison.[16] The passage of time is perhaps what is most relevant about Cervantes's novel, for with time, the genres which were once viewed as trivial, debased, or obscene become classics. This alone constitutes the most cogent argument against censorship, for what one epoch "arrests" becomes "arresting" to the next. The chivalric tales of Froissart, *Orlando Furioso,* and *Amadis of Gaul* were devalued in their own day—as was *Don Quixote,* which, while widely read, conferred few honors on Cervantes in his lifetime. His novel is not only an anatomy of a genre and an age; it is an anatomy of ideology. As Robert Stam argues, quoting Althusser, ideology itself is quixotic: it is "a system of representation based on 'the imaginary relationship of individuals to their real conditions of existence.' The real conditions of Quixote's life include windmills, prostitutes, and genteel poverty, but his lived relation to these conditions involves giants, courtly heroines, and a world unsoiled by material preoccupations."[17] Acker's achievement is to underscore the political implications of ideology while simultaneously capturing the intense yearning for transcendence. She exposes all ideologies that produce ideas without bodies, ideas that only develop at the expense of the body, and instead tries to think out the relationship between the mind and the body as few before her have done.

Great Expectations was followed by *Blood and Guts in High School,* the very title of which emphasizes the visceral aspects of Acker's work, as well as its adolescent sensibility of raw emotional intensity. The novel includes childlike drawings—some explicitly sexual. In one of these drawings a childish hand writes, "I can scrawl and I can crawl," along with a string of obscenities that signify her utter frustration with her own powerlessness and with the world as it is. A cartoon arrow points to the word "I," with the wistful confession, "I wish that there was a reason to believe this let-ter"—by which she means the letter *I,* the idea of a unified self, a coher-ent identity.[18] (Another one of her novels, which plagiarizes Rimbaud and Faulkner, is entitled *In Memoriam to Identity.*) While we are taught to see love as the source of identity, faith, and hope, Acker's characters discover that identity is as contingent and as transient as love is. Above all, fragile identity can be shattered by the cruel and the powerful. The novel is what I call a "traumscrapt"—it combines letters with fragments of scripts, scraps of dreams, memories, fantasies, traumas. *Blood and Guts* reverts to the in-fantile stage of nursery rhymes and nonsense, elevating presocial emotions and the libidinous realm of infantile fantasy. Acker reminds us that fantasy can never be legislated—precisely because it takes root in the polymor-phously perverse pleasures of infancy. As one critic notes, "Acker speaks from a level that is both above and below the urbanity of everyday life."[19]

To return to *Don Quixote:* the critique of mimesis is already ingrained in Cervantes's masterpiece, which defines the novel as a self-reflexive, an-timimetic genre deeply engaged with politics. Cervantes's Quixote, indeed, is a prototypical "performance artist," for he transforms the passive activi-ty of reading into an active mode; he internalizes his experience of books and performs them.[20] Acker shows what happens when one adds pop mu-sic, film, and television to the Don's mania for books: Don Quixote is, af-ter all, the first pop culture junkie. Far from holding the mirror up to na-ture, Cervantes traces "nature" directly back to books.

From Work to Hypertext

The myth of the inviolate body has been a long time dying, and so has the myth of the inviolate literary text. But the seeds of its destruction were evident from its inception. As Robert Coover notes, "Through print's long history, there have been countless strategies to counter the line's power, from marginalia and footnotes to the creative innovations of novelists like Laurence Sterne, James Joyce, Raymond Queneau, Julio Cortazar, Italo Calvino and Milorad Pavic, not to exclude the form's father, Cervantes himself."[21]

Small wonder, then, that Acker uses hypertext to push the boundaries of the anti-aesthetic even further. Acker's gender-bending experiments in *Don Quixote* and other novels mime the indeterminacy of gender in cyberspace. Coover notes that "'hypertext' has given way to 'hypermedia,' combining graphs, photographs, sound, music, animation, and film."[22] Acker also publishes in *Postmodern Culture,* an electronic journal devoted to disseminating new modes of criticism and creative writing.[23] Cyberspace also fulfills the displacement of authorial mastery so long ago predicted by Roland Barthes; computers complete the movement from "Work" to "Text," transforming it into a communal, anonymous, interactive experiment rather than the sole property of one individual. Just as the photograph's and film's reproducibility liquidated the traditional value of the cultural heritage at the beginning of the century, as Walter Benjamin has shown, hypertext liquidates the traditional "moral of the story," substituting simultaneity, multiplicity, indeterminacy.[24] Acker is producing "a new kind of fiction, and a new kind of reading. The form of the text is rhythmic, looping on itself in patterns and layers that gradually accrete meaning, just as the passage of time and events does in one's lifetime."[25]

Twenty-first-Century Epistolarity

I wish I had time to discuss all the ways in which epistolary production is flourishing: electronic mail, fax machines, personal ads, and fan mail are a few that come to mind. Particularly notable are epistolary modes that combine the verbal and the visual, like Ken Burns's television epic on the Civil War, which featured the letters of soldiers, and *Letters Home,* which focused on the correspondence of veterans of the Vietnam War. Personal ads are also especially intriguing because they are written to a fictional addressee: the ideal mate who is "out there" somewhere. Personals advertisers fictionalize themselves too: no one would confess that he or she is primarily interested in sex, for instance. Personals ads encourage us to package ourselves in instantly appealing forms. They exploit the ideal of romantic love, the triumph of hope over experience. They encourage us to create an ideal persona, plot, and setting in ten words or less: *Sleepless in Seattle.*

With the film's plot revolving around *An Affair to Remember,* it is worth noting the enormous impact popular culture has had on epistolary production. Personals advertisers model themselves on Tom Hanks and Meg Ryan, who in turn are reprising the roles of Cary Grant and Deborah Kerr. Pop culture is not merely an influence; it *quixotically* (in both senses of the word!) contributes to the very formation of identity. Earlier I mentioned Acker's fan letters to Susan Sontag and David Antin; fan mail is yet another intriguing extension of epistolarity. What motivates the fan's epistolary address? What processes of identification and projection inspire fans to write to celebrities? In *Fan Mail, Frank Letters and Crank Calls* (1989), Cookie Mueller combines phone sex and fan mail with hilarious results. Nicholson Baker's *Vox* (1991) is another novel that deploys phone sex, yet few have noticed its debt to Jean Cocteau's 1930 *The Human Voice,* one of the first twentieth-century plays to link *ancient* epistolary conventions to a (relatively) new communications technology—the telephone.

Fan mail and other epistolary devices are even beginning to show up in scholarly essays. In "Morphing Identities: Arnold Schwarzenegger—Write Us," Michael Blitz and Louise Krasniewicz publish their own electronic-mail correspondence as they collaborate on a scholarly essay about celebrity. Marveling at how their own stories get mixed up in Arnold's, they both begin dreaming about him. On 20 July 1991, Louise writes Michael about going to the supermarket and coming upon a young couple pretending to be Linda Hamilton and Schwarzenegger in *The Terminator!*[26] Arnold Schwarzenegger is an interface between human and cybernetic hardware, as Krasniewicz and Blitz observe: "In our e-mail work on Schwarzenegger, we have effectively created a dynamic morph among Arnold, our selves, the computer and our culture."[27]

I want to shift gears now and discuss ways in which epistolarity has left letter, paper, envelope, and even e-mail behind. The artist I want to discuss is a woman who has given herself a fictional name of Orlan—a synthetic fabric to match a synthetic identity. Orlan lives in Paris, next to Artaud's studio. She is in the process of turning her face into a composite of the icons of femininity in classical Western painting: the chin of the Botticelli

Venus; the nose of Gerome's Psyche; the mouth of Boucher's Europa; the forehead of the Mona Lisa. She achieves this through plastic surgery; her operations take place in art galleries. Gallery visitors watch the surgery, while satellite and fax hookups put Orlan in contact with well-wishers from far-flung corners of the globe who are also watching. Orlan is awake during the entire procedure, submitting to only local anesthesia.

Orlan is our age's Cocteau, the missing feminist link between the Surrealists' exploration of the unconscious, the Situationists' strategic intervention in a society of spectacle, and Baudrillard's theory of simulation. What interests me most is how Orlan *invents* a new model for epistolarity and simultaneously *performs* it. I am equally interested in how the verbal and the visual intersect, for Orlan's correspondents can *see* as well as hear her, just as she sees, hears and responds to their questions and comments. This takes epistolary communication far beyond the powers even of e-mail. The "correspondence" is *visual, aesthetic, and clinical*—all at the same time. It is *multiple, spontaneous, and staged*—all at the same time.

Orlan's performances reaccentuate numerous epistolary conventions. She exploits three of the codes that underwrite the classic epistolary address: the Codes of Femininity, Beauty, and Pathos. Orlan pays homage to Héloïse's letters to Abélard and to the nun Mariane's *Portuguese Letters* by teasing out the latent subtext of their celebrated letters, just as Kathy Acker distills essential kernels from the novels she "plagiarizes." Well aware that both Héloïse and Mariane were *nuns,* Orlan stages Catholicism as a spectacle of abasement and abjection. In 1971 she baptized herself "Saint Orlan," miming the exaggerated emotionalism of Bernini's *St. Theresa in Ecstasy.* To her, the human body is a *relic*—both in the sense of being "obsolete" and in the sense of *religious* relics. Orlan's art is not only visual but *visceral.*

As grotesque as this may sound, Orlan only takes to an extreme what scores of celebrities like Michael Jackson take halfway. She merely exposes the surgical procedures that celebrities take pains to conceal. Moreover, she infuses the proceedings with campy humor. In keeping with what I said earlier about the carnivalesque, she transforms the operating room into a carnival, complete with a surgical team in designer gowns, men doing stripteases, and all sorts of absurd juxtapositions of skull's heads, pitchforks, and crucifixes, reminiscent of the Surrealists' Exquisite Corps. She turns her own body into one of Marcel Duchamp's readymades. She describes her art as "carnal" art—the body art of the 1990s, which emphasizes process, ritual, the performative.

Even more profoundly, rather than repudiating Freud's famous equation of femininity with narcissism, Orlan literalizes it and acts it out. But in contrast to Freud, Orlan does away with depth psychology. As Peter Sloterdijk notes, "The suspicion bourgeois individuals have of themselves being animals creates the cultural framework for modern depth psychology."[28] That is the framework Orlan attacks through parody. She illustrates that the new model of self is *conceptual* rather than organic. It is, moreover, infinitely rearrangeable; everything can be shuffled and reordered in every way conceivable. When her metamorphosis is complete, she will let an ad agency give her a new name to go with her new identity.

Both Kathy Acker and Orlan strive to restore the aggressive instincts women have been denied. Both present us with a frightening and rare presence—an unsocialized woman. While on the operating table, Orlan actually reads from Kristeva's *Powers of Horror.* She also reads from Artaud, to show how her work spells the end of representational systems and is a logical evolution of the "Theater of Cruelty." She reads from Lacan's "The Mirror Stage" to memorialize the moment in infancy when subjectivity becomes irretrievably fractured. The mirror stage inaugurates a futile and *quixotic* quest. Orlan observes: "Being a narcissist isn't easy when the question is not of loving your own image, but of re-creating the self through deliberate acts of alienation."[29] Orlan highlights the impossible cult of femininity. Art critic Barbara Rose puts it this way: "Orlan's performances might be read as rituals of female submission. . . . But actually she aims to exorcise society's program to deprive women of aggressive instincts of any kind. . . . If the parts of seven different ideal women are needed to fulfill Adam's desire for an Eve made in his image, Orlan consciously chooses to undergo the necessary mutilation to reveal that the objective is unattainable and the process horrifying."[30]

In different ways, Kathy Acker and Orlan are both savage satirists of the idea of "old masters" and "masterpieces." They both interrogate patriarchy, and the patrilineal genealogy of genius, from the classics to the present. Just as Acker transforms the venerable Don Quixote into a woman, (who is on the operating table for an abortion in the novel's opening scene), Orlan describes herself as the first "Woman-to-Woman Transsexual." They both shove our received ideas about sex and gender, interior and exterior, depth and surface down our throats. They confront spectators with their own voyeurism and with their social and psychic investments. While politicians and some feminists strive to ban images and ideas that might cause "harm" to someone somewhere, Acker and Orlan are assaulting the senses with taboos no one else will touch: sadism and masochism, narcissism and voyeurism, abjection and revenge. No "skin magazine" would depict their work. Few art ones would either. Too literal for art, too visceral for porn.

What are the implications of these developments for theorists of epistolarity? Epistolary conventions remain even when the "correspondence" is transformed by technology, as when *The Handmaid's Tale* substitutes a tape cassette for a letter. While the surgeons operate, Orlan opens a window to the world: epistolarity is now international, instantaneous, and interactive. *Epistolarity* has now joined forces with *virtual interactivity* to create the concept of *"Omnipresence,"* which was the title of Orlan's 1993 New York show.

Further, I have used Orlan as a test case to show how much genre theory can illuminate, but I also want to stress the limitations of genre theory. As Ralph Cohen explains: "It should . . . be noted that to attempt to connect literary history with theory of the period is to assume that theory and practice are synchronic. But works innovated in a period often have no theory to explain them. Theories that exist . . . are applicable to texts and genres previously written, not to innovations."[31] I think that is true of Orlan's innovations: her work has no theory to explain it, even though she *reads theory* during her surgical operations! Responses to her work range from amusement to incomprehension and revulsion. As if to suggest the infinite extendibility of epistolarity in time and space, Orlan's appearance at the First Annual Performance Studies Conference in New York City in 1995 provoked a prolonged, antagonistic e-mail debate, which was subsequently published in the *Theater and Drama Review* (fall 1995).

Orlan is Janus: One side faces the past, which memorializes the obsolete body and looks back to epistolary traditions and to a remarkable body of feminist work on beauty, femininity, and spectatorship. The other side faces the cyborg future, when artificial organs and reproductive technologies transport us into the world of tomorrow, which is already being called the epoch of the "Posthuman." Indeed, this world already invisibly envelops us: anyone on Prozac, prosthetics, pacemakers qualifies. This explains why her 1994–95 installation at the "Hors Limites" exhibition at the Pompidou Center in Paris was entitled "Entre" ("In Between Two"): she stands as intermediary between past and future. Orlan traces the passage from Nature to Culture, with specific attention to the *cuts* along the way. Remember, when Orlan's operations are complete, she will not look like the Mona Lisa, the Botticelli Venus, or any other single painting—instead, she will be a composite of them all. Orlan desacralizes our culture's investment in medicine, which she sees as our epoch's religion. That is why she chooses the role of nun, or saint, or intercessor: by seizing control of the medical apparatus, she strips it of mystique. In so doing, she invokes *another* epistolary classic, Mary Shelley's *Frankenstein*. Mary Shelley's mother died giving birth to her; Mary Shelley never lost the uncanny conviction that she had been born of dying parts. Orlan is Frankenstein, the monster, and Bride of Frankenstein all rolled into one.

The aim of transgressive artists like Kathy Acker and Orlan is to stage the emotions by *literalizing* the body. Obsessed with what goes in and comes out of the body, they seize technology (computers, faxes, medical imaging devices) to open it up. They want to show how the image shapes subjectivity, and how the visual intercepts the verbal—a process I have emphasized in this essay. Just as Walter Benjamin documented the transformation of subjectivity as a result of the advent of cinema, subjectivity today has undergone another profound transformation as a result of televisual technologies. A recent essay asks whether television fundamentally *determines* our experience: "Is the television a—or the—dominant but unacknowledged epistemological model of subjectivity? Do we understand ourselves as presentational constructions, moved by prefabricated, precoded information . . . in a strangely evacuated but somehow 'electric' space?"[32] Today, subjectivity does not control the image; instead the image shapes subjectivity, whether the image comes from books, cinema, advertising, or other components of our society of simulation, spectacle, and celebrity.

I see Kathy Acker and Orlan as anatomists who are simultaneously performing and dissecting this idea. All great anatomists are those on whom no genre is lost. Cervantes mocks in turn epic, pastoral, romance, comedy, and devotional literature. Anatomists take high and low materials and tease them into art, often seducing minor genres into brilliance, as

Cervantes did with Renaissance chivalric romance,[33] and as Acker does
with Cervantes. As Richard Kostelanetz notes, "In practice, new fiction
usually rejects or ignores the recently dominant preoccupations of literature to draw selectively upon unmined or unfashionable strains of earlier
work, recording an esthetic indebtedness that may not be immediately apparent. Therefore, thanks to innovative work, certain otherwise forgotten
precedents are revived in literature's collective memory. Furthermore, new
work tends to draw upon materials and structures previously considered
beneath or beyond fiction, as well as upon new developments in the other
arts."[34]

   Italo Calvino, who makes the connection between epistolarity and a
"memo" in *Six Memos for the Next Millennium,* argues that there are two
types of imaginative processes: one that starts with the word and arrives
at the visual image, and the other that starts with the visual image and arrives at its verbal expression. One of Calvino's six memos is entitled
"Visibility"; in it, he exhorts artists to reconnect the external world of scientific knowledge with the inner world of imagination. That is precisely
what all the artists discussed above have been doing for some time. Will
letter writing become extinct in the age of telecommunications and technological wizardry? Obviously not. Derrida declares that *The Post Card*
marks the end of the epistolary genre and the postal epoch, but he cease-
lessly postpones that "end." Similarly, Calvino argues: "I have come to the
end of this apologia for the novel as a vast net. Someone might object that
the more the work tends toward the multiplication of possibilities, the further it departs from that unicum which is the self of the writer, his inner
sincerity and the discovery of his own truth. But I would answer: Who are
we, who is each one of us, if not combinatoria of experiences, information, books we have read, things imagined? Each life is an encyclopedia, a
library, and inventory of objects, a series of styles, and everything can be
constantly shuffled and reordered in every way conceivable."[35] Each of the
artists I have discussed highlight Calvino's idea: they shuffle and reorder
codes and conventions in every conceivable way. The epistolary artists discussed here are translators, for only they can go *beyond* technology to analyze its manifest and latent meaning and import. Some commentators er-
roneously regard new electronic communications systems merely as
transparent tools that bring new efficiencies but maintain the status quo
regarding family, community, state. This view remains circumscribed by

modernity, rather than postmodernity, as Mark Poster points out.[36] By contrast, the artists in these pages are using these technologies to invent new cultural formations, new spaces of knowledge, and new identities. They subvert the utilitarian goal of producing more efficient, productive subjects. They are scrutinizing the *kinds* of subjects emerging, for better or worse, via these new technologies. As Bill Nichols points out in "The Work of Culture in the Age of Cybernetic Systems," "The transgressive and liberating potential which Bataille found in the violation of taboos and prohibitions, and which Benjamin found in the potential of mechanically reproduced works of art persists in yet another form. The cybernetic metaphor contains the germ of an enhanced future inside a prevailing model that substitutes part for whole, simulation for real, cyborg for human. . . . The task is not to overthrow the prevailing cybernetic model but to transgress its predefined interdictions and limits, using the dynamite of the apperceptive powers it has itself brought into being."[37]

Not all postmodern artists are innately transgressive. But the ones discussed here are experimenting with epistolary conventions to construct new models of interactivity. As Kathy Acker's work demonstrates, by exposing the state's invisible power, they are devising a new strain of resistant literature—resistant to idealized visions of the autonomous man, citizen, consumer. Acker and Orlan both demonstrate that—like the myth of the inviolate text—the myth of the inviolate *body* has been a long time dying. They also show how much women stand to gain by dismantling romantic myths of feminine protection. Their work is the product of a profound social anger, a portrait of the sadomasochism of everyday life. Their audacious and original experiments are blueprints for the anti-aesthetic outlined here. These epistolary innovators are cartographers, mapping the fin-de-millennium environment that is invisibly enveloping us.

Postscript by Richard Hardack

A Letter to Linda: Female Quixotism and the School of Sadeian Woman
When Linda S. Kauffman claims in Not a Love Story *that she "hopes the redemptive sex project fails," she strikingly articulates an alternative model of epistolarity; instead of serving as the locus for an unattainable wholeness or healing, sex becomes the site only of representation. At the heart of her essay, Kauffman proposes the dy-*

namic but perhaps inchoate conceit of using epistolarity to develop an antiromantic aesthetic.

It would be useful to read Kauffman's agenda against that of Leo Bersani throughout The Culture of Redemption; *for example, Bersani argues against the pernicious influence of redemptive fictions: he also notes that "Joycean parody simultaneously 'scorches' the other texts to which it refers and reconstitutes them as cultural artifacts within the intertextual designs woven by Ulysses. . . . [W]hat is peculiar is the novel's use of the intertext as a redemptive strategy." Kathy Acker, the central "protagonist" of Kauffman's essay, follows this strategy for different reasons and to different ends, but in some ways her project could also be critiqued along similar lines; in other words, where Kauffman sees sexuality as offering a false liberation, Acker champions intertextuality as subversive and redemptive. Bersani claims that the reader is meant to understand in "Circe" that "language cannot represent desire," and this failure of representation also permeates Acker's text.[1] The arc from Joyce's intertextual "sandblasting" to Acker's plagiarism still reveals a hidden or never fully erased desire to formulate an anti-aesthetic that offers transcendence.*

Poststructuralist theories of intertextuality often displace author and influence in favor of the discursive interaction of texts. As Susan Stanford Friedman argues, American critics tend to retain the author in discussions of intertextuality.[2] Even if we displace the author with the intertext, however, we do not escape the issue of redemptive fictions. One problem with Acker is she has already deliberately dismantled herself as an author(ity), appearing as a series of citations, revisions, and plagiarisms, suggesting either that her subject position has been left only with such options, or that all identity is constructed through such overlays; in an anti-aesthetic, these intertexts themselves, however, become the site of possible redemption.

The intertextual model Kauffman and Acker invoke, however, raises the possibility that we are merely valorizing inversion while trapped within a false dialectic; we face a specious liberal dichotomy, where the only alternatives—which are really mutually defining polarities—are absolute marital fidelity or adultery/pornography, authoritarian models of language and ownership or plagiarism. The aesthetic and ontological lure of inversion becomes Genet's problem, in fact the crucible of most writers in the Sadeian tradition. As Noam Chomsky would suggest in discussing the false opposition between Republicans and Democrats in capitalist Western democracies, we wind up with an entirely manufactured sexual consensus, with all possible positions operating under (or only responding to) the same assumptions; that is, all the Sadeian can finally do is argue that when romance is masochism, we must make masochism itself our romance. Such a move is akin to enjoying sex because the church says it is sinful, but it hardly repudiates the morality of the church; in fact, it only reminds us how inescapable that morality has proven. If, as Kauffman claims, "the anti-aesthetic substitutes the ugly, the perverse, and the antiromantic [as] an antidote to the ideology of romantic love," its ideology is conceived primarily as a response and a substitute—not an ideology of its own desire. It represents a kind of dialectical revenge, limited to a strategy of disavowal and camouflage rather than liberation.

In what ways does Orlan reflect the possibilities and limitations of such an anti-aesthetic? In a sense, this performance artist inhabits the body of de Sade's Justine, becoming or at least impersonating a passive object without desire who is molded by those around her. As Angela Carter—to whom I will return momentarily—describes her, Justine "sees herself only as the object of lust. She does not act, she is. She is the object of a thousand different passions . . . but she is the subject of not a single one."³ As Kauffman situates her, Orlan modernizes this disturbing objectification; her desire is to mirror and thus critique fantasies of beauty, but she can only reify and respond to, rather than actually revise, those fantasies. Orlan presumably enacts and critiques someone else's desire, but cannot formulate one of her own. Who is Orlan, and who does she want to look like or be? Is manipulating and controlling, but still participating in, one's own objectification a form of self-empowerment? Kauffman here might raise the powerful objection that desire can only represent a response to an existing (and hence oppressive?) discourse. One could also validate Orlan's procedure with the old proviso that one must destroy in order to create, for in her case deformation literally cannot be separated from creation: through her surgeons, Orlan destroys her old face as she creates the new one. Either strategy moves us beyond the idea that identity is performative to the idea that identity—whether along gender or racial lines—is transformative; that transformative model brings us back to the epistolary mode, for the letter must not only reach its audience, but elicit a response.

In 1996, I taught a class at Bryn Mawr College that began with Tabitha Tenney's Female Quixotism *(1801) and ended with Kathy Acker's* Don Quixote, Which Was a Dream *(1986); we were in part tracing a gendered metaphysics of transcendentalism in American literature as well as the interplay between romance and masochism in Sadeian discourse. Two of my students, Jennifer Alexander and Julia Parshall, working collaboratively and "intertextually," produced a brilliant research paper on how these texts try to dismantle conventions of epistolarity and romance; especially in a response/letter on epistolarity, it would be helpful to cite a few of their arguments. Their essay, "The Masochistic Nature of Love and Language in Tabitha Tenney's* Female Quixotism *and Kathy Acker's* Don Quixote; The Final Paper for Jennifer Alexander and Julia Parshall [which was a nightmare . . .]," uses the figure of the romantic heroine to trace the constructedness of "innate" desires: "Dorcasina is at a loss for a literary history or role model; she has inherited nothing in this area and so reproduces or recreates herself as a romance heroine and thus an instrument of a value system that immobilizes and silences her." Alexander and*

Parshall begin to intimate that all identity is generated from an intertextual pastiche of codes and references that must create a disparity between romantic image and lived experience, a disparity that can lead to a voluntary self-objectification: "Dorcasina is both a masochist and a plagiarist. . . . She lifts language and scenarios from the romance novels which have constituted her life's textbooks, and tries to pass them off not only as her own work, but as herself." Yet even the anti-aestheticist participates in the process she critiques, and can only hope to redeem herself as intertext.

Tenney, Acker, and Kauffman might all contend that the epistolary tradition of Clarissa *represents a long-extended embrace of masochism in a variety of guises. As Alexander and Parshall continue, "once self-articulation enters into the realm of romance, Acker rearranges power structures by problematizing gender roles; distinctions between male and female are blurred, traditional gender roles are shuffled, and identifying pronouns are confused. The result is that the dominant/submissive structure inherent to romance as created by language is unveiled in the form of the ensuing sado-masochism. . . . [T]he working definition of romance requires that someone act the part of dominator and someone the part of submissant. Thus [for Acker], to participate in romance is an act of masochism." "Intertextual" epistolarity, however, can also foster what Carter notes as the interchangeability of gender roles in the Sadeian school,[4] or what Kauffman sees as the indeterminacy of gender in cyberspace, and such indeterminacies might nullify the hierarchies of romance.*

But Acker does not seek to endorse masochism itself as an anti-aesthetic: as Alexander and Parshall claim, Acker regards *"acts of masochism as a physical manifestation of the philosophy underlying the concept of romantic love," and not "as an artistically preferable alternative to current sexual politics. . . . If Acker holds masochism as a model for her art—'anger turned in on itself'—this is only because she intends her art to express and expose the culture in which she writes."* Orlan, however, goes beyond exposing to reifying the way society constructs gender identity, and this transgression of course may be her point; but anti-aesthetics often remain tied to, even in love with, the systems to which they are opposed. As Acker's Don Quixote remarks, *"If I wasn't loved, I couldn't fit into this marketplace or world of total evaluation."*[5] Acker's character is more ambivalent than Kauffman depicts her, acknowledging that while she refutes masochism as a strategy, she may have come to love her own oppression.

If we agree with Alexander and Parshall that *"the official language of love moonlights as the instrument of female oppression,"* then Acker's need to destabilize all aspects of that language becomes all the more compelling aesthetically and politically. Angela *Carter's* The Sadeian Woman *(1979), a defense of pornography, has eloquently pursued part of the project Kauffman envisions: "to expose the pernicious effects of the ideology of romantic love," Kauffman's critique (via Sloterdijk) of the bourgeois fantasy that we are animals recalls Carter's attack on the feminist valorization of mother goddesses and maternal icons—a demystification of identifications closely tied to the putative "romanticization," and attendant commodification, of women's bodies. In all these studies, de Sade stands as the iconoclast who shatters not just romantic illusions but the structures of power operating in redemptive/romantic identifications. As Carter concludes, "in a society which still ascribes an illusory metaphysics [or, for instance, in Kauffman a sacred quality] to matters which are in reality solely to do with the relations between human beings, the expression of the sexual nature of men and women is not seen as part of human nature."[6] De Sade demystifies and desacralizes sexuality and motherhood, and inverts all aspects of fairy tale and romance; in de Sade, not rape but seduction is the greatest violation of the self—the "material"/psychological root of injustice. As everyone from de Sade to Orwell to Chomsky has suggested, the greatest coercion finally relies on the voluntary submission of the victim. But if romance or a sacred sexuality represent forms of oppression, what do we replace them with? If sex is not sacred, what is? Is it another reification to need or seek a replacement? If we no longer needed to "redeem" sex as part of a highly restrictive reproductive model, could any form of sexual expression become sacred? Would such an extension alleviate or exacerbate the ideology of romance?*

At the center of Kauffman's essay is a call for an anti-aesthetic or antiromance, though it is not entirely clear that such an aesthetic is always exigently connected to epistolarity—that the letter, simply by its nature, can always figuratively serve as a letter-bomb. Of course, many of the definitive tenets of romance are literally and figuratively expressed in letters, but Kauffman might further prove her claim that Acker's uses epistolary strategies even in "combining the masochism of unrequited love with the abjection of orphanhood." Even if Kauffman acknowledges that "the anti-aesthetic cannot be defined solely in relation to a single medium, epistolary or otherwise," it is not always clear how an intertextual epistolarity will necessarily be tied to the principles of the antiromance.

Kauffman's implicit equation of epistolarity with the virtues of dialogism does seem to privilege letter writing. Bakhtin would claim that all writing is dialogical, that "only the mythical Adam, who approached a virginal and as yet verbally unqualified world with the first word, could really have escaped from start to finish this dialogic inter-orientation with the alien world."[7] Indeed, as Kauffman argues, the myth of the inviolate text is linked to the myth of the inviolate body; in some ways, however, Kauffman constructs an alternate myth of the inviolability of the intertextual, or cut-up, letter or body. In other words, anti-aesthetics, from that of de Sade to Deleuze and Guattari, often wind up seeming more "romantic" than the aesthetics they oppose.

Perhaps one could formulate a revised discourse of the Sadeian enterprise in American or new world literatures specifically from a model of epistolarity. I would suggest that we treat the Sadeian tradition as a distinct but intertextual genre: like the School of Caliban, a school of a Sadeian or Quixotic Woman would focus on a figure who is both victim and rebel, and one who destabilizes language and the definition of the human; as Don Quixote's Dog tells us, "here, at the edges of meaning, I'm safe."[8] From Cervantes, we might also trace an inevitable deterioration/progress to de Sade, from romance to sadism to nomadism. Acker's Don Quixote and Orlan undergo complete self-deconstruction: even in male camouflage, Acker's character claims, "I'm no one; I'm no longer a personality."[9] In a variety of registers, the ungendered "no one" is not Ulysses, but the female Quixote. Such a school of inquiry might discover a way for these characters who have constructed themselves from the texts and intertexts of romance and antiromance to exist as part of a new epistolary community.[10] Acker, perhaps also speaking for Orlan, knows that her figure is "born into and part of a male world, [so] she had no speech of her own. All she could do was read male texts which weren't hers"; but she also asks, "has there ever in history, that is, in novels, been a human being such as me?"[11]

In The Female Eunuch (1971), Germaine Greer also addresses many of the issues Kauffman raises. Though some of the assumptions in Greer's book are dated, her arguments remain strikingly relevant. For Greer, romance has often been a cover for masochism, though Greer does not imagine an anti-aesthetic to replace that facade; for Greer, in contemporary Western society, the "ritualization of sex which is the essential character of romance" is necessary "to make sex acceptable."[12] Kauffman has noted, via Laura Mulvey, that women are castrated and turned into fetishes to assuage male fears of castration. Kauffman's reading of Orlan's literal cuts then recalls Greer's project of tracing the ways women are "castrated" in a variety of ways in modern commercial societies; what is disturbing is that Orlan— and perhaps the epistolary tradition as a whole—enacts the very thing she protests; she is like a nun immolating herself to protest violence. Female "adventure" was once supposed to involve falling in love and following the various conventions of romance, but from the Sadeian woman to the female Quixote to the female eunuch, "sexual religion [becomes] the opiate of the supermenial."[13] The real female adventurer abandons the path of romance laid out for her.

Finally, romance is usually a privilege of class; one needs a room of one's own with a view and a bed. Anything outside that view becomes "unredeemed" sex; but valorizing sex for its own sake, or that which inverts the ideology of masochism/romance, can only alert us to the snares of romance, not offer the hope of escape. For critical discourse, perhaps Kauffman's call for an anti-aesthetic, one constructed through a revised notion of epistolarity, could serve as another beginning.

Notes

1. Linda S. Kauffman, *Discourses of Desire: Gender, Genre, and Epistolary Fictions* (Ithaca: Cornell Univ. Press, 1986).

2. Frédéric Deloffre and J. Rougeot, eds., *Lettres portugaises, Valentins, et autres oeuvres de Guilleragues* (Paris: Garnier, 1962), 357.

3. Linda S. Kauffman, *Special Delivery: Epistolary Modes in Modern Fiction* (Chicago: Univ. of Chicago Press, 1992), 103–110.

4. Donald Alexander Downs, *The New Politics of Pornography* (Chicago: Univ. of Chicago Press, 1989), 60.

5. Hal Foster, "Postmodernism: A Preface," in *The Anti-Aesthetic: Essays on Postmodern Culture,* ed. Hal Foster (Post Townsend WA: Bay Press, 1983), ix.

6. Rosalind Krauss, "Sculpture in the Expanded Field," in *The Anti-Aesthetic: Essays on Postmodern Culture,* ed. Hal Foster (Post Townsend WA: Bay Press, 1983), 41.

7. Kathy Acker, *Don Quixote* (New York: Grove Press, 1986), 9. Hereafter cited parenthetically in the text as *DQ.*

8. Richard Walsh, "The Quest for Love and the Writing of Female Desire in Kathy Acker's *Don Quixote,*" *Critique* 32.3 (spring 1991): 154.

9. Ibid., 162–63.

10. Robert Siegle, *Suburban Ambush: Downtown Writing and the Fiction of Insurgency* (Baltimore: Johns Hopkins Univ. Press, 1989), 105.

11. Andrea Juno, "Interview with Kathy Acker," in *Angry Women* (San Francisco: Re/Search Publications, 1991), 179.

12. Walsh, "The Quest for Love," 158.

13. Cited in Siegle, *Suburban Ambush,* 101–2.

14. Kathy Acker, *Great Expectations* (New York: Grove Press, 1982), 64. Hereafter cited parenthetically in the text as *GE.*

15. Catharine A. MacKinnon, *Only Words* (Cambridge MA: Harvard Univ. Press, 1993).

16. Walter Starkie, introduction to *Don Quixote* (New York: New American Library, 1964), 26.

17. Robert Stam, *Reflexivity in Film and Literature: From Don Quixote to Jean-Luc Godard* (Ann Arbor MI: UMI Research Press, 1985), 209.

18. Kathy Acker, *Blood and Guts in High School* (1978; rpt. London, Pan Books, 1984), 109.

19. Ann Haverley, "In the (K)night-time," review of *Don Quixote, Times Literary Supplement,* 23 May 1986, 554.

20. Walter L. Reed, *An Exemplary History of the Novel: The Quixotic versus the Picaresque* (Chicago: Univ. of Chicago Press, 1981), 93.

21. Robert Coover, "The End of Books," *The New York Times Book Review,* 21 June 1992, 1, 23–25.

22. Robert Coover, "Hyperfiction: Novels for the Computer," *New York Times Book Review,* 29 Aug. 1993, 7, 9.

23. In *Postmodern Culture,* see, for example, Robert Coover, "The Adventures of Lucky Pierre," and William Vollmann, "Incarnations of the Murderer," 3.1 (Sept. 1992); and Kathy Acker, "Obsession," 2.3 (May 1992).

24. Walter Benjamin, "The Work of Art in the Age of Mechanical Reproduction," in *Illuminations,* ed. Hannah Arendt, trans. Harry Zohn (New York: Schocken Books, 1969).

25. Carolyn Guyer and Martha Petry, "Izme Pass," in *Writing on the Edge* 2.2 (spring 1991), cited in Coover, "End of Books," 9, 12.

26. Michael Blitz and Louise Krasniewicz, "Morphing Identities: Arnold Schwarzenegger—Write Us," in *Getting a Life: The Everyday Uses of Autobiography,* ed. Sidonie Smith and Julia Watson (Minneapolis: Univ. of Minnesota Press, 1996), 89–107.

27. Ibid., 100.

28. Peter Sloterdijk, *Critique of Cynical Reason,* trans. Michael Eldred (Minneapolis: Univ. of Minnesota, 1987), 262.

29. Cited in Barbara Rose, "Is It Art? Orlan and the Transgressive Act," *Art in America* 81.2 (Feb. 1993): 83–125.

30. Ibid., 125.

31. Ralph Cohen, "Genre Theory, Literary History, and Historical Change," in *Theoretical Issues in Literary History,* ed. David Perkins (Cambridge MA: Harvard Univ. Press, 1991), 85–113.

32. Ted Byfield and Lincoln Tobier, "Television," *Stanford Humanities Review* 2.2–3 (spring 1992): 90–108.

33. See Stam, *Reflexivity in Film and Literature,* 131.

34. Richard Kostelanetz, "New Fiction in America," in *Surfiction: Fiction Now and Tomorrow,* ed. Raymond Federman, 2d ed. (Chicago: Swallow Press, 1981), 86; cited in Siegle, *Suburban Ambush,* 394.

35. Italo Calvino, *Six Memos for the Next Millennium* (Cambridge MA: Harvard Univ. Press, 1988); cited in Cohen, "Genre Theory," 99.

36. Mark Poster, *The Second Media Age* (Cambridge MA: Basil Blackwell 1995), 27.

37. Bill Nichols, "The Work of Culture in the Age of Cybernetic Systems," *Screen* 29.1 (winter 1988): 22–47.

Notes to Postscript

1. Leo Bersani, *The Culture of Redemption* (Cambridge MA: Harvard Univ. Press, 1990), 169, 166.

2. As discussed in Tracy Mishkin, "Theorizing Literary Influence and African American Writers," in *Literary Influence and African American Writers,* ed. Tracy Mishkin (New York: Garland, 1996), 8.

3. Angela Carter, *The Sadeian Woman: An Exercise in Cultural History* (London: Virago, 1979), 49.

4. Ibid, 111.

5. Kathy Acker, *Don Quixote, Which Was a Dream* (New York: Grove, 1986), 115. Or, as Carter notes, de Sade reveals the specific parallels between "a bank balance and a body" (58). The Marquis de Sade, whose presence suffuses almost every page of Acker's novel, even 'appears' as King Sunny Adé, the Nigerian musician (45).

6. Carter, *Sadeian Woman,* 141.

7. Mikhail Bakhtin, "Discourse in the Novel," in *The Dialogic Imagination,* ed. Michael Holquist, trans. Caryl Emerson and Michael Holquist (Austin: Univ. of Texas, 1981), 279. Kauffman ideally would also have the space to historicize some of her claims: when she argues, for example, that tattooing is a means of imprinting the repressed on the body, she universalizes all tattooing, a practice that needs to be treated more contextually; for example, a female British punk's tattoos would not serve the same cultural function as those of an eigh-

teenth-century male Maori warrior. With Orlan, Kauffman also seems to be making a case for the radical difference of the posthuman examples she cites; but why is Prozac posthuman if people have been using mind-altering substances, from wine to opiates to peyote, for thousands of years?

Finally, along these lines, Kauffman might further address how epistolarity is distinct from communication; it is also not entirely clear how an epistolary response is central to Orlan's enterprise.

8. Carter, *Sadeian Woman*, 143.

9. Acker, *Don Quixote*, 66.

10. Kauffman makes the convincing point that epistolarity fosters or is part of a collective mode of storytelling, as evident in parts of the Arab world; work is viewed as a collective rather than individualistic enterprise. After Kauffman, it might also be salient to note that the first name of Avodah Offit, author of *Virtual Love,* means "work" in Hebrew.

11. Acker, *Don Quixote*, 39, 27.

12. Germaine Greer, *The Female Eunuch* (London: Paladin, 1971), 182.

13. Ibid., 188.

∾ Contributors

Nancy Armstrong is Nancy Duke Lewis Professor of Comparative Litera-ture, English, Modern Culture and Media, and Women's Studies at Brown University. She is the author of *Desire and Domestic Fiction: A Political History of the Novel* (1987) and coauthor, with Leonard Tennenhouse, of *The Imag-inary Puritan: Literature, Intellectual Labor, and the Origins of Personal Life* (1992). She has coedited two collections, also with Leonard Tennenhouse, *The Ideology of Conduct: Literature and the History of Sexuality* (1986) and *The Violence of Representation: Literature and the History of Violence* (1989). Her most recent book is entitled *Fiction in the Age of Photography: The Legacy of British Realism* (2000).

Anne L. Bower is an Associate Professor of English at the Ohio State University–Marion. Author of *Epistolary Responses: The Letter in Twentieth-Century American Fiction and Criticism* and *Recipes for Reading: Community Cookbooks, Stories, Histories*, as well as of articles on quilting metaphors in poetry, pedagogical methods, and contemporary fiction, she is currently working on a bibliographic study of twentieth-century letter fiction.

Clare Brant is Lecturer in English at King's College, London. She is the coeditor, with Diane Purkiss, of *Women, Texts and Histories, 1575–1760* (1992). She has published various articles on eighteenth-century letters and is cur-rently writing a major study of a wide range of epistolary writings enti-tled *Eighteenth-Century Letters and British Culture*.

Amanda Gilroy is Lecturer in English at the University of Groningen, where she teaches literature of the long eighteenth-century and feminist theory. She is the editor of *Romantic Geographies: Discourses of Travel, 1775–1844* (2000); coeditor, with Keith Hanley, of *Joanna Baillie: A Selection of*

Poems and Plays (2000), and with W. M. Verhoeven, of *Correspondences: A Special Issue on Letters, Prose Studies* (1996), and *The Emigrants* by Gilbert Imlay (1998).

Richard Hardack was Visiting Professor of English at Haverford and Bryn Mawr Colleges after he received his Ph.D. in American Literature in 1994 from the University of California at Berkeley, where he was a Javits and Phi Beta Kappa Fellow. His work focuses on connections among American transcendentalism, postmodernism, and African American literature. His articles have appeared in *Callaloo, Studies in the American Renaissance, The Arizona Quarterly, ESQ, Literary Influences and African American Writers, Languages of Visuality, Passages, Lit,* and *Social and Secure? Politics and Culture of the Welfare State.* He has completed a book on pantheism, gender, and transcendental identity for Cambridge University Press. He still treasures seeing his first Trystero post horn.

Linda S. Kauffman is the author of *Discourses of Desire: Gender, Genre, and Epistolary Fictions* (1986) and *Special Delivery: Epistolary Modes in Modern Fiction* (1992). She is editor of three collections of feminist theory for Basil Blackwell, including *American Feminist Thought at Century's End* (1993). Segments of the essay for this collection appear in her new book *Bad Girls and Sick Boys: Fantasies in Contemporary Culture* (1998). She is Professor of English at the University of Maryland, College Park.

Donna Landry, who teaches in the English department at Wayne State University in Detroit, is the author of *The Muses of Resistance: Laboring-Class Women's Poetry in Britain, 1739–1796* (1992) and, with Gerald MacLean, of *Materialist Feminisms* (1993). With MacLean, she has coedited *The Spivak Reader* (1996), and with MacLean and Joseph P. Ward, *The Country and the City Revisited: England and the Politics of Culture, c. 1550–1850* (1999). Her current book projects focus on the invention of the English countryside as an index to the waning of hunting and field sports, the significance of fox hunting for English identity, and English women travelers and their bestial loves.

Gerald MacLean is Professor of English at Wayne State University, Detroit. He is the author of *Time's Witness: Historical Representation in*

English Poetry, 1603–1660 (1990), coauthor, with Donna Landry, of *Materialist Feminisms* (1993), editor of Poulain de la Barre's *The Woman as Good as the Man* (1988) and of *Culture and Society in the Stuart Restoration: Literature, Drama, History* (1995), and coeditor of *The Spivak Reader* (1996) and *The Country and the City Revisited: England and the Politics of Culture, c. 1550–1850* (1999). Currently he is editing the English poems on the Stuart Restoration while beginning research on English representations of Ottoman culture.

Martha Nell Smith is Professor of English at the University of Maryland, College Park. She is the author of *Rowing in Eden: Rereading Emily Dickinson* (1992) and has recently completed an editorial, critical, and biographical study of the poet's prolific correspondence, *Open Me Carefully: Emily Dickinson's Intimate Letters to Susanne Huntington Gilbert* (1998). She has also coauthored, with Suzanne Juhasz and Christianne Miller, *Comic Power in Emily Dickinson* (1993). Currently she is working on *Life before Last: Reminiscences of a Country Girl* (an edition of the previously unpublished autobiography by Martha Dickinson Bianchi), *Erotobiographies in American Popular Culture* (essays), and *The Life of Susan Dickinson* (with Ellen Louise Hart).

W. M. Verhoeven teaches American literature at the University of Groningen, and is Director of the American Studies Program. He has published extensively on American and English-Canadian literature, and has edited *James Fenimore Cooper: New Historical and Literary Contexts* (1993) and *Rewriting the Dream: Reflections on the Changing American Literary Canon* (1992); he has coedited, with A. Robert Lee, *Making America/Making American Literature: Franklin to Cooper* (1996), and with Amanda Gilroy, *Correspondences: A Special Issue on Letters, Prose Studies,* (1996), and *The Emigrants* by Gilbert Imlay (1998). He is currently writing a book entitled *Subversive Acts: Performance and Pose in the Radical Fictions of Charles Brockden Brown* and editing *Transatlantic Revolutions: Cultural Crossings, 1775–1815.*

～ Index